WHO'S
WHO IN
POLITICAL
REVOLUTIONS

Editorial and Advisory Boards

WHO'S WHO IN POLITICAL REVOLUTIONS

Seventy-three Men and Women
Who Changed the World

JACK A. GOLDSTONE,
EDITOR

CONGRESSIONAL QUARTERLY, INC.
WASHINGTON, D.C.

Book design and production by Naylor Design Inc., Upper Marlboro, Maryland
Printed and bound in the United States of America

The paper used in this publication meets the minimum requirements of the American National
Standard for Information Sciences—Permanence of Paper for Printed Library Materials, ANSI Z39.48-
1984.

LIBRARY OF CONGRESS CATALOGING-IN-PUBLICATION DATA
Who's Who in political revolutions: seventy-three men and women
who changed the world / Jack A. Goldstone, editor
        p.   cm.
    Includes bibliographical references and index.
    ISBN 1-56802-461-4 (alk. paper)
    1. Revolutionaries—Biography. 2. Heads of state—Biography.
3. Politicians—Biography. 4. Revolutions—History. 5. World politics.
I. Goldstone, Jack A.   II. Congressional Quarterly, Inc.
    D21.3.W485 1999
    909.08'092'2—dc21
    [b]   98-51551

CONTENTS

Preface   vii

Alphabetical List of Articles   ix

Contributors   xiii

Introduction   xvii

Time Line of Revolutionary Events and Leaders   xix

Articles A–Z   1

Credits for Photographs   153

Index   155

PREFACE

These are the stories of men and women who changed the world. They were not inventors; some were not politicians. They were people with ideas and people of action. What they shared was a vision for their societies of greater justice, equality, and freedom.

Many of these men and women will be familiar to you from American or European history—George Washington, Thomas Jefferson, Vladimir Lenin. But there were also heroic liberators in South America (José Martí and Simón Bolívar), Africa (Kwame Nkrumah, Julius Nyerere, Nelson Mandela), and Asia (Mahatma Gandhi and Ho Chi Minh), to name just a few. Of course, as with any human enterprise, in revolution there are tales of tragedy as well as triumph—some of those who sought to save their nations turned out to be terrible tyrants, such as Adolf Hitler and Joseph Stalin. And some of our entries are about philosophers and writers who did not make revolutions but who inspired millions of others to pursue revolutionary dreams (Karl Marx, John Locke, Frantz Fanon).

The revolutionary writers and leaders profiled in this volume came from every walk of life. A few, such as George Washington or Gilbert du Motier de Lafayette, came from privileged backgrounds. Others, including Rosa Luxemburg, Fidel Castro, and Maximilien Robespierre, came from ordinary middle-class or professional backgrounds. Still others, such as Rigoberta Menchú Tum, came from peasant communities or were former slaves, as was François-Dominique Toussaint L'Ouverture. Regardless of their social background, they did not let the customs and habits of their day limit their view of how society could be arranged. Taking great risks, these men and women dared to be unconventional, to seek a different path for themselves and their people. In this book, you will find their stories—the lives of the greatest revolutionary leaders and thinkers of the past five centuries from around the world.

These essays are drawn from the *Encyclopedia of Political Revolutions,* also published by Congressional Quarterly. To learn more about the revolutionary events shaped by these leaders or about important concepts—such as democracy or women and gender issues—and their role in revolution, ask your librarian to help you find that volume. The essays in this book were written by world-renowned experts, under the guidance of a distinguished editorial board. I want to thank all of them for contributing their time and expertise to this project.

The men and women whose lives are described in this book have stirred and fascinated people around the world. I hope that in reading their stories, you too will be moved to think about the world, and your life within it, in new ways.

JACK A. GOLDSTONE
Del Mar, California

Alphabetical List of Articles

Adams, John
David W. Conroy, *Author*

Adams, Samuel
David W. Conroy, *Author*

Anthony, Susan B.
Kathleen Barry, *Pennsylvania State University*

Atatürk, Kemal
A. Holly Shissler, *Indiana University of Pennsylvania*

Biko, Stephen
Kenneth W. Grundy, *Case Western Reserve University*

Bolívar, Simón
Peter Blanchard, *University of Toronto*

Buonarroti, Filippo Michele
William Doyle, *University of Bristol*

Burke, Edmund
Isaac Kramnick, *Cornell University*

Cabral, Amílcar
Ronald H. Chilcote, *University of California, Riverside*

Castro, Fidel
Jorge I. Domínguez, *Harvard University*

Chiang Kai-shek
Parks M. Coble, *University of Nebraska at Lincoln*

Cromwell, Oliver
John Morrill, *Cambridge University*

Deng Xiaoping
Lucian W. Pye, *Massachusetts Institute of Technology*

Fanon, Frantz Omar
Ali A. Mazrui, *State University of New York at Binghamton, University of Jos, and Cornell University*

Franklin, Benjamin
Ralph Ketcham, *Syracuse University*

Gandhi, Mahatma
Stanley Wolpert, *University of California, Los Angeles*

Garibaldi, Giuseppe
John Whittam, *University of Bristol*

Gorbachev, Mikhail
Stephen Kotkin, *Princeton University*

Gramsci, Antonio
Carl Boggs, *National University*

Guevara, Ernesto "Che"
Jon Lee Anderson, *Author and journalist*

Havel, Václav
Sharon L. Wolchik, *George Washington University*

Henry, Patrick
Emory G. Evans, *University of Maryland at College Park*

Hitler, Adolf
Daniel Chirot, *University of Washington*

Ho Chi Minh
William J. Duiker, *Pennsylvania State University*

Hong Xiuquan
P. Richard Bohr, *College of Saint Benedict and Saint John's University, Saint Joseph, Minn.*

Jefferson, Thomas
Lance Banning, *University of Kentucky*

Jinnah, Mohammad Ali
Stanley Wolpert, *University of California, Los Angeles*

Juárez, Benito
John Tutino, *Georgetown University*

Kenyatta, Jomo
Tabitha Kanogo, *University of California, Berkeley*

Khomeini, Ayatollah Ruhollah
Saïd Amir Arjomand, *State University of New York at Stony Brook*

Kim Il Sung
Dae-Sook Suh, *University of Hawaii at Manoa*

King, Martin Luther, Jr.
Clayborne Carson, *Stanford University*

Lafayette, Gilbert du Motier de
Robert Rhodes Crout, *Charleston Southern University*

Lechín Oquendo, Juan
Steven S. Volk, *Oberlin College*

Lenin, Vladimir Ilyich
Stephen E. Hanson, *University of Washington*

Locke, John
John Marshall, *Johns Hopkins University*

L'Ouverture, François-Dominique Toussaint
Alex Dupuy, *Wesleyan University*

Lumumba, Patrice
Crawford Young, *University of Wisconsin at Madison*

Luther, Martin
Thomas A. Brady Jr., *University of California, Berkeley*

Luxemburg, Rosa
Stephen Eric Bronner, *Rutgers University*

Madison, James
Ralph Ketcham, *Syracuse University*

Mandela, Nelson Rolihlahla
Kenneth W. Grundy, *Case Western Reserve University*

Mao Zedong
Lucian W. Pye, *Massachusetts Institute of Technology*

Marat, Jean-Paul
William Doyle, *University of Bristol*

Martí, José
John Kirk, *Dalhousie University*

Marx, Karl, and Friedrich Engels
David McLellan, *Eliot College, University of Kent*

Menchú Tum, Rigoberta
Deborah J. Yashar, *Princeton University*

Mosaddeq, Mohammad
Homa Katouzian, *Exeter University*

Mugabe, Robert Gabriel
Norma Kriger, *Author*

Mussolini, Benito
Daniel Chirot, *University of Washington*

Nasser, Gamal Abdel
Joel Gordon, *University of Nebraska at Omaha*

Nehru, Jawaharlal
Stanley Wolpert, *University of California, Los Angeles*

Nkrumah, Kwame
Jon Kraus, *State University of New York at Fredonia*

Nyerere, Julius Kambarage
Ali A. Mazrui, *State University of New York at Binghamton, University of Jos, and Cornell University*

Orwell, George
Stephen Ingle, *University of Stirling*

Paine, Thomas
Jack Fruchtman Jr., *Towson University*

Robespierre, Maximilien
William Doyle, *University of Bristol*

Rousseau, Jean-Jacques
Carol Blum, *State University of New York at Stony Brook*

San Martín, José Francisco de
Jeremy Adelman, *Princeton University*

Sandino, Augusto César
Thomas W. Walker, *Ohio University*

Sorel, Georges
Stephen Ingle, *University of Stirling*

Stalin, Joseph
Daniel Chirot, *University of Washington*

Sukarno
Daniel Chirot, *University of Washington*

Sun Yat-sen
David Strand, *Dickinson College*

Tito, Josip Broz
Gale Stokes, *Rice University*

Tocqueville, Alexis de
William Doyle, *University of Bristol*

Trotsky, Leon
Mark von Hagen, *Columbia University*

Walesa, Lech
Jan T. Gross, *New York University*

Washington, George
Don Higginbotham, *University of North Carolina at Chapel Hill*

William of Orange (King William III of England)
Stephen B. Baxter, *University of North Carolina at Chapel Hill*

William the Silent
Maarten Ultee, *University of Alabama*

Zapata, Emiliano
John Tutino, *Georgetown University*

CONTRIBUTORS

ADELMAN, JEREMY
Princeton University
José Francisco de San Martín

ANDERSON, JON LEE
Author and journalist
Ernesto "Che" Guevara

ARJOMAND, SAÏD AMIR
State University of New York at Stony Brook
Ayatollah Ruhollah Khomeini

BANNING, LANCE
University of Kentucky
Thomas Jefferson

BARRY, KATHLEEN
Pennsylvania State University
Susan B. Anthony

BAXTER, STEPHEN B.
University of North Carolina at Chapel Hill
William of Orange (King William III of England)

BLANCHARD, PETER
University of Toronto
Simón Bolívar

BLUM, CAROL
State University of New York at Stony Brook
Jean-Jacques Rousseau

BOGGS, CARL
National University
Antonio Gramsci

BOHR, P. RICHARD
College of Saint Benedict and Saint John's University, Saint Joseph, Minn.
Hong Xiuquan

BRADY, THOMAS A., JR.
University of California, Berkeley
Martin Luther

BRONNER, STEPHEN ERIC
Rutgers University
Rosa Luxemburg

CARSON, CLAYBORNE
Stanford University
Martin Luther King, Jr.

CHILCOTE, RONALD H.
University of California, Riverside
Amílcar Cabral

CHIROT, DANIEL
University of Washington
Adolf Hitler
Benito Mussolini
Joseph Stalin
Sukarno

COBLE, PARKS M.
University of Nebraska at Lincoln
Chiang Kai-shek

CONROY, DAVID W.
Author
John Adams
Samuel Adams

CROUT, ROBERT RHODES
Charleston Southern University
Gilbert du Motier de Lafayette

DAE-SOOK SUH
University of Hawaii at Manoa
Kim Il Sung

DOMÍNGUEZ, JORGE I.
Harvard University
Fidel Castro

DOYLE, WILLIAM
University of Bristol
Filippo Michele Buonarroti
Jean-Paul Marat
Maximilien Robespierre
Alexis de Tocqueville

DUIKER, WILLIAM J.
Pennsylvania State University
Ho Chi Minh

DUPUY, ALEX
Wesleyan University
François-Dominique Toussaint L'Ouverture

EVANS, EMORY G.
University of Maryland at College Park
Patrick Henry

FRUCHTMAN, JACK, JR.
Towson University
Thomas Paine

GOLDSTONE, JACK A.
University of California, Davis
Introduction

GORDON, JOEL
University of Nebraska at Omaha
Gamal Abdel Nasser

GROSS, JAN T.
New York University
Lech Walesa

GRUNDY, KENNETH W.
Case Western Reserve University
Stephen Biko
Nelson Rolihlahla Mandela

HANSON, STEPHEN E.
University of Washington
Vladimir Ilyich Lenin

HIGGINBOTHAM, DON
University of North Carolina at Chapel Hill
George Washington

INGLE, STEPHEN
University of Stirling
George Orwell
Georges Sorel

KANOGO, TABITHA
University of California, Berkeley
Jomo Kenyatta

KATOUZIAN, HOMA
Exeter University
Mohammad Mosaddeq

KETCHAM, RALPH
Syracuse University
Benjamin Franklin
James Madison

KIRK, JOHN
Dalhousie University
José Martí

KOTKIN, STEPHEN
Princeton University
Mikhail Gorbachev

KRAMNICK, ISAAC
Cornell University
Edmund Burke

KRAUS, JON
State University of New York at Fredonia
Kwame Nkrumah

KRIGER, NORMA
Author
Robert Gabriel Mugabe

MARSHALL, JOHN
Johns Hopkins University
John Locke

MAZRUI, ALI A.
State University of New York at Binghamton, University of Jos, and Cornell University
Frantz Omar Fanon
Julius Kambarage Nyerere

McLELLAN, DAVID
Eliot College, University of Kent
Karl Marx and Friedrich Engels

MORRILL, JOHN
Cambridge University
Oliver Cromwell

PYE, LUCIAN W.
Massachusetts Institute of Technology
Deng Xiaoping
Mao Zedong

SHISSLER, A. HOLLY
Indiana University of Pennsylvania
Kemal Atatürk

STOKES, GALE
Rice University
Josip Broz Tito

STRAND, DAVID
Dickinson College
Sun Yat-sen

TUTINO, JOHN
Georgetown University
Benito Juárez
Emiliano Zapata

ULTEE, MAARTEN
University of Alabama
William the Silent

VOLK, STEVEN S.
Oberlin College
Juan Lechín Oquendo

VON HAGEN, MARK
Columbia University
Leon Trotsky

WALKER, THOMAS W.
Ohio University
Augusto César Sandino

WHITTAM, JOHN
University of Bristol
Giuseppe Garibaldi

WOLCHIK, SHARON L.
George Washington University
Václav Havel

WOLPERT, STANLEY
University of California, Los Angeles
Mahatma Gandhi
Mohammad Ali Jinnah
Jawaharlal Nehru

YASHAR, DEBORAH J.
Princeton University
Rigoberta Menchú Tum

YOUNG, CRAWFORD
University of Wisconsin at Madison
Patrice Lumumba

INTRODUCTION

In "great man" theories of history, revolutions are presented as the triumph of one or a few individuals whose ideas and devoted efforts changed the course of history. This view was most famously expressed by the German sociologist Max Weber in his depiction of the "charismatic" leader as an exceptional presence who moves people to break free from the normal course of events. This view is often presented in popular histories and biographies and reaches its most profound expression in those revolutionary states that developed "cults" around their leaders. Vladimir Ilyich Lenin in Russia, Mao Zedong in China, Fidel Castro in Cuba, and Ayatollah Ruhollah Khomeini in Iran are just a few of the individuals who have been given heroic, if not divine, attributes as revolutionary leaders.

In contrast, most social scientific analyses of revolutions give much less credit to individual leaders for making revolutions. Focusing instead on the weakness of old regimes, the impact of international conflicts, and the struggles between classes or political factions, social scientific analyses often give leaders the much more limited role of opportunists who step forward to act in a situation that invites, or even impels, revolutionary actions. "Structuralist" social scientists, such as the American scholar Theda Skocpol, hardly mention revolutionary leaders in their analyses. For the structuralists, social-structural factors lead to the rise and fall of regimes, and revolutionary "leaders" are often frustrated, surprised, or confounded by their inability to control events, as they too are swept along by the forces of history.

THE NATURE OF REVOLUTIONARY LEADERS

Studies of revolutionary leaders, such as those by the American political scientists Mostafa Rejai and Kay Phillips, reveal that they are surprisingly diverse and have more in common with conventional political leaders than one might guess. Whereas some leaders, like Castro and Leon Trotsky, are dashing and daring, others are quietly noble, such as George Washington and Václav Havel; still others, like Lenin and Maximilien Robespierre, are puritanical ascetics. In their education (above average for their societies) and family background (professional and middle class), revolutionaries are mostly like conventional political leaders. Drawn to politics from an early age, many of them envisioned careers in conventional politics, only to have a personal crisis wrench them onto a radical path.

Revolutionary leadership, like leadership in general, takes two major forms. Scholars identify these as "people-oriented" leadership, the ability to communicate an ideological vision that will inspire loyalty and persuade people to work for a common cause, and "task-oriented" or organizational leadership, the ability to mobilize people and resources to achieve specific goals. Successful revolutions require both kinds of leadership, whether combined in a single dominant leader or, much more commonly, spread among a key elite of primary leaders. Where leadership groups fail to combine and mesh these skills, revolutionary movements fail. And where both types of leadership are present but divided among different leaders who come into conflict, revolutionary regimes are thrown into turmoil. Examples of the former are Ernesto "Che" Guevara's efforts to create a revolution in Bolivia, which foundered on lack of organizational skills, or the efforts of the liberal Kadets under Alexander Kerensky to create a revolutionary regime in Russia, which collapsed in part through the inability of Kerensky to match Lenin's popular appeal. Examples of the latter are communist China, where recurring conflicts between ideologically devoted Maoists and more pragmatic technocrats periodically disrupted China and led to the tragedies of the Cultural Revolution; and the short-lived New Jewel revolution in Grenada, which extinguished itself through the homicidal conflict between its ideological and organizational leaders.

THE CONTRIBUTION OF LEADERSHIP TO REVOLUTION

The tendency of structuralist social scientists to minimize the role of revolutionary leaders in making revolutions arises in part because what successful revolutionary leaders do best is take advantage of structural weaknesses in an existing regime. Thus successful leadership and structural vulnerability are almost always found together and are easily confounded. It is probably true that revolutionary leaders cannot "will" the destruction of a strong, united existing regime. But that does not mean that their role is modest or incidental. Without outstanding revolutionary leadership, the

fall of an old regime can simply lead to chaos, civil war, or a series of unstable regimes. In France from the fall of Napoleon in 1815 until 1870, in many African and Latin American societies, and in several modern countries in eastern Europe and central Asia, such as Yugoslavia and Tajikistan, vulnerable and collapsing regimes were followed by long and distressing waves of dictatorship, violence, and instability. Revolutionary leadership is crucial to consolidate a new regime, unite various revolutionary factions, and create a new political, economic, and social structure that can endure.

Moreover, the goals and character of revolutionary leaders can place an indelible stamp upon the new regime. India and South Africa are democracies today, despite high rates of poverty, inequality, and racial and ethnic conflict, because the leaders who founded their regimes (Mahatma Gandhi and Nelson Mandela) were devoted to the ideal of democracy. In contrast, autocratic leaders—such as Lenin in Russia, Mao in China, or Castro in Cuba—tend to establish autocratic regimes, whatever their expressed plans for future democracy. Similarly, the choice of a socialist or capitalist path among revolutionary regimes depended greatly on the experience and ideology of revolutionary leaders, not just the disposition of foreign powers or the structure of their prerevolutionary economies.

Revolutionary leaders, then, are indispensable to revolutions. Without talented, balanced, and united revolutionary leadership, even the collapse of states does not automatically bring forth a new regime. And when a new regime is constructed, the choices and vision of revolutionary leaders are crucial to shaping its future.

JACK A. GOLDSTONE

TIME LINE OF REVOLUTIONARY EVENTS AND LEADERS

Many of the individuals profiled in *Who's Who in Political Revolutions* are associated with specific revolutions and movements. These events are organized by geographic region. Within each region, the events are arranged chronologically, and for each event, the name or names of profiled individuals are provided.

	1500	1550	1600	1650	1700	1750	1800	1850	1900	1950	2000

THE AMERICAS

American (U.S.) Revolution (1776–1789)
John Adams, Samuel Adams, Edmund Burke,
Benjamin Franklin, Patrick Henry, Thomas Jefferson,
Gilbert du Motier de Lafayette, John Locke,
James Madison, Thomas Paine,
George Washington

Haitian Revolution of Independence (1791–1804)
François-Dominique Toussaint L'Ouverture

Latin American Revolutions for Independence (1808–1898)
Simón Bolívar, François-Dominique Toussaint
L'Ouverture, José Martí, José Francisco de San Martín

Women's Rights Movement (1848–)
Susan B. Anthony

Mexican Revolution (1910–1940)
Emiliano Zapata

Bolivian National Revolution (1952)
Juan Lechín Oquendo

U.S. Civil Rights Movement (1954–1968)
Martin Luther King, Jr.

Cuban Revolution (1956–1970)
Fidel Castro, Ernesto "Che" Guevara

AFRICA

Ghanaian Independence Movement (1946–1957)
Kwame Nkrumah

South African Antiapartheid Revolts and Reform
(1948–1994)
Stephen Biko, Nelson Rolihlahla Mandela

Kenyan Mau Mau Movement (1952–1960)
Jomo Kenyatta

Congolese/Zairian Upheavals (1960–)
Patrice Lumumba

Guinea-Bissau Independence Revolt (1962–1974)
Amílcar Cabral

Zanzibar Revolution (1964)
Julius Kambarage Nyerere

Zimbabwe Revolt and Reform (1966–1980)
Robert Gabriel Mugabe

EUROPE

German Peasant War (1524–1526) and Protestant
Reformation
    Martin Luther

Netherlands Revolt (1566–1609)
    William the Silent

British Civil Wars and Revolution (1638–1660)
    Oliver Cromwell

British "Glorious Revolution" (1688–1689)
    William of Orange, John Locke

French Revolution (1789–1815)
    Filippo Michele Buonarroti, Edmund Burke,
    Gilbert du Motier de Lafayette, Jean-Paul Marat,
    Thomas Paine, Maximilien Robespierre,
    Jean-Jacque Rousseau

Italian Risorgimento (1789–1870)
    Giuseppe Garibaldi

European Revolutions of 1848 and Paris Commune (1871)
    Karl Marx and Friedrich Engels

Russian Revolution of 1917
    Vladimir Ilyich Lenin, Joseph Stalin, Leon Trotsky

German Revolution (1918)
    Rosa Luxemburg

Italian Fascist Revolution (1919–1945)
    Benito Mussolini

German Nazi Revolution (1933–1945)
    Adolf Hitler

Yugoslav Partisans and Communist Revolution (1941–1948)
    Josip Broz Tito

Czechoslovak "Prague Spring" (1968)
    Václav Havel

Polish Protest Movements and Solidarity Revolution
(1970–1991)
    Lech Walesa

Portuguese Revolution (1974)
    Amílcar Cabral

Czechoslovak "Velvet Revolution" and "Divorce"
(1989–1993)
    Václav Havel

East European Revolutions of 1989
    Mikhail Gorbachev, Václav Havel

USSR Collapse and Dissolution (1989–1991)
    Mikhail Gorbachev

1500   1550   1600   1650   1700   1750   1800   1850   1900   1950   2000

1500 1550 1600 1650 1700 1750 1800 1850 1900 1950 2000

THE MUSLIM WORLD

Iranian Constitutional Revolution (1906–1911) and
Democracy Movement 1949–1965
  Mohammad Mosaddeq

Turkish Revolution (1908–1922)
  Kemal Atatürk

Pakistani Independence Movement (1940–1947)
  Mohammad Ali Jinnah

Indonesian National Revolution (1945–1950)
  Sukarno

Egyptian Revolution (1952)
  Gamal Abdel Nasser

Algerian Revolution (1954–1962)
  Frantz Omar Fanon

Indonesian Upheaval (1965–1966)
  Sukarno

Iranian Islamic Revolution (1979)
  Ayatollah Ruhollah Khomeini

SOUTH AND EAST ASIA

Chinese Taiping Rebellion (1851–1864)
  Hong Xiuquan

Indian Independence Movement (1885–1947)
  Mahatma Gandhi, Mohammad Ali Jinnah,
  Jawaharlal Nehru

Chinese Republican Revolution (1911)
  Sun Yat-sen

Chinese Nationalist Revolution (1919–1927)
  Chiang Kai-shek, Sun Yat-sen

Chinese Communist Revolution (1921–1949)
  Chiang Kai-shek, Mao Zedong

Vietnamese Revolution (1945–1975)
  Ho Chi Minh

Korean Civil War (1950–1953)
  Kim Il Sung

Chinese Cultural Revolution (1966–1969)
  Mao Zedong

Chinese Tiananmen Uprising (1989)
  Deng Xiaoping

WHO'S
WHO IN
POLITICAL
REVOLUTIONS

JOHN ADAMS

John Adams (1735–1826) was a principal theorist and creator of the American Republic. After graduating from Harvard in 1755, he often despaired over his situation as a young lawyer in Braintree, Massachusetts. It was not just that the area men seemed indifferent to his education and intellect, voters also elevated tavern orators to high office. Vice in government seemed rampant. Adams's experience in local politics was a lesson in the evolving character of colonial society that would haunt him as he became a leader of resistance and revolution.

In 1765 he won renown by composing instructions for Braintree's representative to the Massachusetts Assembly to oppose the Stamp Act. He also published his *Dissertation on Canon and Feudal Law*, which linked parliamentary efforts to tighten control over the colonies with repressive systems of law imposed in Europe in the past. In this "enlightened" age, Adams thought, the legitimacy of governments must be judged by their defense of natural rights. Braintree elected him to the Assembly, which in turn sent him to the First Continental Congress in 1774. As "Novanglus," he argued in a newspaper debate the next year that the internal affairs of the chartered colonies were not subject either to Parliament or even to the king in his "politic capacity." Colonists owed only deference to the king's "person."

In Philadelphia, he agitated to create a new center of governmental gravity for the colonies in Congress and its expanding number of committees. He chaired the Board of Military Ordnance after the outbreak of violence in 1775 and pushed for consideration of independence. In May 1776 he wrote the preamble to resolu-

JOHN ADAMS

tions authorizing the colonies to create new governments and helped edit Thomas Jefferson's Declaration of Independence. He explained independence as the mature judgment of not just Congress but of a people mobilized in a descending tier of conventions and committees.

Still, this vocal radical feared that the people at large would fail to maintain the self-effacing virtue that he and many other leaders considered vital to sustaining any republic. Adams insisted in *Thoughts on Government,* published in 1776, that popularly elected legislatures must be checked by a natural social and intellectual elite in control of upper houses and executive authority. In 1778 he drafted such a mixed constitution for Massachusetts, which invested the governor with a veto over legislation.

At the national level, Adams helped consolidate the new nation by winning recognition from the Netherlands in 1782 and securing loans from the Dutch to finance the fledgling republic. With Franklin he helped negotiate the Treaty of Paris, which ended the war in 1783. Congress appointed him ambassador to Britain in 1785, where he continued to press American interests over disputed conditions of the treaty.

Such endeavors never long distracted him from his concern over the stability of the new governments at home. News of Shays's Rebellion in Massachusetts and other unrest stirred him to write *Defence of the Constitutions of the United States* in 1787–1788. Having lost faith that the Revolution had wrought any refinement of American character, he reiterated his conviction that only mixed governments of distinct social orders could check popular passions. Such concerns also influenced the Constitutional Convention's draft of a new national government in 1787.

With his wide experience, Adams won office as George Washington's vice president in 1789 and succeeded him as president in 1796. But Adams's hopes for the consolidation of a natural aristocracy of merit were shattered by the development of popular antipathy toward any such pretensions. Thoroughly disillusioned by his single, turbulent term, he nevertheless helped achieve a constitutionally mandated transition from one political persuasion to another in 1800.

See also *Adams, Samuel.*

DAVID W. CONROY

BIBLIOGRAPHY

Bailyn, Bernard. *Faces of Revolution: Personalities and Themes in the Struggle for American Independence.* New York: Vintage Press, 1992.

Butterfield, Lyman H., ed. *Diary & Autobiography of John Adams.* 4 vols. New York: Atheneum Press, 1964.

Smith, Page. *John Adams.* 2 vols. Garden City, N.Y.: Doubleday Press, 1962.

Wood, Gordon. *The Creation of the American Republic, 1776–1787.* New York: Norton Press, 1972.

SAMUEL ADAMS

Samuel Adams (1722–1803) was a principal organizer of the American Revolution. When he entered Harvard in 1736, he was ranked according to custom by his family's social status. As the son of a justice, Adams ranked sixth. Such hierarchical distinctions, however, diminished in the political culture to which Adams gravitated after graduation. As Boston's tax collector after 1756, Adams began to construct a base of popular support upon which he drew to resist direct taxation by the Crown after 1765. Indifferent to material enrichment, he personified the republican ideal of self-sacrifice for the commonweal.

Adams acted to thwart the implementation of the Stamp Act tax by helping organize the Sons of Liberty in 1765. The Sons sought to arouse opposition to any parliamentary legislation considered to be a violation of colonial rights under the British constitution. They successfully pressured Stamp Agent Andrew Oliver to resign his office by intimidating him through crowd actions like the hanging of his effigy. Such tactics would be used repeatedly during the next ten years. After Adams's elevation to the colonial legislature (1764–1774), he also acted to influence other colonies. In 1767 his Circular Letter appealed to other assemblies to support Massachusetts's opposition to the Townshend duties. Gradually, Adams became convinced of the existence of a British conspiracy to subvert colonial legislative autonomy.

Adams could never completely control popular protest, as when a crowd provoked British sentries to fire and kill five men in 1770. Characteristically, however, he seized on the event to organize a peaceful protest in the form of elaborate funeral processions uniting Bostonians of all ranks. When in 1772 the Crown tried to make royal officials independent of local institutions by paying their salaries directly, Adams motioned the Boston town meeting to create a committee of correspondence to inform every town in the province of this latest threat. Across the province, towns elected their own committees to write replies in accord with Boston. By this device, Adams elicited an outpouring of popular support for the actions of Boston radicals, but with due respect for formal procedure. In 1773 he condoned the dumping of imported tea liable for tax in Boston harbor only after every means had been exhausted to reach some accord with Governor Thomas Hutchinson. By this breach of respect for property, however, Adams risked alienating leaders in other colonies.

Parliament acted to isolate Massachusetts by a series of punitive acts, including closure of the port of Boston. But Adams's election to the First and Second Continental Congresses in 1774–1775 provided him with a platform to promote colonial solidarity through the adoption of the Continental Association for Nonimportation and the authorization of local committees to enforce it. Techniques of resistance developed and refined

SAMUEL ADAMS

which transformed Congress into a national government.

Along with his cousin, John, Samuel Adams became alarmed over deeper democratization in the 1780s. Now that the people had become sovereign over all branches of government, he saw no need for the creation of popular organizations, such as county conventions advocating reform of the courts, to promote particular political agendas. Shays's Rebellion of desperate debtor farmers in 1786 seemed symptomatic of a general collapse in public virtue. Still, he continued to nurture the infant republican institutions of Massachusetts by presiding as lieutenant governor between 1789 and 1794 and as governor from 1794 to 1797. Under his near unassailable eminence, governing institutions absorbed the new shocks of bitter party divisions by establishing peaceful precedents for the transfer of power from one party to another.

See also *Adams, John.*

DAVID W. CONROY

in Massachusetts now became devices to construct national unity. Gradually, Adams helped persuade moderates in Congress that petitions to the Crown were pointless and that the colonies must prepare for war in 1775. The next year Adams signed the Declaration of Independence and helped draft the Articles of Confederation,

BIBLIOGRAPHY

Brown, Richard D. *Revolutionary Politics in Massachusetts: The Boston Committee of Correspondence and the Towns, 1772–1774.* Cambridge, Mass.: Harvard University Press, 1970.

Fowler, William M., Jr. *Samuel Adams: Radical Puritan.* New York: Longman Press, 1997.

Maier, Pauline. *From Resistance to Revolution: Colonial Radicals and the Development of American Opposition to Britain, 1765–1776.* New York: Vintage Press, 1972.

SUSAN B. ANTHONY

nthony (1820–1906), the most controversial and steadfast leader of the
woman's rights movement in the nine-
teenth-century United States, was born in western Massachusetts to a Quaker family and into a
generation of women who would reshape the
destinies of American women. She grew up during the Industrial Revolution with Quaker egalitarianism as her faith and creed. Her industrious
father was one of the first mill owners in the

industry that changed the United States from an
agrarian to an industrial society.

Although the Industrial Revolution extended
the exploitation of labor from the home to the
workplace, it also opened a public sphere of work
and the potential for an independent economic
existence to women. Anthony was among the first
to take advantage of these new possibilities. With
little advanced education she became a school
teacher when the male domination of that field

SUSAN B. ANTHONY

was only beginning to yield. By her late twenties, she found herself in a unique position—economically self-sufficient, employed outside the home, with legal rights that were denied her married sisters, and free to chart her own life. She followed her own interests and turned away from teaching and into social reform movements. Her Quaker family did not discourage her independence, which brought her into the leadership of the anti-slavery, temperance, and woman's rights movements by mid-century.

During the 1850s Anthony became a leader of the radical Woman's Rights Movement, having teamed up with feminist reformer Elizabeth Cady Stanton, who had called the 1848 Seneca Falls Convention. Simultaneously, she was a vigorous campaigner against slavery, insisting on the immediate emancipation of all slaves, and she crusaded for women's right to co-education, their entry into the profession of teaching, property rights, the right to divorce for married women, and suffrage. She quickly became known for the courage of her convictions, and as she uncovered wrongs against women, sought the most radical change that would root out the conditions that produced them.

During the Civil War, Anthony organized and led the Women's National Loyal League, petitioning President Abraham Lincoln to emancipate all human beings from slavery. But after the Civil War, when slavery was abolished, the abolitionist men with whom she had worked turned against women by securing a constitutional amendment guaranteeing all *men,* black and white, the right to vote. This dramatic turning point in women's struggle for emancipation found Anthony refusing to compromise. She would not support any law that would exclude one-half of the African American population and all women from the most fundamental right of citizenship. Anthony campaigned for the rest of the century from the conviction that until women had the power to legislate in their own behalf, they would always be in serfdom. Despite criticism and abuse, she was unwavering in her commitment to women's self-determination. She was equally committed to petitioning Congress and to grassroots organizing of women in village after village that she visited throughout the second half of the nineteenth century.

By the 1870s Anthony, both loved and hated, was the recognized leader of the Woman's Rights Movement throughout the country. She was considered dangerous by many because she could not be made to compromise on women's rights. But for throngs of women she was their charismatic leader. They looked to her for hope. In her lifetime she became a symbol of what was possible for women.

In 1872 when she was arrested because she voted for president of the United States, her crime—being a woman who voted—was treated as a capital offense. Many other women defied the U.S. Constitution by voting in that election, but Anthony's case became a national issue. When she was arrested, she refused bail and insisted that she be subjected to the full power of the unjust law. Her case took bizarre twists that defy rationality in the history of American jurisprudence. Her friend and lawyer posted her bail because he—chivalrously—could not see her going to jail. But by doing so, he prevented her case from going before the Supreme Court. Then in a jury trial that she condemned as one not of her legal peers as guaranteed to her by the Constitution—in that the jurors were all men with rights denied to her—the judge, who had prepared a decision before the trial began, instructed the jury to read it and convict her. Anthony was fined but refused to pay it, and the court refused to jail her for not paying it. She was more convinced than ever that until women had the power of the ballot, they would be subservient to men's power.

In the 1880s Anthony took the issue of women's rights to Europe and went from one country to the next, building an international woman's rights movement just as she had in the United States. Through the 1890s she solidified the movement for the struggle that she had come to realize would not be won in her lifetime. She was determined to leave a united and well-organized movement behind to carry the struggle to victory. Anthony's radical egalitarianism did not waver, even in her later years, and her charisma was an ongoing force galvanizing the movement, but the movement itself had changed. Women who entered the movement in the 1880s and 1890s no longer appreciated the original reasons for focusing the movement on suffrage. A more-educated generation of women who now for the first time had access to college fought for their suffrage as an individual right, not a claim for self-determination of women.

Anthony's dream of women with full citizenship was not realized in her lifetime. Thirteen years after her death women achieved the right to vote, but it would be eighty-five years and the 1990s before they would begin to vote as a gender block. Anthony's heroic, lifetime commitment to struggle for woman's rights has left her as a symbolic image of women's hoped-for emancipation.

KATHLEEN BARRY

BIBLIOGRAPHY

Barry, Kathleen. *Susan B. Anthony: A Biography.* New York: New York University Press, 1988.
Harper, Ida Husted. *The Life and Work of Susan B. Anthony.* 3 vols. Indianapolis: Bowen-Merrill, 1899, 1908.

KEMAL ATATÜRK

An Ottoman army officer, Atatürk (1881–1938) emerged as the principal leader of the national resistance movement in Anatolia after World War I. After securing the evacuation of Allied troops and establishing national sovereignty over most territories in Ottoman possession at the time of the October 1918 Armistice of Mudros, he concentrated power in his own hands, abolished the sultanate, and established the Republic of Turkey. As president of the new republic, he carried out wide-ranging reforms aimed at transforming Turkish society and creating a modern nation-state. Although these reforms were not new in their nature or methods but continued efforts at modernization dating from the reign of Sultan Mahmud II (1808–1839), the rapid and uncompromising manner in which Atatürk carried them out was revolutionary.

Born in Salonika, Atatürk was the son of a low-level bureaucrat. He graduated from the General Staff College in 1905, one of the new state-sponsored military high schools and colleges, and, like many officers of his generation influenced by Western ideas encountered during their education, joined the secret Committee for Union and Progress and participated in the Young Turk Revolution of 1908. Though he remained a member of the movement, an uneasy relationship with the committee's most prominent military leader distanced him from the regime after 1913. He was nevertheless active during World War I, serving on the Caucasian and Syrian fronts, as well as at Gallipoli (1915), where he won fame and promotion to the rank of brigadier.

In May 1919, as Greek forces landed at Izmir, Atatürk left Istanbul to join the national resistance then forming in Anatolia. There he forged its disparate elements into a more unified movement and established his own leadership by coalescing support around two fundamental assertions—that sovereignty resided in the nation and that it should be exercised without any limitation in those territories under Ottoman control at the time of the armistice. To give legitimacy to the national movement, he convened a number of congresses (Erzurum, Sivas), culminating in the election of a nationalist majority to parliament in late 1919. That body adopted these principles as the National Pact.

THE SECULAR STATE

The nature of the nation and the future role of the sultan-caliph were matters Atatürk carefully left vague in the early days of the struggle. After the defeat of the Greek forces, however, he no longer needed to compromise with religious conservatives or liberal moderates. The sultanate was abolished (1922) just before the Lausanne meetings to renegotiate the terms of the peace ending World War I opened, forcing Allied recognition of the Ankara government. In 1923 Atatürk consolidated his political control by dis-

KEMAL ATATÜRK

First he secularized the state and brought religious institutions under its control. In 1924 Turkey abolished the caliphate, the Office of the Seyhulislam (the chief Muslim jurisconsultant and his staff), the Ministry of Pious Foundations, and remaining religious schools and courts. Religious education and the supervision of pious foundations were severely reduced and brought within the purview of government ministries. The Sheikh Said Rebellion, a Kurdish uprising in the southwest with religious and nationalist overtones (February–April, 1925), provided Atatürk the opportunity to quell political opposition and impose further reforms. These measures were designed to break down religious custom and instill in the populace a secular mentality. Among the more important measures, Sufi orders and sites of pilgrimage were closed; fezzes and turbans were banned and the European brimmed hat imposed (more than six hundred people were executed by special Independence Tribunals for resisting these laws); a secular civil code was adopted; and in 1928 a phonetic Latin alphabet replaced the Arabic-Persian script.

solving the assembly and calling new elections with carefully prepared lists of candidates. The subsequent founding of the People's Party, encompassing all members of the new assembly, formed the basis of his one-party state, and a republic was declared in October. With a national political organization established and the assembly brought into line, Atatürk set in motion a vast chain of reforms that would change the face of Turkey in a startlingly short time.

SOCIAL REFORM

The worldwide depression of the 1930s posed new challenges for the Atatürk regime. After a brief flirtation with introducing a second political party, Atatürk responded with the political doctrine of Kemalism, embodied in six points:

nationalism, republicanism, populism, statism, secularism, revolution. In practice this amounted to state intervention in the economy in the form of developing industry and supporting agricultural prices—and the creation of a strong Turkish national identity. The regime promoted interpretations of philology and history that emphasized the pre-Islamic past and cast ancient Turkic peoples as the source of most great civilizations. A language reform was attempted, rooting out words of Persian and Arabic origin and replacing them with Turkish neologisms. Even the Qur'an was translated, and mosque prayers were conducted in Turkish. Together with the change in alphabet, these reforms constituted a major break with the past.

Atatürk also worked to expand literacy, and education generally, and to alter radically the position of women. He campaigned for an end to veiling, promoted women's entrance into the workforce and professions, and gradually introduced coeducational classrooms. Monogamous civil marriage was made law in 1926, and women achieved full political rights in 1934.

When Atatürk died, power passed to his longtime associate, Ismet Inonu, who continued to push for Westernization of Turkish society.

A. HOLLY SHISSLER

BIBLIOGRAPHY

Berkes, Niyazi. *The Development of Secularism in Turkey.* Montreal: McGill University Press, 1964.

Landau, Jacob M., ed. *Atatürk and the Modernization of Turkey.* Boulder, Colo.: Westview Press, 1984.

Lord Kinross (Patrick Balfour). *Atatürk: The Rebirth of a Nation.* Nicosia and London: K. Rustem and Brother, 1981.

Shaw, Stanford J., and Ezel Kural Shaw. *History of the Ottoman Empire and Modern Turkey.* Cambridge: Cambridge University Press, 1977.

Zürcher, Erik Jan. *The Unionist Factor: The Role of the Committee of Union and Progress in the Turkish National Movement, 1905–1926.* Leiden: E.J. Brill, 1984.

STEPHEN BIKO

Biko (1946–1977) was the charismatic leader of the black consciousness movement in South Africa and a founder of and intellectual inspiration behind the South African Student Organization (SASO). Although the Soweto uprising of 1976 was not formally organized by the black consciousness movement, Biko's influence largely triggered the protests and the widespread resistance to apartheid that immediately followed.

Biko, a medical student at the University of Natal (black section), was involved in student politics. Dissatisfied with the way white liberals dominated student politics nationally, he led African and Indian students to quit the National Union of South African Students. In 1968–1969 they organized SASO, with Biko as president. In 1970 they began using the more positive term "black" instead of the negative "nonwhite." The question of race, definitions of South African and African nationalism, and the role of whites in the struggle against apartheid had long been subjects of intense debate among blacks. The Africanist posture of the Pan-Africanist Congress attracted many black intellectuals. The Pan-Africanist Congress had broken away from the African National Congress in 1958, criticizing the ANC's close association with non-Africans and its collaboration with the Communist Party of South Africa.

Biko's arguments against collaboration with whites were more psychological than political.

He thought it necessary to liberate blacks from their own attitudes of inferiority and sub-servience before political rights could be achieved, and thus he sought to exclude whites from the movement in order to encourage black self-reliance. Although he rejected a role for whites in the struggle, his conception of black unity included Indians and coloreds (mixed race) as well as Africans. To Biko, "being black" meant being excluded from power by state-imposed categories of race. But Biko went further to say that once liberation had been won and apartheid ended, race would no longer be the central organizing principle of the polity.

Biko at first maintained that white power would somehow collapse as blacks asserted their unwillingness to abide by it, regardless of the intentions of those in power or the balance of forces. Later he came to see the need for a united front against the state and to realize the likelihood of a protracted struggle. With the black consciousness movement's deemphasis of confrontation, military power, and materialism, the state at first regarded the movement as no threat. But after the Africanist rhetoric of the movement began to appeal to the urban poor and Biko started to reach out successfully to the ANC in exile and to other resistance groups, the state crushed the movement. The authorities feared a unified black opposition.

Biko was detained on August 18, 1977, interrogated, beaten to near death by the police in

STEPHEN BIKO BECAME A MARTYR OF THE ANTIAPATHEID MOVEMENT. IN SEPTEMBER 1987, ACTIVISTS GATHER IN HIS HOMETOWN OF GINSBERG TO COMMEMORATE THE TENTH ANNIVERSARY OF HIS DEATH.

Port Elizabeth, and then driven to Pretoria, where he died, in a cell, on September 12. Five weeks after Biko's death, on October 19, the government banned seventeen black consciousness and affiliated organizations. Many of their 14,000 supporters who had fled South Africa during and after the Soweto uprising joined the ANC. Black consciousness was effectively silenced.

An official inquest, conducted in November–December 1977, exonerated the police and state medical officials from responsibility for Biko's death. That inquest has since been totally discredited, and Biko is a martyr in the democratic struggle. In 1997 several police officers, to avoid subsequent prosecution for his murder, sought amnesty from the Truth and Reconciliation Commission, a state body trying to determine the facts about human rights violations under apartheid.

See also *Mandela, Nelson.*

KENNETH W. GRUNDY

BIBLIOGRAPHY

Arnold, Millard, ed. *Steve Biko: Black Consciousness in South Africa.* New York: Random House, 1978.

Biko, Steve. *I Write What I Like.* San Francisco: Harper and Row, 1986.

Gerhart, Gail M. *Black Power in South Africa: The Evolution of an Ideology.* Berkeley: University of California Press, 1978.

Pityana, Barney, ed. *Bounds of Possibility: The Legacy of Steve Biko and Black Consciousness.* Cape Town: David Philip, 1991.

Woods, Donald. *Biko.* New York: Vintage, 1979.

Simón Bolívar

The most famous of the leaders of the Latin American independence struggles, Simón Bolívar (1783–1830) was the "Liberator" of six Latin American countries: Venezuela, Colombia, Panama, Ecuador, Peru, and Bolivia. Born into one of the oldest and wealthiest families in Caracas, Venezuela, he became an adherent to the cause of independence at an early age. His outlook was a result of the influence of his family and teachers, who introduced him to the writers of the European Enlightenment, as well as colonial policies that discriminated against the American-born. His early life was shaped also by travels in Europe and by personal tragedy, particularly the death of his young wife in Venezuela in 1803. After her death, he returned to Europe and while in Rome dedicated himself to his country's freedom.

Bolívar's reputation as well as many of his political ideas were created out of years of military struggle. A skilled but not brilliant general, he succeeded as a result of his passionate belief in the rightness of his cause; his strategy of continuous attack; his appeal to individuals who provided the military skills, recruits, and supplies that kept his armies in the field; and his personal ties with his soldiers. He first came to public attention in 1810 as one member of the group that took over the government in Caracas following the Napoleonic invasion of Spain. He participated in the unsuccessful defense of the first Venezuelan republic, established himself as a military commander in Colombia, and declared the second Venezuelan republic in 1813. Its collapse forced him to reconsider his strategy. He returned to the field in 1816 and led a campaign that secured the independence of Colombia and, eventually, Venezuela. Realizing that success required the freeing of the entire continent, he marched south through Ecuador to Peru and Upper Peru, where his armies had destroyed the remaining royalist forces by 1825. In reward for his accomplishments in Upper Peru, the new republic was named Bolivia in his honor.

Bolívar's letters, addresses, and constitutional proposals reveal a man committed to republicanism, centralism, and reformism. His views regarding the nature of the newly independent states gradually changed over time in response to the realities he faced. The chaos and disorder that accompanied his military campaigns and dogged the new states after independence confirmed his belief in the need for strong central authority. Politically conservative, he was socially liberal, introducing measures to improve the conditions of the region's Indian population and to end slavery. Yet his liberalism was tempered by pragmatism and the need to maintain elite support, a fact that explains the inconsistencies and contradictions in his actions and writings.

Although Bolívar was the most powerful and influential man in Spanish America in the mid-1820s, his desire to create a large, centralized political entity came into conflict with less imag-

SIMÓN BOLÍVAR

inative, more regionally focused individuals. The target of growing criticism, opposition, and even assassination attempts, Bolívar managed to maintain a position of political importance in Colombia until the late 1820s, when, embittered and disillusioned, he decided to leave South America. However, he died of tuberculosis near Santa Marta, Colombia, on December 17, 1830.

See also *San Martín, José Francisco de.*

PETER BLANCHARD

BIBLIOGRAPHY

Bolívar, Simón. *Selected Writings of Bolívar.* Compiled by Vicente Lecuna. Edited by Harold A. Bierck Jr. 2 vols. New York: Colonial Press, 1951.

Bushnell, David, ed. *The Liberator Simón Bolívar.* New York: Knopf, 1970.

García Márquez, Gabriel. *The General in His Labyrinth.* Harmondsworth, England: Penguin Books, 1990.

Masur, Gerhard. *Simón Bolívar.* Rev. ed. Albuquerque: University of New Mexico Press, 1969.

Salcedo-Bastardo, J. L. *Bolívar: A Continent and Its Destiny.* Edited and translated by Annella McDermott. Atlantic Highlands, N.J.: Humanities Press International, 1977.

FILIPPO MICHELE BUONARROTI

Participant in, and most authoritative chronicler of, the first attempt in history to bring about a communist revolution, Buonarroti (1761–1837) remained until his death a tireless organizer of revolutionary conspiracies. Despite consistent lack of success, the model of revolution through conspiracy that he promoted had a profound influence on later revolutionaries.

A Tuscan nobleman (from the same family as Michaelangelo), Buonarroti studied law in Florence during the enlightened regime of Grand Duke Leopold. Reading Jean-Jacques Rousseau and other French radical thinkers left him dissatisfied with the limited reforms possible under absolute monarchy, and instead of following the expected administrative career, Buonarroti wrote radical pamphlets and frequented Masonic lodges. Excited by the experimental possibilities offered by the French Revolution, he crossed to Corsica in 1789, where his loud anticlericalism won him appointment as an administrator of confiscated church lands. A conservative uprising, however, forced him back to Tuscany, from where he traveled to Paris and applied for French citizenship. By the time he received it in 1793, he had become a follower of Maximilien Robespierre, and his connections secured him appointment in 1794 as administrator of Oneglia, a tiny north Italian principality occupied by French troops. Here he harassed nobles and clerics and enforced eco-

nomic controls in the face of a popular hostility that he found inexplicable. Belatedly identified as a Robespierrist, Buonarroti was recalled and imprisoned seven months after Robespierre's fall. During his imprisonment (March–October 1795), he met Gracchus Babeuf (1760–1797) and others who would agitate over the subsequent winter for a restoration of social reforms associated with the memory of Robespierre and for the introduction of the abandoned democratic constitution of 1793.

When in the spring of 1796 the alarmed executive Directory took steps to crush the agitation, Babeuf and Buonarroti went underground and began to plan an uprising whose ultimate aim was the abolition of private property. An initial dictatorship of enlightened leaders would carry out the destruction of the old order before handing over power to the sovereign people. The "Conspiracy for Equality" was betrayed, however, and the leading conspirators were arrested (May 10, 1796). Babeuf was later executed, Buonarroti merely imprisoned. He remained in custody until 1802, and was under some sort of surveillance for much of the rest of his life. But surveillance did not deter him from trying to organize secret revolutionary networks, first against Napoleon, then against the restored Bourbons and the post-Napoleonic fragmentation of Italy. His networks were Masonic in inspiration and ritual and always sought to work through secret, subversive hierarchies. They were repeatedly betrayed and broken up, only to be re-formed under new names.

Buonarroti, however, remained dedicated to the ideals that he thought had come so near to achievement between 1793 and 1796. In 1828 he set them out in his celebrated account, the *Conspiracy for Equality*. Translated into English in 1836 and devoured by the French left for a half century, and not least by Karl Marx and Friedrich Engels, the book received a new lease on life in the twentieth century during the heyday of Soviet communism. A celebration as much of Robespierre's lost "republic of virtue" as of the communistic ideals of the 1796 conspirators, *Conspiracy of Equality* was also a handbook of how (and how not) to bring about an egalitarian revolution and a martyrology of ideological ancestors for all future socialist revolutionaries.

See also *Robespierre, Maximilien; Rousseau, Jean-Jacques.*

WILLIAM DOYLE

BIBLIOGRAPHY

Buonarroti, Filippo Michele. *Buonarroti's History of Babeuf's Conspiracy for Equality.* Translated by Bronterre O'Brien. London: Hetherington, 1836.

Eisenstein, Elizabeth L. *The First Professional Revolutionist. Filippo Michele Buonarroti, 1761–1837.* Cambridge, Mass.: Harvard University Press, 1959.

Rose, Barry. *Gracchus Babeuf. The First Revolutionary Communist.* London: Edward Arnold, 1978.

Talmon, Jacob L. *The Origins of Totalitarian Democracy.* London: Secker and Warburg, 1952.

EDMUND BURKE

EDMUND BURKE

Burke (1729–1797) was a British statesman and writer whose book *Reflections on the Revolution in France* (1790) remains to this day the classic antirevolutionary manifesto. Born in Dublin, Burke moved to London to study law and then pursued a literary and political career. He was a member of the House of Commons from 1765 to 1794, and in his speeches and pamphlets he addressed both the American and French Revolutions, defending the former and denouncing the latter.

The Americans were in the right, he argued, because they defended traditional practices and principles, the rights of Englishmen, against the disruptive innovations represented by George III's trade and taxation policies. His conservative preference for the status quo led Burke to see the French Revolution in reverse terms, with bloody revolutionaries recklessly subverting the traditional social and political order that embodied the wisdom and experience of the past.

While most of his British contemporaries applauded the revolutionary developments in France, Burke warned that with the events of 1789 "the age of chivalry is gone . . . and the glory of Europe extinguished forever." What Burke particularly despised about the French revolutionaries was their urge to change social institutions in the name of abstract ideas and ideals. Their mistakes were the direct result of their "faith in the dogmatism of philosophers," he wrote, which led them to place too much confidence in reason and speculation. They sought to remake the world in the name of abstract, a priori principles of natural right, freedom, and equality. He contrasted the French attitude with what he considered a native British antirevolutionary disposition. The English had no illusions of rapid political change; they understood the complexity and fragility of human nature and human institutions. They were "not converts of Rousseau" or "disciples of Voltaire." Their instinct was to repair incrementally the walls of the constitutional edifice, not destroy its very foundations in the name of constructing an ideal new structure.

Revolutionaries, according to Burke, misguidedly assumed that people had the ability to reform society according to rational principles thought up by "learned and speculative men." He was convinced, on the contrary, that the power of human reason was severely limited and that custom, tradition, and habit played a much more important role in politics. Revolutionaries thus wove rational schemes of reform and improvement far beyond the power of a flawed human nature to implement. He believed that people lived less by reason than by "untaught feelings" and "old prejudices"; indeed, they loved their "old prejudices" the longer they lasted. Monarchy, aristocracy, and established religion, ancient ideals and institutions that had stood the test of time, were being uprooted by irreverent revolutionaries.

Burke's *Reflections on the Revolution in France* has inspired legions of antirevolutionaries since 1790 who agree with him that people "are not morally at liberty, at their pleasure, and on their speculations of a contingent improvement" to destroy traditional hierarchical and deferential arrangements in the name of abstractions like freedom, justice, and equality. To do so, Burkeans contend, leads inevitably to "unsocial, uncivil, unconnected chaos."

ISAAC KRAMNICK

BIBLIOGRAPHY

Burke, Edmund. *Reflections on the Revolution in France.* Harmondsworth, England: Penguin Books, 1968.

Kramnick, Isaac. *The Rage of Edmund Burke.* New York: Basic Books, 1976.

Ritchie, Daniel E., ed. *Edmund Burke, Appraisals and Applications.* New Brunswick, N.J.: Transaction Publishers, 1990.

O'Brien, Conor Cruise. *The Great Melody: A Thematic Biography of Edmund Burke.* Chicago: University of Chicago Press, 1992.

Amílcar Cabral

From his birth in 1924 in the Portuguese colony of Guinea-Bissau to his tragic death by assassination on January 20, 1973, Cabral achieved recognition as poet, agronomist, theorist, revolutionary, and political organizer. He was one of few Africans to study at a Portuguese university and receive a doctorate, and his work as an agronomist led to agricultural surveys and analyses that served as a foundation for planning the economy of his homeland. As a theorist, he was one of Africa's original, independent Marxist thinkers. As a political organizer, he formed a vanguard party and organized the social and political life of liberated areas as he led a revolutionary guerrilla struggle against Portugal and its imperial and colonial legacy, contributing significantly to the 1974 coup within Portugal that ended a half-century of dictatorship. Most of his life was dedicated to eliminating the Portuguese presence in the colonies and to undermining imperialism in the broader international context.

All evidence depicts Cabral as a mobilizer of people around him. During the late 1940s he participated in student and youth political movements in Lisbon. As an agronomist during the 1950s he was involved in the early political opposition to Portuguese rule in Guinea-Bissau and Cape Verde; founded the African Party for the Independence of Guinea and Cape Verde (PAIGC) on September 19, 1956; encouraged his Angolan comrades to organize a movement to liberate that country from Portuguese control; and helped form a broad anticolonial movement among dissident activists in the Portuguese African colonies.

During the 1960s he was instrumental in the armed struggle. He influenced strategy away from protest in urban areas and toward the organization of the peasant masses in the countryside, and he pushed his movement from political opposition to national insurrection. He was instrumental in launching the guerrilla war in January 1963. Once his movement had succeeded in consolidating control over much of Guinea-Bissau, he began to organize the liberated areas and to build a government independent of the colonial form. A rudimentary administrative structure evolved to perform such tasks as increasing production, ensuring diversification of crops, improving distribution systems, establishing peoples' stores, improving education, building schools, and establishing health-care clinics.

Cabral also envisaged how to deal with the problem of assimilating the new structures in liberated zones with those in the Portuguese colonial enclaves. Village committees, people's courts, people's stores, health clinics, and rural schools founded in the liberated zones were to serve as models for the new integrated society, whereas the land, the Portuguese-controlled trading companies, and the few factories would be brought under national direction. A self-centered development rather than a state bureaucratic model would be emphasized at the outset of independence. The revolutionary party was decisive in establishing in liberated areas a state parallel to the colonial state. At the first PAIGC congress held within Guinea-Bissau, in February 1964, the party was decentralized so that power could devolve to local bodies and special administrative committees in the liberated zones.

As theoretician, disciplined intellectual, and productive scholar, Cabral effectively assimilated old and new ideas and thinking to revolutionary conditions. His thought can be segmented into perspectives on colonialism and imperialism, showing that dominated African peoples are denied their historical process of development under colonialism and that imperialism associates with the expansion of capitalism; revolutionary nationalism and national liberation, with an emphasis on how the armed revolutionary struggle emanates from culture based on history and the successes of resistance and struggle; class and class struggle, in an analysis aware of contradictions everywhere in society, involving races, religions, ethnic groups, and social classes; and a rudimentary theory of state and development.

Cabral showed how a vanguard party in the revolutionary period can govern and provide for basic human needs in liberated areas. His original thinking and independent Marxist analysis demonstrated that success was dependent not on old formulas and revolutionary situations but on unique, particular conditions. Finally, his personal commitment and example as organizer and unifier served to influence and motivate the mass revolutionary movement in achieving independence.

RONALD H. CHILCOTE

BIBLIOGRAPHY

Cabral, Amílcar. *Unity and Struggle: Speeches and Writings.* Translated by Michael Wolfers. New York: Monthly Review Press; and London: Heinemann, 1979.

Chabal, Patrick. *Amílcar Cabral: Revolutionary Leadership and People's War.* African Studies Series, no. 37. Cambridge: Cambridge University Press, 1983.

Chilcote, Ronald H. *Amílcar Cabral's Revolutionary Theory and Practice: A Practical Guide.* Boulder, Colo.: Lynne Rienner Publishers, 1991.

Davidson, Basil. *The Liberation of Guiné: Aspects of an African Revolution.* Baltimore, Md.: Penguin Books, 1969.

Rudebeck, Lars. *Guinea-Bissau: A Study of Political Mobilization.* Uppsala: Scandinavian Institute of African Studies, 1974.

FIDEL CASTRO

Born to a prosperous family in rural eastern Cuba and educated at the country's best Jesuit schools, Fidel Castro (1926–) obtained a law degree from the University of Havana. On March 10, 1952, Fulgencio Batista and some military associates overthrew Cuba's constitutional government. Castro joined the opposition, and on July 26, 1953, he led an unsuccessful attack on the Cuban army's Moncada barracks and soon founded the anti-Batista Twenty-sixth of July Movement. He served two years in prison, went into exile, and, in December 1956, led an expedition from Mexico that landed in eastern Cuba. A guerrilla insurgency followed in the Sierra Maestra Mountains. Batista's ineptly led forces retreated and eventually disintegrated. On December 31, 1958, Batista fled to the Dominican Republic.

Castro emerged from the guerrilla war a hero to many Cubans. A gifted public speaker, he made extensive and nearly continuous use of radio and television to build extraordinary public support. He roamed the country, con-

solidating his popularity. Between 1959 and 1961 Castro's policies transformed Cuba. His government expropriated all the means of production (except some peasant agricultural plots) and turned all the private schools, hospitals, and charitable entities into state agencies as well. Castro broke with the United States and re-created and mobilized Cuban nationalism, bringing it to a fever pitch. In later years he sought to reduce the role of market forces and the autonomy of civil society. He urged citizens to work for the sake of the nation, not for the rewards of "vile money."

FIDEL CASTRO

In 1961 Castro launched a massive literacy campaign, followed by years of sustained and successful efforts to raise the population's educational level. He instituted free and universal health care, which lengthened life expectancy. Also in 1961, for the first time in his life, Castro proclaimed himself a communist. The Communist Party is the only party legally authorized to operate in Cuba.

During the 1960s Castro ordered the execution of thousands of his opponents and jailed not fewer than tens of thousands of people, many merely for the "crime" of expressing opposition. Relative to its population, Cuba had a rate of political imprisonment in the 1960s among Latin America's highest. More than one million Cubans emigrated between 1959 and 1980.

A U.S.-sponsored brigade of Cuban exiles landed at Cuba's Bay of Pigs in April 1961 but was defeated within three days. The following year Castro secretly requested the deployment of Soviet missiles and nuclear warheads to Cuba as a deterrent to an expected U.S. invasion. In October 1962 he recommended a Soviet first-use of nuclear weapons to respond to a U.S. conventional attack on Cuba, and he subsequently obstructed the missile crisis settlement that the United States and the Soviet Union had negotiated. The Soviet-Cuban alliance strengthened in the 1970s and continued until the collapse of the Soviet Union in 1991. Particularly in the 1970s and 1980s, Cuba received vast economic subsidies from the Soviet Union.

From the 1960s to the early 1990s Castro supported insurgencies in several dozen Latin American and African countries, with few successes. In the 1970s and 1980s, however, he won three international wars. In 1975 he dispatched 36,000 troops to Angola to fight off a South African invasion. In 1977 he sent more than 10,000 troops to defend Ethiopia from a Somali invasion. And in 1987 he raised the number of Cuban troops in Angola to about 50,000 to combat a new South African invasion.

In the 1990s, after the loss of Soviet subsidies, Cuba's economy plunged. Castro enacted some limited market reforms, especially welcoming foreign investment, but sought to prevent extensive political change. Defiant still in his relations with the United States, Castro is one of very few extant communist leaders.

See also *Guevara, Ernesto "Che."*

JORGE I. DOMÍNGUEZ

BIBLIOGRAPHY

Lockwood, Lee. *Castro's Cuba, Cuba's Fidel.* Rev. ed. Boulder, Colo.: Westview, 1990.

Quirk, Robert. *Fidel Castro.* New York: Norton, 1993.

Szulc, Tad. *Fidel Castro: A Critical Portrait.* New York: Morrow, 1986.

CHIANG KAI-SHEK

Chiang Kai-shek (1887–1975) was China's paramount leader from 1927 until 1949. He rose to power in Sun Yat-sen's Kuomintang (Nationalist) movement and was one of the "Big Four" Allied leaders in World War II.

Chiang Kai-shek began training for a military career in China and continued his training in Japan from 1908 until 1911. He joined Sun Yat-sen's movement while in Japan and returned to China to serve in Shanghai during the 1911 revolution. When Sun faced defeat at the hands of the Beijing militarists, Chiang supported his attempts to establish a new revolutionary base in the south.

The turning point in Chiang's career came when Sun established a Kuomintang army with assistance from the Soviet Union. In 1924 Sun appointed Chiang to head the new Whampoa Military Academy near Guangzhou (Canton), in south China. As leader of the academy, Chiang supervised a new generation of officers, who formed the core of the Kuomintang military and the foundation of Chiang's later military and political power. Temporarily allied with the Soviet Union and the Chinese Communists, the Kuomintang prepared to launch a Northern Expedition to unite China.

When Sun Yat-sen died suddenly in 1925, Chiang gained control of the Kuomintang movement. In a deft series of moves he weakened opponents on the right and left. As the Northern Expedition began, Chiang became deeply suspicious of the Communists. In April 1927 Chiang hit the Communists swiftly with a "white terror" in which thousands were executed, gutting their organization and leading to a long civil war. Chiang established his capital at the central city of Nanjing in 1928 and solidified his political claims by marrying the sister of Sun Yat-sen's widow.

CHIANG KAI-SHEK

In alliance with regional militarists nominally loyal to the Kuomintang, Chiang then completed the Northern Expedition in 1928. Over the next decade Chiang gradually weakened these militarists, but his other rivals, the Communists, proved elusive as they moved into rural base areas. A third force, Japanese imperialism, ultimately proved to be the gravest threat to the Nanjing government. In September 1931 Japanese military forces seized northeast China, creating a puppet state of Manchukuo. Japan gradually encroached on north China over the next several years, forcing a showdown at the Marco Polo Bridge outside Beijing (then known as Beiping) in July 1937.

The war with Japan was a disaster for Chiang. His best forces were destroyed in the battle for the Shanghai area. After retreating to the interior city of Chongqing (Chungking) in 1938, Chiang's position deteriorated under conditions of hyperinflation, corruption, and supply shortages. The Communists, meanwhile, developed a powerful political and military organization in north China.

Ironically, Chiang's domestic weakness coincided with his greatest international prestige. When he met with Franklin Roosevelt and Winston Churchill during the war, he was acknowledged as one of the key leaders of the Allied powers. After World War II ended in August 1945, Chiang was defeated by the Chinese Communists in a bloody civil war. Retreating to Taiwan, he set up a rival Chinese government that received American and United Nations' recognition as the government of China until the 1970s. After his death in 1975, Chiang Kai-shek was succeeded as president of the Republic of China on Taiwan by his son, Chiang Ching-kuo.

See also *Sun Yat-sen.*

PARKS M. COBLE

BIBLIOGRAPHY

Ch'en Chieh-ju. *Chiang Kai-shek's Secret Past: The Memoir of His Second Wife.* Edited by Lloyd E. Eastman. Boulder, Colo.: Westview Press, 1993.

Coble, Parks M. *Facing Japan: Chinese Politics and Japanese Imperialism, 1931–1937.* Cambridge, Mass.: Harvard East Asian Monographs, 1991.

Crozier, Brian. *The Man Who Lost China.* New York: Scribner, 1976.

Eastman, Lloyd E. *The Abortive Revolution: China under Nationalist Rule, 1927–1937.* Cambridge: Harvard University Press, 1974.

Loh, Pinchon P. Y. *The Early Chiang Kai-shek: A Study of His Personality and Politics, 1887–1924.* New York: Columbia University Press, 1971.

OLIVER CROMWELL

OLIVER CROMWELL

Cromwell (1599–1658) made several distinctive contributions to the British revolutions of 1638–1660 as soldier, religious radical, and Lord Protector, the nonroyal head of the British state. He was a brilliant soldier whose command of cavalry contributed to the parliamentarian defeat of Charles I in the first civil war (1642–1646). He took part in more than thirty battles and in many major sieges and assaults on towns and fortified houses, and he never experienced defeat. In the second civil war he stamped out the royalist uprisings in Wales, and he defeated a Scottish army at the battle of Preston (August 1648); and as Lord General of the forces of the English Commonwealth, he achieved what no English monarch or general had ever achieved—the complete military subjugation of Ireland (1649–1650) and Scotland (1650–1652)—and he defeated Charles II at the battle of Worcester (September 1651).

Cromwell's conquest of Ireland and Scotland led to the fullest political integration of the islands of Britain and Ireland ever achieved and to a permanent and disastrous transfer of almost half the land mass of Ireland from the established (Catholic) population to English (Protestant) colonists. As a political leader, his late but convinced conversion to the cause of regicide was crucial to stiffening the will of his colleagues in the army and a minority of civilian politicians to put King Charles I on trial for treason against the people of England, for securing his conviction, and for carrying out the public execution (January 30, 1649). As head of the army, Cromwell carried out a series of coups d'état, and he set up a series of constitutional experiments whose common purposes were the establishment of "liberty for all varieties of Protestants" and social justice.

Although in the autumn of 1653 he seems to have avoided taking personal power, by the end of the year he had consented to being made head of state, under the title Lord Protector. He was later to decline a parliamentary offer of the Crown, but his regime increasingly took on the outward trappings of monarchy. He was driven by an absolute conviction that he was God's chosen instrument, called like Gideon or Moses in the Old Testament from a humble background on the fringes of gentry. He once said that he was not "wedded and glued to forms of government," and he clearly believed that all existing political and ecclesiastical structures were infected by the "corruptions of the flesh" and that it was God's will that they be overthrown and replaced by new forms that God would reveal to the "saints," men (and perhaps women) who represented "the various forms of godliness in this nation." As a result, Cromwell was committed to permitting freedom of religious worship and expression. His credentials as one wholly committed to the destruction of ancient constitutionalism and of the principle that membership in the national church was a duty of citizenship are undoubted; the extent to which personal ambition and social conservatism weakened his commitment to the more democratic and egalitarian aspects of the 1649 revolution remains highly contentious.

JOHN MORRILL

BIBLIOGRAPHY

Gaunt, Peter. *Oliver Cromwell.* Oxford: Blackwell, 1995.

Morrill, John S. *Oliver Cromwell and the English Revolution.* Harlow: Addison Wesley Longman, 1990.

Roots, Ivan A. *The Speeches of Oliver Cromwell.* London: Everyman Classics, 1989.

DENG XIAOPING

Deng (1904–1997) was a leading figure in the Chinese communist revolutionary movement for more than fifty years, serving as China's paramount ruler from 1978 to 1997. He introduced pragmatic economic reforms that gave China one of the world's most impressive growth rates and raised the living standards of more people in less time than in all of history. Politically he broke with the radical ideological politics of Mao Zedong's era, although he steadfastly resisted any changes that would have weakened the Communist Party's monopoly on power or challenged China's official ideology of Marxism-Leninism. His resistance to political liberalization culminated in his decision to order the Chinese army to fire on the students and workers demonstrating peacefully in Tiananmen Square on June 4, 1989.

Deng was the eldest son of the leading family of a rural town in Sichuan Province. His father, who wanted his son to have a modern education, sent Deng when he was only twelve years old to Chongqing for tutoring. Four years later Deng was selected to go to France to participate in a work-study program. There he lived with fellow Chinese students, including Zhou Enlai, who were among the founders of the Chinese Communist Party. As a sixteen-year-old he was by far the youngest among them, but he insisted on assuming adult responsibilities as a working member of their communist cell. Deng's introduction to communism thus differed significantly from that of other first-generation Chinese communists. Many of them came to communism as a consequence of their quests for solutions to China's modernization problems, while for Deng, communism was largely a pragmatic matter of fitting into an established group and skillfully performing one's assigned tasks. Thus, from the outset, Deng adopted a pragmatic, nonideological approach to communism.

After Paris, and a further year of training in Moscow, Deng returned to China to become a full-time party worker, first in the underground organization in Shanghai and then in the guerrilla base camp Mao Zedong had established in the Jiangxi Mountains. During the Long March of 1934–1935, when the Chinese communist armies retreated to their Shaanxi Province stronghold, Mao came to appreciate Deng's quick and practical mind. Deng spent much of the war against Japan as a leading political commissar in the guerrilla headquarters of the communist Eighth Route Army.

After the communists came to power in 1949, Deng quickly demonstrated his administrative skills. During inner-party factional struggles he was purged three times, but each time he was called back because of his recognized administrative abilities. Deng was out of favor when Mao Zedong died in 1976, but he was quickly rehabilitated by Hua Guofeng, Mao's designated successor, and called to Beijing to help run the country. Deng easily superseded Hua and quick-

DENG XIAOPING

ly reversed the national course by opening China to the outside world and initiating pragmatic economic policies, which turned out in many respects to be more revolutionary than Mao's ideological politics.

The hallmark of Deng's rule was pragmatism in the economic realm, crystallized in his famous dictum: It doesn't matter whether the cat is white or black as long as it catches mice. The cornerstone of his economic reforms in agriculture was the decision to break up the collective communes and replace them with a "family responsibility system" in which each family worked its own plot of land and was allowed to sell for personal profit any production above a set quota. In industry the major shift was away from the huge state-owned enterprises and toward either privately or collectively owned enterprises and joint ventures with foreigners. Deng also encouraged advances in science and technology, especially by allowing thousands of Chinese students to go abroad to study. He further demonstrated his pragmatism by his formula of "one country, two systems" for the reversion of Hong Kong to Chinese rule, which pledged that the people of Hong Kong could continue their capitalistic system for fifty years.

The secret of Deng's revolutionary reforms was that he allowed the Chinese people to assume greater responsibility for their economic life, while he held to a gradualist approach in policy changes. The elimination of the rural communes was rather abrupt, but in industry he followed a more cautious path. Consequently, at the time of his death the state-owned enterprises had not been fully reformed, leaving questions as to the sustainability of China's economic modernization. On balance, however, Deng's policies, although labeled only as "reforms," transformed China in ways that seem at least as profound as the numerous other revolutions in modern Chinese history.

See also *Mao Zedong.*

LUCIAN W. PYE

BIBLIOGRAPHY

Evans, Richard. *Deng Xiaoping and the Making of Modern China.* London: Hamish Hamilton, 1993.

Franz, Uli. *Deng Xiaoping.* Boston: Harcourt Brace and Jovanovich, 1988.

Goodman, David, S. G. *Deng Xiaoping.* London: Cardinal Press, 1990.

Yang, Benjamin. *Deng, A Political Biography.* Armonk, N.Y.: M.E. Sharpe, 1998.

Frantz Omar Fanon

Fanon (1925–1961) is regarded by many as the most original black political thinker of the twentieth century. Born in Martinique, a Caribbean island that was already becoming part of metropolitan France, he was destined to fight one day to prevent Algeria from being similarly absorbed into metropolitan France.

Fanon was educated in Martinique and France, finally qualifying in medicine and psychiatry at the University of Lyon. From 1953 to 1956 he served as head of the psychiatry department of Blida-Joinville Hospital in Algeria, which was then officially regarded as part of France. Yet he was from 1954 secretly committed to a movement in favor of Algeria's independence.

He joined the National Liberation Front (FLN) of Algeria in opposition to French rule. In 1956 he became editor of the FLN newspaper, *El-Moudjahid,* which was published in Tunis. In 1960 the FLN's Provisional Government appointed Fanon its ambassador to the recently independent Republic of Ghana. There is some speculation that Fanon's exposure to Kwame Nkrumah's Ghana three years after Ghana's independence deepened Fanon's understanding of the temptations of power for the postcolonial elite, and the resulting malaise of aggrandizement and alienation.

Fanon's main contributions to political thought are in the role of violence, the impact of cultural alienation and dependency, the nature of anticolonial nationalism, and the malaise of the postcolonial elites.

On the role of violence as redemption, Fanon's views need to be studied alongside the Christian concept of the crucifixion. Fanon was convinced that anticolonial violence was a healing experience for the colonial freedom fighter. "At the level of individuals, violence is a cleansing force. It frees the native from his inferiority complex, from his despair and inaction" *(The Wretched of the Earth,* 94). Although the crucifixion of Jesus was an act of violence, it was also doctrinally an act of atonement and redemption. There is a convergence between Fanon's thought and Christian doctrine in this respect.

Although he died a few months before Algeria gained independence, Fanon had acted out some of his ideas by participating in the Algerian anticolonial war (1954–1962) on the side of the Algerian revolutionaries. Fanon studied at close quarters the psychology of violence generated by a clash of nationalisms—French and Algerian. As a psychiatrist he also studied trauma cases of the brutal war, which in the end cost more than a million lives.

And yet Fanon was among the first to identify the dual malaise of postcolonial elites. One part of the dual malaise is externally oriented— a constant effort to imitate the bourgeoisie of the former colonial power, thus manifesting acute cultural dependency (the "Black Skin, White

Mask" syndrome). As a psychiatrist Fanon prefers to see this cultural dependency as a neurosis and a form of alienation. The second part of the dual malaise is self-oriented—the pursuit of self-aggrandizement and elite-promotion. The old anticolonial fighters become what Fanon calls "that company of profiteers impatient for the returns."

Cultural dependence and cultural alienation may also take the form of excessive reliance on the language of the imperial power. Fanon lamented the supreme status accorded the French language in Algeria by France. But he lamented even more the Algerian elite's complicity in this linguistic servitude. Fanon regarded the imperial language as an index of power. He himself was a child of Martinique, and was therefore a product of such a configuration between language and power. Fanon was sensitive to the positive role that women often play in revolutions. By being underestimated by the enemy, women can penetrate enemy ranks more easily. A woman can turn her own weakness into a weapon. Fanon draws attention to how Algerian Muslim women used the veil as camouflage for grenades.

Fanon's most influential book, *Les Damne's de la terre* (1961), was published in English as *The Wretched of the Earth* (1965). This book established Fanon not only as a social thinker but also as a prophetic figure. He was widely interpreted as urging colonized peoples to submit themselves to "collective catharsis" through revolutionary violence against colonialism.

ALI A. MAZRUI

BIBLIOGRAPHY

Fanon, Frantz. *Black Skin, White Masks.* New York: Grove Press, 1967.
———. *A Dying Colonialism.* New York: Grove Press, 1967.
———. *Toward the African Revolution.* New York: Grove Press, 1969.
———. *The Wretched of the Earth.* New York: Grove Press, 1968.

BENJAMIN FRANKLIN

B enjamin Franklin (1706–1790), printer, postmaster, scientist, essayist, politician, and diplomat, led the movement to defend the rights of the British colonies in North America, 1757–1775, and then signed the Declaration of American Independence, 1776; the French Alliance, 1778; the peace treaty with Great Britain, 1783; and the Constitution of 1787. He was the only American to sign all four basic documents.

The first fifty years of Franklin's life, described in his famous autobiography, though suffused with apparent loyalty to the British Empire in which he lived, in fact placed him firmly on the road to revolution. As a youth growing up in Puritan Boston and then as a rising tradesman in Philadelphia, he was a self-made, independent-minded man used to managing his own life and accustomed to the opportunity available in what was for its day an unusually open society. Reading such writings as Plutarch's *Lives,* John Locke's works, the *Cato's Letters* of John Trenchard and Thomas Gordon placed Franklin's thinking squarely in the civic republican and radical Whig outlooks well-known in Boston and Philadelphia. Thus in thought and lifestyle he was ill-prepared to be a contented resident of a colony of a distant and increasingly controlling mother country.

His active life as a foe of tyranny began in Pennsylvania in the 1750s, when he led opposition to the efforts by the proprietary Penn fam-

BENJAMIN FRANKLIN

ily to impose its will on the colonial legislature of which he was a member. There he recruited and led militia forces that were unsanctioned by the Penns' executive authority in Pennsylvania. Thomas Penn wrote from London that Franklin was "a dangerous man . . . I should be very glad he inhabited another country, as I believe him a very uneasy spirit, . . . a sort of Tribune of the People." When Franklin left for London in 1757 to explain his dispute with the proprietors to British authorities, he was already in a rebellious frame of mind.

Living in London, 1757–1775, Franklin opposed first proprietary tyranny in Pennsylvania (ironically trying to substitute for it Royal government of the province) and then the measures of the British government that from the Stamp Act (1765) to the so-called Coercive Acts (1774) increasingly and forcefully imposed British authority from New England to Georgia. Franklin at first sought relief from Parliament and from the king's ministers, but, ignored and humiliated by those in power, by 1775 he had become so disgusted with "the extreme corruption prevalent among all orders of men in this old rotten state" that he feared "more Mischief than Benefit from a closer Union" with the realm of George III. He left England in 1775 ready for independence.

Back in America, in his seventies, Franklin busied himself with the affairs of what he hoped would be an independent nation. He helped plan details of supply and training for Pennsylvania's militia regiments, took part in debates in the Continental Congress, made a winter journey to Canada to seek (without success) its participation in the Revolution, drafted articles of confederation for the colonies, drew guidelines for revolutionary diplomacy in Europe, and served on the Committee to Draft the Declaration of Independence, which he signed in July 1776. Declared a traitor with a price on his head by George III, Franklin remained steadfast in his revolutionary stance, asserting, in accord with Thomas Paine's *Common Sense,* that the cause of the new United States was "the cause of all Mankind." Along with Thomas Jefferson, Paine, and John Adams, Franklin's was the authentic voice of the American Revolution.

A perilous sea voyage across the North Atlantic in December 1776 brought Franklin to France, where for nine years he sustained the Revolution. As minister to France, he negotiated the important French alliance of 1778 and managed repeatedly, with great tact, to persuade Foreign Minister Charles Gravier Vergennes of France to loan the vital cash that kept George Washington's armies in the field. Then with John Adams and John Jay, he negotiated the favorable 1783 treaty of peace with Great Britain, granting the United States standing as a fully independent nation whose western border was the Mississippi River. Heralded on both sides of the Atlantic as, along with Washington, the foremost hero of the Revolution, he had completed the most successful diplomatic mission in American history.

Home in Philadelphia, eighty years old and suffering from a painful bladder stone, Franklin nonetheless concluded his revolutionary career by taking an active part in nation-building. He was elected president of Pennsylvania, attended every day of the Constitutional Convention of 1787, making crucial conciliatory proposals, took part in the ratification contest, and spent his last public energies opposing slavery. He died in April 1790, a few months after having congratulated a French friend on the beginning of their revolution in favor of the principles of the American Revolution.

See also *Adams, John; Jefferson, Thomas; Locke, John; Paine, Thomas.*

RALPH KETCHAM

BIBLIOGRAPHY

Ketcham, Ralph, ed. *The Political Thought of Benjamin Franklin.* Indianapolis, Ind.: Bobbs-Merrill, 1965.

Labaree, Leonard, et al., eds. *The Papers of Benjamin Franklin.* New Haven, Conn.: Yale University Press, 1959. 31 vols. to date (papers of 1708–1780).

Van Doren, Carl. *Benjamin Franklin.* New York: Viking Press, 1938.

Wright, Esmond. *Franklin of Philadelphia.* Cambridge, Mass.: Harvard University Press, 1986.

MAHATMA GANDHI

Gandhi (1869–1948) was the greatest leader of India's national movement and one of the great world revolutionaries of the twentieth century. Born in Gujarat, Mahatma ("Great Soul") Mohandas Karamchand Gandhi went to London to study law at the Inner Temple and was called to the bar in 1891. After returning home he accepted a job in South Africa, representing a Muslim firm there. He suffered harsh racial discrimination, including being thrown out of a first-class train carriage by an English officer. That violent act transformed him into a revolutionary leader of the entire South African Indian community. Gandhi spent two decades in South Africa, where he developed and tested his *satyagraha* ("hold onto the truth") technique of nonviolent noncooperation, later used with great success against the British in India.

Satya means "truth," and to Gandhi, "truth is God." He also asked his followers in every struggle to accept *ahimsa* ("nonviolence"), arguing that if *satya* is joined to *ahimsa,* "we can move the world," for the positive side of *ahimsa* is "love." Gandhi's other important Yogic method of struggle, also harking back to ancient India's Vedic and Upanishadic times, was *tapas* ("self-imposed suffering"). Yoga is the oldest form of religious and philosophic thought in India. Great soul and yogi that he was, Gandhi pitted his powers of truth, love, and suffering against those of the mightiest empire on earth at the time, and he won.

His first nationwide *satyagraha* movement was launched against British India's "Black" Acts, imposing extensions of martial law after World War I upon the land that had done so much to help the British win that war. The Punjab, scene

MAHATMA GANDHI

of a massacre by British troops in April 1919, became the crucible of revolutionary Indian nationalism, and Mahatma Gandhi its new national hero and revered leader. The cold-blooded killing of hundreds of unarmed Indians and the gross atrocities that followed British imposition of martial law throughout Punjab Province convinced Gandhi of the "satanic" nature of British rule and modern Western industrial society, which were built on violence and oppression. He called for a return to ancient rural Indian values, to India's village communities, *ashrams,* several of which he started and which survive to this day as exemplars of Gandhian communism, where each contributes what he or she does best for the benefit of all.

Sarvodaya ("the uplift of all") was the name Gandhi gave to his method of social reform. He helped revive interest in and use of Indian handicrafts and made daily spinning and weaving of cotton an integral part of his life and the lives of his followers. He was also determined to put an end to Hindu "untouchability" and struggled against orthodox upper-caste Hindu Brahman leaders to get them to open temples to "untouchables" and to open their homes as well, as he always did. Gandhi's crusade against untouchability bore fruit; it was abolished by law in India's constitution after 1950, and in 1997 India's first ex-untouchable was inaugurated as the country's tenth president. Gandhi never called for the abolition of India's caste system, however, insisting that people were born with differing strengths and weaknesses, some to preach and teach, others to engage in business, and still others to perform hard physical labor.

Gandhi's most famous *satyagraha* movement was his campaign against the British tax on salt, which he led in 1930. His last campaign was his call on the British to "quit India" in 1942, which resulted in his last long incarceration. Gandhi never accepted the idea of partition between Pakistan and India, calling it "vivisection of the mother," and his last years of life were mostly bitter, ending in his tragic assassination at the hands of a hate-crazed Brahman, who called the saintly Father of India "Mohammad," instead of Mahatma, since he read passages from the Qur'an at several of his evening prayer meetings. But to Mahatma Gandhi, all great religions taught much the same truth, for each appealed to God, as he did, trying to make the world a safer, saner, more loving place in which all peoples could work together helping one another survive and enjoy longer life.

See also *Jinnah, Mohammad Ali; Nehru, Jawaharlal.*

STANLEY WOLPERT

BIBLIOGRAPHY

Brown, Judith M. *Gandhi: Prisoner of Hope.* New Haven, Conn.: Yale University Press, 1993.

Erikson, Erik H. *Gandhi's Truth: On the Origins of Militant Nonviolence.* New York: Putnam, 1969.

Gandhi, M. K. *An Autobiography: The Story of My Experiments with Truth.* Boston: Beacon Press, 1993.

Tendulkar, D. G. *Mahatma: Life of Mohandas Karamchand Gandhi.* 8 vols. Bombay: Jhaveri and Tendulkar, 1952–1954.

GIUSEPPE GARIBALDI

During his lifetime (1807–1882) Garibaldi, a guerrilla fighter and revolutionary, became a popular, almost legendary figure because of his heroic exploits in South America and his leading role in the unification of Italy.

Born in Nice, then part of the Italian kingdom of Sardinia and Piedmont, Garibaldi led the adventurous life of a merchant seaman as a young man. In 1833, however, he met Giuseppe Mazzini, leader of the republican organization Young Italy, and dedicated himself to the creation of a united Italy. Implicated in a republican conspiracy against the king, he fled to South America and was sentenced to death in his absence. From 1836 to 1848 he led a contingent of Italians fighting for liberty for Brazil and Uruguay. The poncho he wore in Montevideo (and later the red shirt) became his distinctive style of clothing and an integral part of his personality cult.

He returned to Italy to participate in the revolutions that swept Europe in 1848. Despite his republicanism, he was prepared to support the king of Piedmont against a threat from Austria, which controlled northeastern Italy. Garibaldi was never a rigid idealist like Mazzini but a man of action. Rebuffed by the royalists, he fought with his volunteers until the king signed an armistice with Austria. He then went to Rome to defend Mazzini's short-lived Roman republic. Although Garibaldi was defeated in the summer

GIUSEPPE GARIBALDI

of 1849, his heroism and epic retreat won him lasting fame.

Exiled again, he worked briefly in a New York candle factory before resuming his career as a merchant captain. Disillusioned with Mazzini, he returned to Italy in 1858, where he began an uneasy relationship with Camillo Cavour, the Piedmontese premier. When war with Austria broke out in 1859, he led his volunteers in a successful guerrilla campaign in the Alps. Cavour's surrender of Nice to France, Piedmont's ally, embittered Garibaldi.

In May 1860, with most of central and northern Italy liberated, Garibaldi launched a famous expedition of his red-shirted volunteers, known as "The Thousand," rapidly conquering Sicily and Naples. Proclaiming himself temporary dictator, he promised social reforms that led millions of southern peasants to revere him as a savior. Fearful of Garibaldi's radicalism and his plan to seize Rome, which was defended by a French garrison, Cavour sent Victor Emmanuel II and the royal army south to confront him. Civil war was avoided when Garibaldi agreed to surrender his conquests to Victor Emmanuel, now king of an almost unified Italy. Garibaldi then retired to the island of Caprera, which he had purchased, declining President Abraham Lincoln's offer of a command in the American Civil War.

He made abortive attempts to capture Rome in 1862 and 1867. Ironically, these failures only enhanced his prestige. In 1866 he again fought against Austria and in 1870 supported republican France against Prussia. That same year Rome was finally captured by the new Italian state but, like Mazzini, Garibaldi could only deplore the methods used to create the new Italy. The people had been largely marginalized by politicians, generals, and diplomats.

JOHN WHITTAM

BIBLIOGRAPHY

Hearder, Harry. *Italy in the Age of the Risorgimento, 1790–1870.* London: Longman, 1983.

Hibbert, Christopher. *Garibaldi and His Enemies.* London: Penguin, 1987.

Mack Smith, Denis, ed. *Garibaldi: A Portrait in Documents.* Florence: Passigli Editori, 1982.

———. *The Making of Italy, 1796–1870.* New York: Harper and Row, 1968.

MIKHAIL GORBACHEV

Gorbachev (1931–), born in the village of Privolnoye in Stavropol Province, a fertile land of the north Caucasus, inadvertently helped bring the 1917 Russian Revolution to an early close. The father of Soviet *perestroika,* or restructuring, he experienced a life trajectory resembling that of millions of his compatriots: a middling-peasant family background; the somersault of the rural social order with collectivization; the arrest (and release) in the Terror of his collective-farm-chairman grandfather; the (brief) deportation to Siberia of his other grandfather; the World War II front for his father (who somehow survived); the Nazi occupation for the women and children left behind in the village; and Communist Youth League (Komsomol) service, migration to the city, and Communist Party membership for Mikhail. He rose, and despite the devastating hardships the country rose along with him—he just got further than most, only to bring everything down.

Like his father and grandfather, Gorbachev might have become a farmer, but Stalin's upheavals of the 1930s brought—besides death and destruction—expanded educational opportunities. Mikhail completed eight grades in the village, two more in the district center twenty kilometers away, and set his sights on a university education, aiming not for the local ones but for Moscow. With a peasant-worker background, a pupil's silver medal, a high state award for help-

ing bring in the harvest, and precocious candidate membership in the party, Gorbachev was accepted, and in 1950 made the leap to the Soviet capital. During his five years at Moscow State University's law faculty, the Stavropol hayseed came into contact with a handful of erudite professors as well as members of the Moscow cultural elite, met and married Raisa Titorenko, mourned the death of Stalin, and wrote a thesis setting out socialism's superiority to capitalism. Posted upon graduation to the Stavropol procu-

MIKHAIL GORBACHEV

racy, Gorbachev switched almost immediately to a position in the Komsomol bureaucracy and set about organizing discussion groups in remote settlements in order, as he explains in his autobiography, to "fling open a window to the world." As he climbed the Komsomol ladder, Nikita Khrushchev's de-Stalinization provided a boost. But Gorbachev writes that survivalist functionaries sabotaged the Moscow-instigated reforms. In 1964 the top party elite removed Khrushchev in a conspiracy.

Khrushchev became a memory, local officials advanced higher, and Gorbachev was shifted in 1966 to the party bureaucracy. By 1970 he had climbed to first secretary for Stavropol Province. Because his fief happened to be a southern region where the central elite maintained sanatoria, he played host to many top figures in the leadership, including KGB chief Yuri Andropov. It was Andropov who in 1978 arranged Gorbachev's transfer to Moscow as the new chief of the Central Committee agricultural department. This assignment was followed in 1980 by promotion to full membership in the Politburo. Andropov, who succeeded Leonid Brezhnev in 1982, placed Gorbachev in charge of new appointments, allowing his protégé to congratulate personally those marked for elevation. Andropov was ill, however, and upon his death in 1984 the old guard blocked Gorbachev's path. Yet once the invalid Konstantin Chernenko also passed away, in 1985, the surviving septua- and octogenarians had little choice but to anoint the one relative youth in their midst. With the support of the KGB (Andropov's old power base) as well as officials in the Central Committee and economic ministries whose appointments he had overseen, the fifty-four-year-old Gorbachev became general secretary for what looked like a very long time.

As head of the party, and later Soviet president, Gorbachev led the country on a quest for reformed socialism, but his program of *perestroika* culminated in the autoliquidation of both socialism and the USSR. Unable to control or counter the forces he had helped set in motion, he officially disbanded the USSR and stepped down in December 1991. However, Gorbachev left the deepest of impressions on his times, above all, in the area of disarmament.

STEPHEN KOTKIN

BIBLIOGRAPHY

Brown, Archie, ed. *The Soviet Union: A Biographical Dictionary.* London: Weidenfeld and Nicholson, 1990.
Gorbachev, Mikhail. *Memoirs.* New York: Doubleday, 1995.
Medvedev, Zhores. *Gorbachev.* New York: Norton, 1986.
Wieczynski, Joseph, ed. *The Gorbachev Bibliography, 1985–1991.* New York: Norman Ross, 1996.

ANTONIO GRAMSCI

G ramsci (1891–1937), one of the greatest Marxist theorists, labor activists, and political journalists of the twentieth century, was born in the small town of Ales in Sardinia. Influenced by Karl Marx, Benedetto Croce, and the Italian Marxist Antonio Labriola, he joined the Italian Socialist Party in 1913.

During World War I he became deeply radicalized, investing the bulk of his energies in the militant Turin working-class movement associated with both the emergent council formations and the Italian Socialist Party. As a party journalist, Gramsci hoped to articulate the theories of the spontaneous popular movements of Turin. Sharply disillusioned when party leadership failed to take advantage of revolutionary opportunities during 1916–1919, Gramsci and other leading Italian radicals founded the Italian Communist Party in 1921, with Gramsci as one of its guiding intellectual and political figures.

In 1922 Gramsci went to Moscow to serve as the Italian Communist Party representative to the Comintern. He returned to Italy just as fascism was consolidating power, and in May 1924 he was elected to parliament as a party delegate. With the right on the ascendancy, Gramsci was arrested by the regime of Benito Mussolini in November 1926. From late 1926 until just before his death in April 1937 Gramsci was confined to prison, often kept in isolation, where he suffered mounting ill health, loneliness, and detachment from the world of everyday politics.

ANTONIO GRAMSCI

Despite the ordeal of prison, Gramsci was able to read and write—and he indeed wrote prolifically. It was during these years that Gramsci compiled his various notes, which were eventually smuggled out by his sister-in-law, Tatiana Schucht. Systematically assembled only after World War II, these notes would come to be known as the *Prison Notebooks,* a collection of treatises that would soon be famous around the world. International pressure mounted for Gramsci's release, and he was finally given his freedom in Rome in April 1937. But by this time he was so physically and mentally broken that he died just five days after his release.

The body of Gramsci's intellectual contribution includes his early writings from the Italian Socialist Party and the journal *The New Order* (1914–1920), his prolific interventions during the Italian Communist Party years (1921–1926), and above all the *Prison Notebooks*. The *Notebooks,* which have been translated into every major language, covered amazingly diverse topics—Italian history, political affairs, education, culture, philosophy, theory of the state, and his illuminating discourses into the realm of (Marxist) political strategy. A major theme underlying his otherwise fragmented notes was the task of forging a Marxist theory and strategy adequate to the requirements of socialist transformation in the advanced industrial setting.

In the late twentieth century Gramsci became probably the most widely known of the Western Marxists who sought to free classical Marxism of its economism and determinism and who looked to a more democratic, egalitarian revolutionary process than was typical of the Soviet and other Leninist experiences. Gramsci's most famous concept was that of ideological hegemony, which pointed toward the complex forms of ideological and cultural domination that helped reproduce capitalism, especially in highly industrialized societies. To combat the spread of capitalism, Gramsci insisted on the necessity of a broad cultural war of position designed to renew civil society—that would join the more conventional war of position associated with the struggle for political and economic power. Gramsci expected influential critical thinkers immersed in the everyday life of workers to lead the struggle.

Gramsci's legacy is a powerful and multifaceted one that lives on within and without the Marxist tradition. Throughout the 1980s and 1990s Gramscian discourse entered into and helped shape a number of modern academic disciplines, including sociology, history, film studies, literature, urban planning, and anthropology. Gramsci's ideas have spread throughout the world, far outlasting the regime that sought to silence him.

See also *Marx, Karl, and Friedrich Engels.*

CARL BOGGS

BIBLIOGRAPHY

Adamson, Walter. *Hegemony and Revolution.* Berkeley: University of California Press, 1980.

Boggs, Carl. *The Two Revolutions: Antonio Gramsci and the Dilemmas of Western Marxism.* Boston: South End Press, 1984.

Fiori, Giuseppe. *Antonio Gramsci: Life of a Revolutionary.* New York: E. R. Dutton, 1971.

ERNESTO "CHE" GUEVARA

ERNESTO "CHE" GUEVARA ADDRESSES THE INTER-AMERICAN ECONOMIC AND SOCIAL CONFERENCE IN PUNTA DEL ESTE, URUGUAY, AUGUST 8, 1961.

G uevara (1928–1967) was born in Rosario, Argentina. A charismatic Marxist revolutionary, he was instrumental in helping Fidel Castro seize power and install a socialist system in Cuba. As a radical minister in Castro's government, he advocated the spread of socialism and sponsored numerous armed guerrilla campaigns against U.S.-backed governments in Latin America before leaving Cuba to spearhead efforts himself in Bolivia, where at the age of thirty-nine he was killed by his military captors.

The eldest of five children born to a middle-class Argentine family, Ernesto Guevara de la Serna studied medicine and obtained a medical degree in 1953, but after leaving Argentina and witnessing the 1954 U.S.-backed military overthrow of Guatemala's leftist president, Jacobo Arbenz Guzmán, he was drawn to radical politics. He joined the 1956–1958 revolutionary war led by Castro against Cuba's dictator, Fulgencio Batista, became one of Castro's closest aides, and earned renown as the guerrilla commander known as "Che."

Following the rebel victory in January 1959, Guevara helped consolidate Castro's power by presiding over revolutionary purge trials of the defeated security forces and organizing Cuba's new Revolutionary Armed Forces, civilian National Militias, and state security apparatus. He also played a leading role in brokering Castro's eventual political alliance with the Cuban Communist Party and in drafting the agrarian reform that nationalized large private landholdings and foreign-owned properties, paving the way for a state-run Cuban economy.

An early advocate of Castro's confrontation

with the United States, which wielded sweeping economic and political influence in Cuba, Guevara was also a principal catalyst of the new links forged between Havana and Moscow. He traveled widely as Castro's emissary, seeking trade and diplomatic ties in meetings with such leaders as Nikita Khrushchev, Mao Zedong, Gamal Abdel Nasser, and Jawaharlal Nehru. As Cuba's national bank president Guevara increased state control of the economy, and as minister of industries he lobbied for the island's rapid industrialization in order to reduce its reliance on sugar exports.

By the mid-1960s, however, faced with Cuba's increasing dependency on the Soviet Union and thwarted in his ambitious industrialization campaign, Guevara had soured on the Soviet model of socialism. In a February 1965 speech he accused the Kremlin of engaging in "exploitative" relationships with developing nations and called for a new socialist "solidarity" in the common struggle against the capitalist West. In his essay, *Socialism and the New Man in Cuba,* published after his personal break with the USSR, Guevara extolled the notion of "heroic" self-sacrifice as a means of creating a true socialist consciousness. During this time he also developed the *foco* theory of guerrilla warfare and revolution, based on his reading of the Cuban events of 1956–1958.

In April 1965 Guevara left Cuba to assist Marxist-led revolutionaries fighting for power in the former Belgian Congo, but his forces were quickly routed. In 1966 he traveled to Bolivia to spark what he hoped would become a "continental revolution" in Latin America. Instead, after an abortive eleven-month guerrilla campaign, he was wounded, captured, and on October 9, 1967, executed on the orders of the Bolivian president, Gen. René Barrientos, in the tiny mountain hamlet of La Higuera.

See also *Castro, Fidel.*

JON LEE ANDERSON

BIBLIOGRAPHY

Anderson, Jon Lee. *Che Guevara: A Revolutionary Life.* New York: Grove Press, 1997.

Castaneda, Jorge G. *Companero: The Life and Death of Che Guevara.* Translated by Marina Castaneda. New York: Alfred A. Knopf, 1997.

Guevara, Ernesto Che. *The Bolivian Diary of Ernesto Che Guevara.* Edited by Mary-Alice Waters. New York: Pathfinder Press, 1994.

———. *Episodes of the Cuban Revolutionary War, 1956–1958.* Edited by Mary-Alice Waters. New York: Pathfinder Press, 1996.

Taibo, Paco Ignacio, II. *Ernesto Guevara: Also Known as Che.* New York: St. Martin's Press, 1997.

VÁCLAV HAVEL

avel (1936–), playwright and former dissident, became president of Czechoslovakia following the fall of communism and of the Czech Republic after the dissolution of Czechoslovakia. A long-term advocate of human rights, Havel played a key role in bringing about the end of communism in Czechoslovakia in 1989.

Havel was born to a wealthy family in Prague. After the establishment of communist rule in Czechoslovakia in 1948, however, this was a stigma. Due to his family background he was forced to take night courses while working to finish high school. He studied briefly at a technical university and completed his education as an external student in the Theatre Department of the Academy of Fine Arts. He worked as a stage hand at the ABC Theatre in Prague and later at the Theatre on the Balustrade. There his plays, including *The Garden Party, The Memorandum,* and *The Increased Difficulty of Concentration,* were an important part of Prague's developing theater of the absurd. In the mid-to-late 1960s Havel was active in trying to liberalize the official Writers Union.

After the Warsaw Pact invasion of Czechoslovakia in August 1968, Havel could no longer work as a playwright. His plays were banned in Czechoslovakia. However, some of his plays gained acclaim abroad. Havel also wrote several politically oriented books, including *Living in Truth* and *Letters to Olga.*

VÁCLAV HAVEL

In 1977 Havel became one of the founders of the human rights movement Charter 77 and the Committee for the Defense of the Unjustly Persecuted. He continued to be a leading figure in the opposition in Czechoslovakia in the 1970s and 1980s. Havel was arrested numerous times and served several jail terms. Sentenced to four and a half years in jail in 1979, he was released in March 1983. He was again jailed for several months in the spring of 1989 for participating in a peaceful demonstration in January 1989 in honor of the Czechoslovak student, Jan Palach, who burned himself to death in January 1969 in protest against the Soviet invasion.

When mass demonstrations developed in Czechoslovakia after the November 17, 1989, beating of peaceful student demonstrators, Havel and other dissidents took the lead in founding Civic Forum, the organization that led mass protests and negotiated the end of communist rule with the regime. Havel quickly emerged as the main symbol of the so-called Velvet Revolution that peacefully ousted the communist system. Seen as the moral voice of his country, he was elected president of Czechoslovakia in December 1989 by the parliament, which still had a majority of Communist deputies.

As a political leader, Havel attempted to put his ideals into practice. The effort was noticeable in his support of Czechoslovakia's return to Europe and focus on regional cooperation with other central European countries. Under his leadership, Czechoslovakia became a member of the Council of Europe and signed an association agreement with the European Union. Havel negotiated the withdrawal of Soviet troops from Czechoslovak territory and worked to restore good relations with the United States. Originally an advocate of a pan-European security structure, he became an ardent supporter of NATO membership.

Havel was unable to prevent the break-up of Czechoslovakia. Unwilling to preside over the break-up of the Czechoslovakian federation, he resigned as president of Czechoslovakia after the Slovak government declared Slovakia's sovereignty in July 1992.

Havel was elected president of the Czech Republic in February 1993 and was reelected in January 1998. Although the powers of the Czech presidency are not as great as those of his previous position, Havel's stature as a world figure has allowed him to have more influence in Czech affairs than the formal powers of the Czech presidency alone would suggest.

Sharon L. Wolchik

BIBLIOGRAPHY

Havel, Václav. *Disturbing the Peace.* New York: Vintage Books, 1990.

Kriseová, Eda. *Václav Havel: The Authorized Biography.* New York: Pharos Books, 1993.

PATRICK HENRY

Henry (1736–1799), revolutionary leader, lawyer, and orator, was born in Hanover County, Virginia, the son of John Henry, a planter and middle-level member of the Virginia gentry. His schooling was limited, and in the 1750s he failed at storekeeping and farming. He then pursued a career in the law, and in 1760, after brief study, he was authorized to practice law in the county courts. Henry was almost immediately successful.

In 1763 he took on a case that later was called the "Parsons' Cause." He appeared for the defense and invoked compact theory, asserting that the original compact between the king and people, protection on the one hand and obedience on the other, had been broken when George III, by disallowing a good law, the Two Penny Act, had forfeited the right to his subjects' compliance. The argument was popular, and it was enhanced by the young lawyer's oratorical gifts.

The Parsons' Cause brought him recognition and was, no doubt, crucial in his 1765 election to the House of Burgesses in the midst of the Stamp Act controversy. Parliament was levying for the first time a direct tax on its American colonies. The tax was widely opposed on the grounds that Parliament could regulate trade but not impose internal taxes—a view expressed strongly when the House of Burgesses adopted Henry's Stamp Act Resolves. In supporting the resolves he declared that Caesar had his Brutus, Charles I his

Cromwell, and George III might profit by their example. Only four of the original seven resolutions were approved, but all were published widely in colonial newspapers, and Henry emerged as an unremitting opponent of British policies.

In 1773 Henry was one of those who worked to establish intercolonial committees of correspondence. He was elected in 1774 and 1775 as

PATRICK HENRY

one of Virginia's delegates to the Continental Congress. Thereafter he held no continental or national offices, but in Virginia he remained active. In March 1775 he pushed through the second Virginia Convention resolutions providing for military preparedness and reportedly concluded one speech with his famous remark "give me liberty or give me death." In May 1776 his version of a resolution proposing independence was approved by the fifth Virginia Convention, and soon thereafter he was elected the new state's first governor, a post he held from 1776 to 1779 and from 1784 to 1786. He was Virginia's most popular politician.

Henry was a localist. Unlike Thomas Jefferson and James Madison, Henry had no national vision. He resisted measures to strengthen the Articles of Confederation; declined to serve in the Constitutional Convention of 1787; and opposed the new constitution. Henry feared a powerful, centralized government, which he believed would be too far removed from its citizens. In his last years he became a Federalist, expressing a desire for "order" in government, but he declined offers of national posts. He died in 1799 at his estate in Charlotte County, Virginia.

Henry's role in the American Revolution was substantial. An unmatched orator who closely identified with the people, he contributed to making the Revolution a more popular movement. And his opposition to strong central government still resonates in American political culture.

See also *Adams, Samuel.*

EMORY G. EVANS

BIBLIOGRAPHY

Beeman, Richard R. *Patrick Henry: A Biography.* New York: McGraw Hill, 1974.

Henry, William Wirt, ed. *Patrick Henry, Life Correspondence and Speeches.* 3 vols. New York: Charles Scribner's Sons, 1891.

Mayer, Henry. *A Son of Thunder: Patrick Henry and the American Republic.* Charlottesville: University Press of Virginia, 1991.

Meade, Robert D. *Patrick Henry.* 2 vols. Philadelphia: Lippincott, 1957–1969.

Adolf Hitler

Hitler (1889–1945) was guided in his political life by his pseudo-scientific understanding of race. His goal was to create a biologically pure, strong Germanic race that would use the rest of the world's races as its servants and slaves. Undesirable and inferior people would be exterminated. The Jews, in his view, were the most dangerous and polluting of all races because the Jews could infiltrate and mix with other races to weaken and destroy them.

Hitler was born in Austria and had an ordinary childhood. In 1907 he went to Vienna to become an artist but failed to get into the Academy of Fine Arts. Reduced to poverty, he picked up the anti-Semitic, German nationalist views then current in Vienna and came to blame Jews, who occupied many prominent positions in Vienna's high cultural life, for his failure. In 1913 he moved to Munich, Germany. When World War I broke out in 1914, he joined the German army. He was an exceptionally courageous, highly decorated soldier. After the defeat of 1918, he joined a small ultranationalist movement in Munich, the National Socialist German Workers' (Nazi) Party. His extraordinarily persuasive speeches and ability to attract followers quickly gained him the party's leadership.

The Nazis wanted to end the democracy imposed on Germany by the victorious allies and to regain German greatness. To do this it was necessary to rid Germany of those whom German rightists viewed as the traitors who had ruined it in 1918, particularly Jews and social democrats. The party organized uniformed gangs of street fighters, the Brown Shirts, to demonstrate and rally support for their cause. The unsettled political conditions in Germany and economic instability that led to ruinous inflation in 1923 swelled the ranks of the malcontent and fearful, and the Nazis benefited.

In 1923 Hitler attempted a coup, but the authorities in Munich held firm, and he was jailed. While in prison in 1924, he wrote his autobiographical political program, *Mein Kampf* (My Struggle). Along with ridding Germany of Jews, he called for expansion of German territory to provide living space and resources. He proposed to create a more youthful, dynamic, and warlike Germany where opportunity would be open to all pure Germans, no matter what their class origins. His vision (except for the anti-Semitism) resembled Benito Mussolini's Italian fascism in that it promised to end the alienation, class-based disputes, and corruption of modern capitalist democracy. The fascist future would be more wholesome, vigorous, and natural.

Out of jail, from 1925 to 1929 he slowly built up Nazi Party membership throughout all of Germany. The Great Depression, which began in 1929, gave him his chance. With over a quarter of the German work force unemployed, Nazi strength rose rapidly. In 1928 the Nazi Party won 3 percent of the vote in parliamentary elections; in 1930, 18 percent; and in July 1932, 37 percent,

ADOLF HITLER (FAR RIGHT), WHO BECAME CHANCELLOR OF GERMANY IN 1933 THROUGH LEGAL MEANS, TRANSFORMED GERMANY INTO A FASCIST DICTATORSHIP.

to become Germany's largest single party. Though the party's vote fell in a second election in 1932, to 32 percent of the electorate, Hitler, allied to other nationalist parties, became chancellor (prime minister) in January 1933. The combination of continuing street violence carried out by both his Brown Shirts and by communist thugs, the demand for economic and political stability, and the inability of the other parties to unite convinced German conservatives that they had no alternative to Nazi control of government.

Hitler quickly banned all opposition, ended democracy, and turned Germany into a totalitarian police state with himself as *fürher,* or leader.

State and party control was gradually imposed on industries and all key social institutions. Rearmament and a huge road-building project ended the depression. Once Hitler had stabilized Germany, Jews, the feeble minded, and homosexuals (all deemed "racially inferior") began to be herded into concentration camps, and some were killed.

But it was only in 1939, when Hitler launched World War II, that his nightmarish plan was fully implemented. His armies conquered and enslaved most of Europe: six million Jews and hundreds of thousands of Gypsies were exterminated. More than ten million Slavic (and therefore, according to Nazi doctrine, also "racially inferior") Poles, Russians, Ukrainians, and others in Eastern Europe were slaughtered or died of starvation and disease. Millions more died elsewhere in Europe.

By the end of 1941, only the Soviet Union and Great Britain held out against him. But the entry of the Americans into the war against him in 1942 and the Soviet victory at Stalingrad in the winter of 1943 turned the tide. In June 1944 the Americans and British landed in France and began to push toward Germany. Dissident German army officers tried to assassinate Hitler in July 1944 but failed.

The allies invaded Germany from east and west in 1945. On April 30, 1945, with the Soviet army a few blocks from his Berlin bunker, Hitler committed suicide after urging the world to continue the struggle against "international Jewry" and calling for Germany to "win territory in the East."

The totalitarian Nazi Germany that Hitler created had much in common with Joseph Stalin's communist state. Both leaders were guided by a revolutionary vision for a new world based on what we know to have been false science. Both deified the leader, created police states, and militarized their societies. Both exterminated their enemies by the millions. Hitler's particular legacy was at least thirty-five million civilian and military deaths and a ruined Europe.

See also *Mussolini, Benito.*

DANIEL CHIROT

BIBLIOGRAPHY

Arendt, Hannah. *The Origins of Totalitarianism.* New York: Meridian, 1958.

Bullock, Alan. *Hitler: A Study in Tyranny.* Rev. ed. New York: Harper Torchbooks, 1964.

Burleigh, Michael, and Wolfgang Wippermann. *The Racial State: Germany 1933–1945.* Cambridge: Cambridge University Press, 1991.

Fest, Joachim C. *Hitler.* New York: Vintage Books, 1975.

Kershaw, Ian. *Hitler.* London: Longman, 1991.

HO CHI MINH

Few political figures have had as much influence on the twentieth century as the Vietnamese revolutionary Ho Chi Minh (1890–1969). Born in a small village in central Vietnam at a time when his homeland was under French colonial rule, Ho became a member of the French Communist Party in the early 1920s. After studying in Moscow, he founded the first communist party in Vietnam and became the chief agent of the Comintern, an organization established in Moscow in 1919 to promote the cause of world revolution, in Southeast Asia. After World War II he led the Communist-dominated Vietminh Front (the popular name for the League for the Independence of Vietnam) in a long struggle that led to the withdrawal of the French in 1954 as a result of the Geneva Conference.

The Geneva Conference temporarily divided Vietnam into two zones—a Communist North and a non-Communist South. Ho was elected president of the Democratic Republic of Vietnam in the North, with its capital in Hanoi. The Geneva agreement called for national elections to reunify the country in 1956, but the government in the South, with U.S. backing, refused to carry them out. In response, Ho and his colleagues launched an insurgent movement in South Vietnam, which won wide popular support from the local population. In 1965 President Lyndon B. Johnson ordered the dispatch of U.S. combat troops to prevent a total Communist victory. Ho died in 1969 while the war was still under way.

By his own admission, Ho (whose real name was Nguyen Tat Thanh) was initially attracted to communism by Vladimir Ilyich Lenin's famous "Theses on the National and Colonial

HO CHI MINH (CENTER) TOURS ANTIAIRCRAFT BATTERIES IN SUBURBAN HANOI, DECEMBER 20, 1966. TO HIS RIGHT IS DEPUTY CHIEF OF STAFF GEN. VAN TIEN DUNG.

Questions" (1920), which urged support by Soviet Russia for anticolonialist movements around the world against the common enemy of Western imperialism. Like his Chinese contemporary Mao Zedong, Ho rejected the Marxist orthodoxy assigning primacy to urban insurrections and argued that revolutionary movements in Asia could not succeed without support from the oppressed rural masses in the region. Ho's distinctive approach to waging revolution—using a combination of nationalism and populism while downplaying issues related to class struggle and proletarian internationalism—was often criticized by European Marxists. But it became the foundation of Vietnamese revolutionary strategy and is widely viewed as the key to the party's final victory over the South in 1975. His personal charisma (because of his avuncular and self-effacing style, he was widely revered by many Vietnamese as "Uncle Ho") was also a major contributing factor in that victory.

In addition to his role as the guiding force behind the Vietnamese revolution, Ho Chi Minh was a leading figure in the international communist movement. He gave vocal support to the revolutionary cause throughout Asia, Africa, and Latin America, and he worked tirelessly to prevent, or minimize the impact of, the Sino-Soviet dispute, which split the communist world into contending factions during the last decade of his life.

WILLIAM J. DUIKER

BIBLIOGRAPHY

Duiker, William J. *The Communist Road to Power in Vietnam*. 2d ed. Boulder, Colo.: Westview Press, 1996.
Halberstam, David. *Ho*. New York: Knopf, 1987.
Hémery, Daniel. *Ho Chi Minh: De l'Indochine au Vietnam*. Paris: Gallimard, 1990.
Lacouture, Jean. *Ho Chi Minh: A Political Biography*. Translated by Peter Wiles. New York: Vintage, 1968.

HONG XIUQUAN

Hong (1814–1864) envisioned and led China's millenarian Taiping Rebellion (1851–1864). A member of south China's oppressed Hakka ethnic minority, Hong aspired to upward mobility through government service. Instead, his repeated failures in the state examinations and exposure to missionary Christianity in Guangzhou (Guangdong's provincial capital) precipitated, in 1837, a powerful dream. In Hong's dream, God identified Hong as Christ's younger brother and commissioned him to replace Confucian China with an egalitarian "Heavenly Kingdom of Great Peace" *(Taiping Tianguo).*

In subsequent sermons and essays, Hong claimed that the biblical God was also China's creator and emperor, who had reigned over an ancient utopia of "great peace and equality" *(taiping)*. As "brothers" and "sisters," God's worshipful children had shared equally in the fruits of His creation. But, Hong lamented, Confucius left God out of his compilation of China's classical texts. And China's emperors usurped God's rule, attributed His sustaining powers to "lifeless" Daoist and Buddhist idols, and abandoned universal love for Confucius's "partial love," which exalted emperor over subject, family over individual, and male over female.

Hong concluded that the result of China's apostasy was social conflict, which he blamed for the Hakka's suffering. Indeed, following the Opium War (1839–1842), population pressures and foreign encroachment intensified unemployment, landlord greed, banditry, opium smuggling, ethnic polarization, famine, and plague throughout south China's Guangzhou delta and neighboring Guangxi Province. During the late 1840s Hong preached moral revival among his "God Worshipper" congregations, which honeycombed throughout southeastern Guangxi. He insisted that these congregations were the vanguard of the biblically promised Heavenly Kingdom *(Tianguo)* come to earth. To prepare for the new dispensation, Hong wove Christian baptism, the Ten Commandments, and Chinese sectarian ideals into compelling ritual, an ascetic, universalist morality, and a communal "Sacred Treasury," which incorporated Hakka customs of property-sharing and gender equality.

Alarmed by the God Worshippers' loyalty to a transcendent God, the Qing (Manchu) emperor unleashed troops against Hong's flock in the summer of 1850. On January 11, 1851, Hong announced the inauguration of the Taiping Heavenly Kingdom. He invited all Chinese to unite as one "Chosen People," whom God, now restored as China's legitimate ruler, would deliver from Manchu despotism and Confucian injustice. Militant faith and an all-embracing theocratic leadership enabled one million Taipings to capture Nanjing, the former imperial capital near the mouth of the Yangzi River, in March 1853.

Christening the city "New Jerusalem," Hong made Nanjing his Heavenly Capital. Proclaiming himself the reincarnated Melchizedek (the Bible's messianic priest-king) as well as China's Heavenly King (God's earthly vice regent), Hong used ceaseless worship and a strict moral code to maintain discipline. He assaulted Confucianism by abolishing female footbinding, concubinage, arranged marriage, and prostitution, and by decreeing women's equal access to schooling, the examinations, public office, military service, and landholding. Hong also substituted the Bible and his own writings for Confucian texts as the basis of universal public education and the examinations and guaranteed economic security and social welfare through property-sharing at a level of government never before proposed in China: the "congregation" of twenty-five families.

A fratricidal power struggle in 1856 between Hong and his chief deputy crippled theocratic control. After that, Hong's plans to link Taiping China with the Christian West were sabotaged by the missionaries' condemnation of his "heretical" religion and by Western military support of Qing forces, who crushed "New Jerusalem" in the summer of 1864.

Hong was a leader without parallel in Chinese history. Believing that China could be saved by fusing Chinese and biblical ideals, he developed a bold millennial blueprint that far surpassed the aims and scope of traditional rebels, especially in its efforts to make Chinese women equal partners of men in carrying out the Heavenly Father's mandate to transform China. In fact, Hong's religious vision presaged China's twentieth-century revolutions, which—while also inspired by a unique synthesis of Chinese and foreign sources—succeeded through exclusively human means.

P. RICHARD BOHR

BIBLIOGRAPHY

Bohr, P. Richard. "The Politics of Eschatology: Hung Hsiu-ch'üan and the Rise of the Taipings, 1837–1853." Ph.D. dissertation, University of California, Davis, 1978.
———. "The Theologian as Revolutionary: Hung Hsiu-ch'üan's Religious Vision of the Taiping Heavenly Kingdom." In *Tradition and Metamorphosis in Modern Chinese History: Essays in Honor of Professor Kwang-Ching Liu's Seventy-fifth Birthday*. 2 vols. Edited by Yen-p'ing Hao and Hsiu-mei Wei. Taipei: Institute of Modern History, Academia Sinica, 1998.
Spence, Jonathan D. *God's Chinese Son: The Taiping Heavenly Kingdom of Hong Xiuquan*. New York: W. W. Norton, 1996.
Wagner, Rudolph G. *Reenacting the Heavenly Vision: The Role of Religion in the Taiping Rebellion*. Berkeley: University of California, Institute of East Asian Studies, 1982.

Thomas Jefferson

Jefferson (1743–1826) was a central figure in two democratic revolutions: the American and the French. A member of the Virginia House of Burgesses by 1769, he soon identified himself with the colony's resistance to recent British measures. When illness prevented his own election to the First Continental Congress, he drafted "A Summary View of the Rights of British America" (1774) as a proposed set of instructions for Virginia's delegates. It was one of the earliest revolutionary pamphlets to maintain that the colonies were connected to Great Britain only by way of a compact with the king. In 1776 his reputation as a theorist and penman led to his selection to draft the Declaration of Independence, after which he returned to Virginia to serve two terms as wartime governor and to lead the infant state in an ambitious republican revisal of its laws. His *Statute for Securing Religious Freedom,* one of the great landmarks in the American separation of church and state, was a leading feature of the revision.

Jefferson returned to Congress in 1783, serving long enough to draft the Land Ordinance of 1784, thus pioneering the concept of a gradual extension of a union of equal, self-governing states across the North American continent. In 1785 he succeeded Benjamin Franklin as U.S. minister to France and strengthened his reputation as a philosopher as well as a revolutionary statesman by publishing his *Notes on the State of*

Virginia, which powerfully condemned both slavery and the insufficiently democratic, poorly balanced early revolutionary constitutions. Jefferson continued in Paris through the early stages of the French Revolution and participated, with Gilbert du Motier de Lafayette and other friends among the liberal nobility, in discussions leading to a constitutional revision and the drafting of the Declaration of the Rights of Man. He returned to the United States in October 1789 and reluctantly accepted an appointment as secretary of state in the new administration of George Washington.

As minister to France, Jefferson had been unable to participate in framing the new American Constitution, although he filled his correspondence with influential appeals for the addition of a bill of rights. By 1792, however, he was moving to the head of an emerging opposition to the financial program, foreign policy, and broad interpretation of the Constitution promoted by Alexander Hamilton, the secretary of the Treasury. Jefferson resigned from Washington's administration at the end of 1793 but continued to lead the first organized political party. Elected vice president in 1796, he nevertheless secretly drafted the Kentucky Resolutions of 1798, which laid a groundwork for later claims that the states, as parties to the compact that had created the Constitution, retained a right to interpose against "unconstitutional" measures such as the Alien and Sedition Acts of

THOMAS JEFFERSON

that year. Jefferson considered his defeat of John Adams in the presidential election of 1800 to be "as real a revolution in the principles of our government as that of 1776 was in its form." As Jefferson perceived it, his victory permitted the Jeffersonian Republicans to correct the pro-British slant of Federalist foreign policy, to end the danger of a close and corrupt connection between the federal government and a moneyed few, and to withdraw that government within the bounds originally envisioned by the framers and ratifiers of the Constitution.

As a proponent of limited government, a skeptic about urbanization and industrialization, a lifelong slaveholder, and a philosopher who expressed a strong suspicion that blacks might be inferior to whites, Jefferson has recently become a favorite target for critics of the limitations of American revolutionary thought. For much of American history, however, he has seemed perhaps the best exemplar of the American democratic spirit and the most eloquent spokesman for the democratic and libertarian ideals enunciated in the Declaration of Independence and developed in his messages, writings, and correspondence. During the age of democratic revolutions, certainly, he had few peers as an effective champion of popular rule within the confines of respect for constitutional charters, civil liberties, and inherent natural rights.

See also *Lafayette, Gilbert du Motier de.*

LANCE BANNING

BIBLIOGRAPHY

Malone, Dumas. *Jefferson and His Time.* 6 vols. Boston: Little, Brown, 1951–1981.

Onuf, Peter S., ed. *Jeffersonian Legacies.* Charlottesville: University Press of Virginia, 1993.

Peterson, Merrill D. *Thomas Jefferson and the New Nation: A Biography.* New York: Oxford University Press, 1970.

MOHAMMAD ALI JINNAH

Jinnah (1876–1948) was the "Great Leader" who founded Pakistan ("Land of the Pure") and served as its first governor general from August 14, 1947, until his death. Born in Karachi, Jinnah went to London, where he studied law at Lincoln's Inn, and became one of the most successful barristers of British India by the eve of World War I.

Jinnah launched his political career as a member of India's National Congress Party. A liberal Anglophile leader who worked for Hindu-Muslim unity, Jinnah initially brought the Congress and the Muslim League together in their nationalist demands, which he drafted in 1916. After 1919, however, when Mahatma Gandhi revolutionized the hitherto moderate Congress's program, Jinnah was driven out of that party. He turned more to his legal practice but also helped build up the Muslim League, demanding greater electoral representation for India's Muslim minority on all newly expanded legislative councils.

In 1935 Jinnah was chosen to serve as permanent president of the Muslim League by his disciples and admirers, and five years later he presided over the party's most famous session, in Lahore. "The Musalmans are a nation," Jinnah told his cheering followers that March of 1940, insisting that the problem of India was not intercommunal but international. The next day, the Muslim League adopted its famous Pakistan Resolution, calling for the creation of auto-

MOHAMMAD ALI JINNAH

nomous and sovereign Pakistan, to be carved out of British India's northwest and northeast zones, in which the Muslims were a majority. Despite his tenacious insistence on his League's Pakistan demand, however, Jinnah was wise enough to accept the British cabinet mission's confederal plan of 1946, by which the British would transfer their imperial power to a single confederal Indian Dominion. Congress also agreed to that plan, but then Jawaharlal Nehru took back the position of Congress president, which he had turned over to

Maulana Azad throughout World War II, and at his first press conference Nehru insisted that India's Constituent Assembly would not be bound by any prior formula or agreement, since it would be a sovereign body. Jinnah considered that a betrayal and immediately called on the Muslim nation to prepare for direct action, saying for the first time in his life, "good-bye to constitutionalism." In his last years, conservative, legalist Jinnah became the leader of a Muslim revolution in South Asia, and the response to his call was mass violence over the next year throughout British India, slaughter that started in Calcutta and spread swiftly to the northwest frontier. By April 1947 the British saw no other solution to their greatest imperial headache than to transfer power to two dominions, India and Pakistan, rather than one, and that summer the partition lines were drawn through Punjab and Bengal, which turned into rivers of blood in late August and September.

Though Great Leader Jinnah presided over the birth of South Asia's first Muslim nation, he never totally abandoned his own admiration for British law and the secular ideals of parliamentary government. In early August 1947 he addressed Pakistan's first Constituent Assembly in Karachi, advising his countrymen to forget the past and concentrate on the well-being of the people, especially the poor. He urged all Pakistani citizens to abjure the poisons of bribery, corruption, black-marketing, and nepotism. He was, however, fatally afflicted by that time with both tuberculosis and cancer of the lungs, and he lacked the strength to enforce his will on less enlightened followers. Instead of prospering and developing its economy and polity, Pakistan fell victim to all the divisive forces within its tribal and provincial society and could not long retain the allegiance of its eastern half, which in 1971 gained independence as Bangladesh, with Indian military assistance.

See also *Gandhi, Mahatma; Nehru, Jawaharlal.*

STANLEY WOLPERT

BIBLIOGRAPHY

Ahmad, Riaz. *The Works of Quaid-i-Azam Mohammad Ali Jinnah.* 2 vols. Islamabad: National Institute of Pakistan Studies, 1996–1997.

Allana, G. *Quaid-E-Azam Jinnah: The Story of a Nation.* Lahore: Ferozsons, 1967.

Mujahid, Sharif al. *Quaid-i-Azam Jinnah: Studies in Interpretation.* Karachi: Quaid-i-Azam Academy, 1978.

Wolpert, Stanley. *Jinnah of Pakistan.* New York: Oxford University Press, 1984.

BENITO JUÁREZ

Preeminent leader of Mexico's liberal reforms, Juárez (1806–1872) remains a symbol of Mexican nationalism. Born a Zapotec Indian, he moved at age twelve to the city of Oaxaca. Educated first at a seminary, in 1828 he entered the Oaxaca Institute of Sciences and Arts and took up liberal politics. After completing his legal studies, Juárez held office as Oaxaca city councilman in 1832, Oaxacan state legislator in 1833, and judicial magistrate in 1834. With the end of liberal rule in 1835, Juárez turned to legal work, often aiding Oaxaca's immigrant merchant community.

In 1846, as war with the United States began, liberals reclaimed power and Juárez became a deputy in the national congress. He returned to Oaxaca in 1847 as the elected state governor. He aimed to support the war effort but faced rebellion among the Zapotecs of the Isthmus of Tehuantepec, who demanded political autonomy and opposed liberal laws that privatized community lands and coastal salt beds. Juárez defended the liberal state, private property, and commercial production, sending troops to defeat the rebels in a conflict that consumed much of his term as governor.

The conservative regime of Antonio López de Santa Anna forced Juárez into exile in New Orleans in 1853. He was there when Juan Alvarez led the revolt of Ayutla, bringing the liberals to national power in 1855. Juárez became minister of justice in Alvarez's cabinet. In November 1855 they issued the Ley Juárez ending the separate legal jurisdictions enjoyed by the clergy and the military. Early in 1856 Juárez was again elected governor of Oaxaca.

In October 1857 Juárez became president of the Supreme Court, which also made him successor to the presidency. After President Ignacio Comonfort defected to the conservative opposition, Juárez became president of a beleaguered liberal regime in January 1858. For three years he roamed Mexico, finally leading liberal forces to

BENITO JUÁREZ

victory over the conservatives late in 1860. In 1861 he was elected president, but conservatives had asked Napoleon III of France to support their fading cause. A French force landed in 1862, only to be defeated by Juárez's liberal armies on May 5, the celebrated Cinco de Mayo. French reinforcements forced Juárez into a nomadic, five-year defense of the liberal regime, culminating in the capture and execution in 1867 of the imposed emperor, Maximilian of Habsburg.

Juárez, elected president a second time in the fall of 1867, asserted national power, completed the nationalization of church properties begun in 1856, and pressed forward the privatization of community lands. The power of conservatives and the church was broken, but regional elites and peasant villagers rebelled repeatedly in the late 1860s. Juárez's troops slowly defeated the fragmented opposition and consolidated the liberal regime, allowing his reelection in 1871.

President Juárez died in July 1872. He had led Mexico's liberals in defeating conservatives, dis-possessing the church, and ending the French intervention. His regime had challenged the landed, political, and cultural autonomy of peasant communities and the central role of Catholicism in Mexican culture. The conflicts that defined Juárez's liberal era persisted into the revolutionary confrontations of the early twentieth century. For his political achievements, and as a symbol of nationalism, the Zapotec president holds a pivotal place in Mexican history.

JOHN TUTINO

BIBLIOGRAPHY

Bazant, Jan. *Alienation of Church Wealth in Mexico: Social and Economic Aspects of the Liberal Revolution, 1856–1875.* Cambridge: Cambridge University Press, 1971.

Hale, Charles. *Mexican Liberalism in the Age of Mora, 1821–1853.* New Haven, Conn.: Yale University Press, 1968.

Hamnett, Brian. *Juárez.* London: Longman, 1994.

Sinkin, Richard. *The Mexican Reform, 1855–1876: A Study in Liberal Nation-Building.* Austin: University of Texas Press, 1979.

Weeks, Charles. *The Juárez Myth in Mexico.* Tuscaloosa: University of Alabama Press, 1987.

JOMO KENYATTA

Founder and first president of independent Kenya, and popularly referred to as *Mzee* ("wise elder"), Kenyatta (ca 1888–1978) was born Kamau Muigai in Ngenda, Central Province, Kenya. He received his early education at Thogoto Mission, Kikuyu, between 1909 and 1914. Baptized Johnstone, he dropped all three names and adopted Jomo Kenyatta upon leaving school.

Kenyatta launched his political career in 1928, when he became secretary general of the Kikuyu Central Association (KCA), a regional political party established in 1924, and editor of *The*

JOMO KENYATTA

Reconciler, a journal that articulated African grievances. In 1929 and again in 1931 Kenyatta was sent to London by the KCA to represent African grievances, especially the conveyance of "White Highlands" (the "stolen lands") by the colonial government to European settlers; lack of political representation; forced labor and low wages; racial discrimination; and inadequate social amenities, including schools and hospitals. His second visit lasted until 1946 and included studies at the London School of Economics, where he completed a diploma in Anthropology. His dissertation was published in 1937 under the title *Facing Mount Kenya.*

In 1946 Kenyatta returned to Kenya and assumed the presidency of the Kenya African Union (KAU), a party established in 1944 that transcended ethnic groups. Steering national politics, Kenyatta focused on dismantling colonialism. Extensive impoverishment among peasants and urban workers, deplorable working conditions, and land hunger precipitated widespread agitation. Although he was not privy to the rapid radicalization of the KAU and trade union movement, which by 1951 was administering the "Batuni" platoon oath committing the partakers to violence against the colonial state, Kenyatta himself adopted an openly radical political stance in his public pronouncements between 1948 and 1952.

On October 19, 1952, Kenyatta and more than 150 other African leaders were arrested. The colonial state accused Kenyatta of leading the clandestine Mau Mau movement. The Mau Mau were associated with sporadic violence in rural Central Province, among Kikuyu squatter laborers on settler plantations, and in such urban areas as Nakuru and Nairobi. At his trial at Kapenguria, Kenyatta denied the charge. Nonetheless, he was detained at Lokitaung Prison in Lodwar until 1961. To the extent that the Mau Mau idealized and idolized Kenyatta and anticipated independence under his leadership, he was guilty of managing the Mau Mau movement. By 1955 the guerrillas had been militarily defeated.

Although Kenyatta was in detention while crucial constitutional changes were introduced between 1954 and 1960, his name was constantly evoked. Released in August 1961, Kenyatta accepted the presidency of the Kenya African National Union (KANU), the stronger and more militant of the two major parties contending for leadership at independence. Overcoming ethnic tension and suspicion, KANU emerged victorious to lead an independent Kenya in December 1963.

Under the *harambee* ("self-help") concept that Kenyatta created, the Kenyatta era (1963–1978) ushered in a phenomenal expansion of health services and primary and secondary schools. The White Highlands and civil service were Africanized. Despite these changes, issues of ethnicity and socioeconomic and regional inequality continued to plague the country. As practiced under Kenyatta, African socialism was capitalist. Kenyatta pursued a conservative political strategy, and in 1969 Kenya became a single-party state. He died in office on August 22, 1978.

TABITHA KANOGO

BIBLIOGRAPHY

Arnold, Guy. *Kenyatta and the Politics of Kenya*. London: Dent, 1974.
Aseka, Eric Masinde. *Jomo Kenyatta: A Biography*. Nairobi: East African Educational Publishers, 1992.
Kenyatta, Jomo. *Facing Mount Kenya: The Tribal Life of the Kikuyu*. New York: Vintage Books, 1965.
———. *Suffering Without Bitterness: The Founding of the Kenya Nation*. Nairobi: East African Publishing House, 1968.
Murray-Brown, Jeremy. *Kenyatta*. 2d ed. Boston: George Allen and Unwin, 1979

AYATOLLAH RUHOLLAH KHOMEINI

The charismatic leader of the Islamic revolution of 1979 in Iran, Khomeini (1902–1989) began his career as a revolutionary leader quite late in life, after he had attained the clerical rank of grand ayatollah (literally "sign of God"), the highest Shi'ite honorific title. His political campaign culminated in the overthrow of the monarchy of Mohammad Reza Shah Pahlavi on February 11, 1979. Although the rhetoric of his Islamic revolution was directed against the shah and the United States, Khomeini's formation predated both the last shah and the appearance of the United States on the Iranian scene. It can be argued that Khomeini was taking on no less than the twentieth-century ideas of modernization.

PREREVOLUTIONARY CAREER

Khomeini was a child during the Constitutional Revolution (1906–1911), which ushered in the era of modern politics in Iran. Shi'ite religious leaders appeared in the forefront of the first popular protests but were divided during that revolution, and one of them, Shaikh Fazlullah Nuri, led a traditionalist movement against the constitution in 1907–1908. The policies of centralization and secularization under Reza Khan (Reza Shah Pahlavi after 1925), the builder of Iran's modern state, were opposed by a few clerics in the 1920s and 1930s, but this opposition remained ineffective.

The reign of Reza Shah (1925–1941) encompassed Khomeini's formative years. Khomeini chose to specialize in mystical philosophy, which was highly suspect in the legalistic scholarly community of Qom. In the 1930s, while teaching mystical philosophy to a small number of students, he also began teaching courses in ethics for a much larger audience, which first brought him to the attention of the police.

Khomeini never forgot the loss of clerical power that resulted from secularization and the modernization of the state and the humiliation of clerics by Reza Shah. He transferred his hostility to the latter's son, Mohammad Reza Shah (1941–1979), whom he contemptuously referred to as "the son of Reza Khan" throughout the revolutionary struggle.

Although Khomeini had frequented the clerical activists in the 1920s and 1930s, his public career began in the 1940s with a tract against an anticlerical pamphleteer and a clerical advocate of reform of Shi'ism. Khomeini first appeared on the national political scene in 1963 as an outspoken critic of the shah and his reform program. He was imprisoned and, after demonstrations by his supporters were violently suppressed in June, exiled to Iraq. It was during his decade and a half of exile in Iraq that Khomeini began to prepare a beleaguered Shi'ite hierarchy to take over a secularizing state. By the late 1970s he had enlisted the loyalty of many of the ablest and most energetic Shi'ite clerics. The militant clerics rallied behind him in opposition to Western cultural domination and to the shah's policies, which they considered a threat to the integrity of Islamic religious institutions.

To launch the revolutionary movement for the establishment of Islamic government, Khomeini assumed the title of *imam*—a title hitherto reserved in Iranian shi'ism for the Twelve Holy Imams. The leading militant clerics, who later came to occupy the highest positions of power in the Islamic Republic, were mostly his former students. Khomeini also mobilized many younger clerics from humbler rural and small-town backgrounds who preached his revolutionary message in mosques and religious gatherings. Other groups, too, became vocal in their opposition to the shah when he tried to liberalize his regime in 1977. As massive demonstrations and strikes paralyzed the government in 1978, all of the political groups that formed the revolutionary coalition against the shah accepted the leadership of Khomeini.

Khomeini's themes of American imperialism and U.S. control of the shah were already popular with nationalists and leftists, including youth and students. Khomeini was also helped by a popular reaction to changes that had hurt or uprooted various segments of Iranian society, and by the prior work of Islamic ideologues and groups such as Ali Shariati, Al-e Ahmad, the Liberation Movement of Iran, and even the leftist Mojahedin-e Khalq.

LEADERSHIP OF THE ISLAMIC REVOLUTION

While in exile, Khomeini had formulated a new theory of theocratic government. The Shi'ites believe that their Twelfth Imam went into hiding in the ninth century and will remain there until the end of time. Khomeini had argued that, dur-

AYATOLLAH RUHOLLAH KHOMEINI

ing the "Occultation of the Twelfth Imam," the right to rule belonged to clerical jurists.

Upon the victory of the Islamic revolution, Khomeini treated the property confiscated from the Pahlavi family and other industrialists of the old regime as war booty according to religious law and used it to endow several foundations, including the Foundation for the Disinherited. Most of the foundations were put under the direction of clerics. Khomeini also appointed Mehdi Bazargan, the leading member of the liberal and nationalist elements in the revolutionary coalition, as prime minister of a provisional government. A clerically dominated Assembly of Experts, elected in place of a constituent assembly at Khomeini's behest, rejected the draft constitution that had been prepared by the provisional government and proposed a theocratic government, as advocated by Khomeini, with an elected parliament and president. The theocratic constitution was approved by a referendum in December 1979, shortly after the occupation of the American embassy and the taking of its staff as hostages, which resulted in the toppling of Bazargan's government. By backing the taking of hostages, Khomeini caused a major international crisis.

In the course of the ensuing power struggle among the partners in the revolutionary coalition, Khomeini sanctioned the violent suppression of the leftist and secular elements in Iranian politics. After the revolutionary power struggle ended with the complete victory of his supporters, Khomeini sought to maintain unity between the conservative and the radical clerics.

Khomeini opposed ending the increasingly unpopular war with Iraq (1980–1988) but was finally persuaded to accept a ceasefire in view of the gravity of the military situation. In the last year of his life, Khomeini caused another international crisis by issuing, on February 14, 1989, an injunction sanctioning the death of Salman Rushdie, a non-Iranian writer who lived in England.

Khomeini died on June 3, 1989, a charismatic leader of immense popularity. Millions of Iranians had massed to welcome him when he returned from exile in 1979, and a million or more joined his funeral procession.

SAÏD AMIR ARJOMAND

BIBLIOGRAPHY

Algar, H. "Imam Khomeini: The Pre-Revolutionary Years." In *Islam, Politics and Social Movements.* Edited by E. Burke III and I. M. Lapidus. Berkeley: University of California Press, 1988.

Arjomand, S. A. *The Turban for the Crown: The Islamic Revolution in Iran.* New York: Oxford University Press, 1988.

Khomeini, Ruhollah. *Islam and Revolution.* Translated by H. Algar. Berkeley, Calif.: Mizan Press, 1981.

KIM IL SUNG

Kim Il Sung (1912–1994) was a revolutionary who ruled the northern half of Korea for nearly a half century. He was general secretary of the Workers' Party of Korea and president of the Democratic People's Republic of Korea. Born the eldest of three sons of a poor peasant in Pyongyang, Korea, Kim Il Sung fought for his country's liberation from Japanese colonialism and for a socialist system of government in Korea.

KIM IL SUNG

As a young man in colonial Korea, Kim Il Sung fled his home and attended Korean and Chinese secondary schools in northeastern China. He left school after being jailed for participating in underground communist activity, and he joined the Chinese communist guerrilla force known as the Northeast Anti-Japanese United Army to fight for Korean independence from Japan and for the cause of communism in Korea. He fought well against the Japanese, but when the United Army was defeated by a Japanese expeditionary force, he fled to the Russian Maritime Province and joined a special military unit of the Soviet Far Eastern Command. When Japan was defeated at the end of World War II, he became the leader of North Korea at the age of thirty-three.

The United States and the Soviet Union withdrew their occupation forces after creating separate governments, each claiming legitimacy across the entire Korean Peninsula. In his effort to unify the divided country, Kim Il Sung launched a military attack from the north in June 1950, thus starting the Korean War. It ended in 1953 a stalemate. Kim consolidated his political power after the war by eliminating his political rivals. By the time of the Fourth Party Congress in 1961, he had recovered economically and politically from the war.

North Korea encountered trouble in the 1960s when its closest allies, the Soviet Union and China, split. Because of the historical ties that Kim Il Sung and his revolutionaries had with the Chinese communist movement, North Korea sided with the Chinese, straining Soviet-North Korean relations. During the Chinese Cultural Revolution (1966–1969), however, the Chinese Red Guards criticized Kim Il Sung and his leadership in North Korea. Kim decided to become independent of both the Soviet Union and China and declared a self-reliance policy. North Korea established diplomatic relations with more than one hundred developing countries and joined the nonaligned movement.

Kim Il Sung created his own political ideology for North Korea, the idea of self-reliance called *chuch'e*. He advocated that North Korea become politically self-reliant, economically self-sustaining, and militarily self-defending. Armed with this idea, he began to promote his own cult of personality, which easily surpassed those of Joseph Stalin in the Soviet Union and Mao Zedong in China. He revised the constitution to justify his rule, and his rule was so absolute that the socialist republic he had labored so long to build looked more like his kingdom than a haven for the workers and peasants. His indoctrination of the people was so complete that when he appointed his son to succeed him, the people accepted it without question. He claimed that he had built a socialist system that the people could enjoy for generations, but his "self-sustaining" economic system collapsed after his death, and his once proud political system was reduced to the status of international mendicant.

DAE-SOOK SUH

BIBLIOGRAPHY

Party History Research Institute. *History of Revolutionary Activities of the Great Leader Comrade Kim Il Sung.* Pyongyang: Foreign Languages Publishing House, 1983.

Suh, Dae-Sook. *Kim Il Sung: The North Korean Leader.* Rev. ed. New York: Columbia University Press, 1995.

MARTIN LUTHER KING, JR.

King (1929–1968), a Baptist minister and proponent of Gandhian concepts of nonviolent social change, became the most widely known leader of the African-American civil rights movement. He was also a consistent and outspoken supporter of anticolonial revolutionary movements throughout the world.

King was born in Atlanta, Georgia, the son of the Reverend Martin Luther King Sr. and Alberta Williams King. From his childhood during the Great Depression, King was influenced by the African-American social gospel tradition, which combined Christian egalitarianism with political activism. In addition to his father and grandfather, King's role models for politically engaged religious leadership included educator Benjamin E. Mays, who served as president of Morehouse College during King's undergraduate years (1944–1948). During his senior year at Morehouse, King was ordained as a minister and decided to attend Crozer Theological Seminary (1948–1951) in Pennsylvania, where he deepened his understanding of liberal theology. He then undertook graduate studies in systematic theology at Boston University (1951–1955), where he received his doctorate.

In December 1955, soon after King accepted his first pastorate at Dexter Avenue Baptist Church in Montgomery, Alabama, Rosa Parks, secretary of the local chapter of the National Association for the Advancement of Colored People (NAACP), was jailed for refusing to obey racial segregation laws. When black residents formed the Montgomery Improvement Association (MIA) to coordinate a bus boycott movement, King became president and main spokesman for the new organization. After the U.S. Supreme Court overturned Alabama's bus segregation laws late in 1956, he assumed the presidency of a new regional group, the Southern Christian Leadership Conference (SCLC). King emerged as a major spokesperson for an expanding African-American civil rights movement. His speeches often linked that movement to anticolonial movements in Africa and Asia and, more generally, to worldwide struggles against racism and oppression. King attended the 1957 independence celebration of Ghana. In 1959 he increased his understanding of Gandhian precepts of nonviolence during a month-long visit to India as a guest of Prime Minister Jawaharlal Nehru.

After leaving Montgomery to return to Atlanta early in 1960, King participated in numerous major protest movements, most notably civil rights campaigns in Albany, Georgia (1961–1962); Birmingham, Alabama (1963); St. Augustine, Florida (1963–1964); and Selma, Alabama (1965). These campaigns spurred passage of the 1964 Civil Rights Act and the 1965 Voting Rights Act. After achieving these civil rights reforms, King sought to confront economic issues in a major series of protests in

MARTIN LUTHER KING, JR. DELIVERS HIS "I HAVE A DREAM" SPEECH AT THE AUGUST 28, 1963, MARCH ON WASHINGTON.

Chicago (1966–1967) and in the Poor People's Campaign (1968), which intended to bring large numbers of protesters to Washington, D.C. During this period, he became more outspoken in his insistence that major economic reforms were necessary to achieve social justice in the United States.

Although King was reluctant to risk his prestige as a civil rights leader by opposing the Vietnam War, he publicly criticized President Lyndon Johnson's war policies as immoral and as a harmful diversion of funds from antipoverty programs. On April 4, 1967, in his first major public statement against the war, King told an audience at New York's Riverside Church "that if we are to get on the right side of the world revolution, we as a nation must undergo a radical revolution of values." King's advocacy of conscientious objection to military service and his call for a unilateral cease-fire in Vietnam decreased his political influence in the United States, but he nonetheless remained an internationally recognized advocate of world peace and militant nonviolence until his assassination on April 4, 1968.

CLAYBORNE CARSON

BIBLIOGRAPHY

King, Martin Luther, Jr. *Stride toward Freedom: The Montgomery Story.* New York: Harper and Row, 1958.
———. *Where Do We Go from Here? Chaos or Community?* New York: Harper and Row, 1967.
———. *Why We Can't Wait.* New York: Harper and Row, 1964.

GILBERT DU MOTIER DE LAFAYETTE

Lafayette (1757–1834), though remembered today mostly as a prominent military figure in the American and French Revolutions, served in the late eighteenth and early nineteenth centuries as a symbol of the military and political struggles for liberal republicanism and constitutionalism in North America, Europe, and Latin America. He was the descendant of a noble family that had served France since the Middle Ages. The deaths of his parents early in his life left Lafayette a young man of independent means. A chance encounter in 1775 at Metz with British king George III's brother, the Duke of Gloucester, stirred his interest in the American cause. He purchased a ship in the spring of 1777 and sailed for America despite family and governmental opposition. Though the Continental Congress usually rejected applications from foreign officers, Lafayette received the rank of brigadier general. George Washington took an interest in the young nobleman and rewarded him with a field command. Lafayette served through the final campaign of the war and developed a strong following among most Americans.

After his return to France in 1782, Lafayette supported greater political, economic, and religious liberty and the reduction of governmental regulation on trade. In March 1789 the nobility of Riom chose him to serve in the Estates-General. In the new National Assembly, he proposed a declaration of rights as a preamble for a forthcoming written constitution. After the fall of the Bastille in July, the Paris municipal government named him commander of its bourgeois militia, which he renamed the Paris National Guard and reorganized to maintain order. After 1790 Lafayette found his efforts around Paris increasingly challenged by radical Jacobins and royalist reactionaries. With the completion of the new constitution in August, he resigned his command on October 8, 1791, to retire to his farm—much as his republican idols Washington and Cincinnatus had.

Lafayette's retirement was short-lived. He was named commander of one of three armies formed in December 1791 to defend the Revolution against neighboring absolutist monarchies. He led his army into battle against Austria in May 1792. As a result of Paris violence in June, Lafayette briefly returned to the city to criticize political factionalism in time of national crisis. This caused him to be attacked by Jacobins in the Assembly and in the press. The fall of the constitutional monarchy on August 10 to radical republicans led Lafayette to rally his troops to continue supporting the constitution, which brought about his removal from command; on August 19 he was declared a rebel. That day, Lafayette and his staff crossed the border to flee to America. Austrian authorities intercepted him and imprisoned him until October 1797.

Lafayette returned to France in December 1799. In 1802 he opposed Napoleon's bid for

a Nation Française assistée de M. De la Fayette terrasse le Despotisme et les Abus du Regne Feodal qui terrassaient le Peuple.

IN THIS PERIOD DRAWING, LAFAYETTE IS DEPICTED AS ASSIST-
ING THE FRENCH NATION (MARIE) IN TRAMPLING FEUDAL
RULE JUST AS THE LATTER HAD TRAMPLED THE PEOPLE.

lifetime consulship and requested his retirement from the army. During the remainder of Napoleon's regime, Lafayette found himself under surveillance. With the restoration of the Bourbon monarchy in France, Lafayette continued under close government scrutiny. Nonetheless, he remained publicly active, serving in the Chamber of Deputies from 1818 to 1824 and from 1827 until his death. He served as an icon for republican and revolutionary movements and liberal causes and was the frequent recipient of

visits from reformers tied to the movements in Italy, Spain, Great Britain, the Austrian and Russian empires, and Latin America. His American tour of 1824–1825 was partially an effort to urge Americans to support the struggles for republicanism and liberal causes elsewhere in the world. By the time of the revolution of July 1830, he was the most widely recognized symbol of reform in France. Assured of his commitment to liberal principles, Lafayette publicly endorsed Louis-Philippe, Duke of Orleans, to be constitutional monarch and accepted the rank of commander of the French National Guard. Soon disappointed by the new king's violation of his promises, Lafayette bitterly resigned in December 1830 and became a leading opposition figure in the Chamber of Deputies.

Lafayette continued during his last years to support such causes as Greek and Polish independence, public education and libraries, the abolition of slavery, prison reform, and women's rights—all outgrowths of the ideas he had espoused from youth.

ROBERT RHODES CROUT

BIBLIOGRAPHY

Idzerda, Stanley J., et al., eds. *Lafayette in the Age of the American Revolution. Selected Letters and Papers, 1776–1790.* 5 vols. to date. Ithaca, N.Y.: Cornell University Press, 1977– .

Idzerda, Stanley J., Anne C. Loveland, and Marc H. Miller. *Lafayette, Hero of Two Worlds: The Art and Pageantry of His Farewell Tour of America.* Hanover, N.H.: Queen's Museum, 1989.

Kramer, Lloyd S. *Lafayette in Two Worlds: Public Cultures and Personal Identities in an Age of Revolutions.* Chapel Hill: University of North Carolina Press, 1996.

Neely, Sylvia. *Lafayette and the Liberal Ideal, 1814–1824: Politics and Conspiracy in an Age of Reaction.* Carbondale: Southern Illinois University Press, 1991.

JUAN LECHÍN OQUENDO

Lechín (1914–) led the powerful Bolivian tin miners and Bolivia's central labor confederation for most of their existence. The tin miners, in particular, stood at the center of the Bolivian Revolution of 1952, one of the most radical proletarian-peasant-nationalist revolutions in Latin American history.

Bolivia's trade unionists, particularly the miners in this country long dependent on tin, developed a militant theory and practice. The Bolivian Federation of Miners (FSTMB), founded in 1944, was shaped ideologically by Trotskyist and Leninist thought; the Bolivian Workers Central (COB), founded shortly after the successful revolution of 1952, was long influenced by Communists, Trotskyists, and left-wing nationalists. Juan Lechín stood at the center of these organizations, as executive secretary of the FSTMB from its founding until his resignation in June 1986, and as general secretary of the COB from its founding until July 1987.

Lechín, of Lebanese ancestry, was born in the mining town of Corocoro. He attended the American Institute run by the Methodist Church, but family debts prevented him from pursuing his studies. He was hired as a clerk in the Catavi tin mines in 1929. After service in the Chaco War (1932–1935) against neighboring Paraguay, he was appointed to a municipal government post in a mining district, and he quickly became involved in local union affairs.

Lechín's ideological flexibility (alternatively interpreted as a lack of theoretical discernment or, more likely, a keen sense of political pragmatism) allowed him to serve as a key intermediary among the parties that worked intensively in the politically crucial mining sector. Influenced by the Trotskyist Revolutionary Labor Party (POR), he provided early backing for militant miners, supporting their frequent occupation of the mines and calls for general strikes. Yet Lechín was never fully comfortable with socialist ideology, and in the late 1940s he broke with the POR and moved over to the Nationalist Revolutionary Movement (MNR), the populist party that won power in April 1952.

Representing the MNR's left flank, Lechín influenced the new government's adherence to a number of radical measures including nationalization of the mining industry, worker cogovernment (with a specified number of COB-nominated ministry seats), and comanagement of the new state mining corporation. But if Lechín helped nudge the MNR to the left, he also acted to prevent more radical forces from gaining control of national policy. Thus, he called for the nationalization of the mines, but also for payment of compensation. He supported worker control in the mines, but not the election of delegates subject to recall by the workers they represented. He prevented Hernán Siles Zuazo (president from 1956 to 1960) from turning the COB into a state-controlled institution, but he also won the COB's support of Siles's stabiliza-

Juan Lechín Oquendo

tion plan, which was detrimental to the workers.

Often promised the presidency on the MNR ticket, Lechín had to settle for the vice presidency under Víctor Paz Estenssoro in 1960, only to be forced out soon after the election on a trumped-up cocaine charge. Long uneasy with both Trotskyists and communists and abandoned by the MNR, Lechín founded the Revolutionary Party of the Nationalist Left, which served as his base for a number of unsuccessful presidential runs. His support of strike calls during numerous military governments after 1964 and his near legendary stature as Bolivia's top labor leader led him to jail and exile on dozens of occasions.

Lechín's advancing age and inability to halt the neoliberal reforms of the mid-1980s finally marginalized him from the labor movement, and, since 1987, he has had little influence either in labor or national politics.

STEVEN S. VOLK

BIBLIOGRAPHY

Cajias, Lupe. *Juan Lechín: Historia de una leyenda.* 3d ed. La Paz: Editorial Los Amigos del Libro, 1994.

Dunkerley, James. *Rebellion in the Veins. Political Struggle in Bolivia, 1952–82.* London: Verso, 1984.

Klein, Herbert S. *Bolivia: The Evolution of a Multi-Ethnic Society.* 2d ed. New York: Oxford University Press, 1992.

Malloy, James M., and Eduardo Gamarra. *Revolution and Reaction: Bolivia, 1964–1985.* New Brunswick, N.J.: Transaction Books, 1988.

VLADIMIR ILYICH LENIN

L enin (1870–1924) was the founder of the Bolshevik Party and one of the most influential revolutionary theorists of the twentieth century. Vladimir I. Ulyanov was born in Simbirsk, Russia; his father was a provincial official. In 1887 Vladimir's older brother Alexander was executed after being found guilty of taking part in a terrorist conspiracy to murder the tsar. As a result, the entire Ulyanov family began to be treated with suspicion by the authorities, and Vladimir was expelled from law school after taking part in a student demonstration. While continuing his legal studies through correspondence courses, he began to study Marxism. In 1895 he was arrested for attempting to publish a socialist newspaper and spent the next five years in prison and in Siberian exile.

In Siberia Ulyanov devoted himself to developing Marxist theory and revolutionary strategy in the context of Russian social conditions. His first book, *The Development of Capitalism in Russia* (1899), endeavored to show that the traditional Russian agrarian economy, based upon the peasant commune, had already been irreversibly undermined by the increasing marketization of agricultural production. In 1900 he left Russia to join the leading Russian Marxists, Georgii Plekhanov, Pavel Axelrod, and Vera Zasulich, in Switzerland, where, along with Leon Trotsky, they founded the newspaper *Iskra* ("Spark"). In 1901 Ulyanov began to sign his articles "Lenin."

Throughout the prewar period Lenin considered himself an orthodox Marxist in the mold of Karl Kautsky, the chief theoretician of the German Social Democratic Party. Indeed, Lenin's famous treatise *What is to be Done?* (1902) was built upon Kautsky's argument that the proletariat could never create a revolution without leadership by committed Marxist intellectuals. However, Lenin went beyond Kautsky in asserting that the working class could be successfully organized only by a strictly disciplined party of professional revolutionaries. Lenin's insistence on this model of organization at the second congress of the Russian Social Democratic Workers' Party (held in 1903) played an important part in the subsequent split between the Bolsheviks, or "those in the majority"—so named because of Lenin's success in getting a bare majority of delegates present to vote to prohibit part-time party membership—and the Mensheviks, or "those in the minority," who resisted Lenin's leadership. By 1904 Plekhanov and his followers had also left Lenin's group to protest what they saw as the latter's dictatorial tendencies—ironically leaving the Bolsheviks very much a minority among Russian Marxists before 1917.

All of this infighting left both the Bolsheviks and Mensheviks almost totally unprepared for the Russian Revolution of 1905—an event that nevertheless demonstrated the increasing instability of Nicholas II's autocracy and the genuinely revolutionary orientation of the Russian working class. Lenin returned to Russia to help promote the Bolshevik cause but arrived a month after Nicholas II had succeeded in stabilizing his regime through the introduction of a limited constitutional order. In 1907 Lenin was again forced into exile in western Europe. The years 1907–1914 were bleak for him, as the Russian economy experienced steady growth and his own movement fragmented into warring splinter groups.

However, the outbreak of World War I in 1914, which both discredited global capitalism and rapidly undermined the legitimacy of the tsarist regime, revived the Bolsheviks' fortunes. As Lenin argued in his essay *Imperialism* (1916), the support by European socialist parties for their governments' participation in the war appeared to demonstrate that even supposedly "orthodox" European Marxists had been hopelessly corrupted by payoffs from capitalist imperial expansion. The proletarian revolution, he concluded, was therefore more likely to begin in Russia, the periphery of what had become a truly global capitalist system, than in the developed countries of the West, despite the weakness of Russian capitalism and the relatively small size of the Russian working class.

The opportunity to act on this theory arose when Nicholas II's sudden abdication in March 1917 left Russia in near anarchy. A Provisional Government made up of former Duma deputies tried, with Allied support, to continue the war against Germany, but in the cities actual power devolved, as in 1905, to local soviets (councils) of workers and soldiers. In the countryside, peasant revolts spread. Lenin returned to Petrograd (now St. Petersburg) in April, advocating the overthrow of the Provisional Government, the establishment of a socialist republic based upon the soviets, and the immediate cessation of the war.

While the radicalism of these proposals at first stunned many of his own closest supporters, by the summer mounting war casualties and the disintegrating economy had turned the tide of opinion among workers and soldiers in the Bolsheviks' favor. On November 7 Lenin and his supporters successfully seized state power and quickly subordinated all other organized political forces within the territory they controlled.

However, Lenin's theoretical expectation that Bolshevik victory would spark socialist revolutions throughout the imperialist world turned out to be unfounded. From 1918 to 1920 Lenin and Trotsky directed an enormously destructive and bloody civil war against various supporters of tsarism, liberalism, anarchism, and anti-

VLADIMIR ILYICH LENIN

Bolshevik socialism. But after having reconquered most of the territory of the former Russian Empire, Lenin began to realize that the final global proletarian victory might be delayed indefinitely. In March 1921, in an attempt to revitalize the ruined Russian economy, Lenin introduced the New Economic Policy, which freed grain prices from state control and allowed small-scale capitalist trade in the cities; simultaneously, however, he further strengthened one-party rule through a ban on "factions," meaning open dissent within the party would no longer be tolerated. In 1922 he promoted Joseph Stalin to the new position of general secretary of the Communist Party, entrusted with the task of ensuring party discipline through control over personnel decisions.

Shortly thereafter Lenin suffered the first in a series of strokes that ultimately left him incapacitated. During brief periods of activity during the last two years of his life he wrote a series of articles in which he struggled—sincerely if rather unsuccessfully—to make Marxist theoretical

sense of the dictatorial semicapitalist Soviet state he had founded. He also bitterly denounced Stalin, whom he began to see as a dangerously powerful "great Russian chauvinist" prone to abusive treatment of non-Russian communists and as a man "too rude" to be entrusted with the position of general secretary. Lenin died in January 1924, having failed to dislodge Stalin from the institutional position he was to occupy for the next three decades.

See also *Stalin, Joseph.*

STEPHEN E. HANSON

BIBLIOGRAPHY

Hanson, Stephen E. *Time and Revolution: Marxism and the Design of Soviet Institutions.* Chapel Hill: University of North Carolina Press, 1997.

Harding, Neil. *Lenin's Political Thought.* 2 vols. New York: St. Martin's Press, 1977.

Lewin, Moshe. *Lenin's Last Struggle.* New York: Pantheon, 1968.

Ulam, Adam. *The Bolsheviks: The Intellectual and Political History of the Triumph of Communism in Russia.* New York: Macmillan, 1965.

Williams, Robert C. *The Other Bolsheviks: Lenin and His Critics, 1904–1914.* Bloomington: Indiana University Press, 1986.

JOHN LOCKE

L ocke (1632–1704) was an English gentleman, philosopher, and political theorist who defended rights of resistance to absolute government in his *Two Treatises of Government* (1689). His ideas later became influential in American revolutionary arguments.

Locke argued that in terms of political rights all men are born naturally free and equal. Government is created to secure individuals' property, meaning their rights to life, liberty, and estate, and individuals consent to join political society for that purpose. According to Locke, each individual possesses a natural right to self-defense by using force against unjust force; any individual can use that right against a government that threatens his and others' life, liberty, and estate. Resistance is justified against a government or any part of a government that violates its "trust," for instance, by altering the forms of government established by the people to secure their rights; by preventing part of the government—such as Parliament—from meeting when it is needed to ensure the safety of the people; and by failing to act as an impartial umpire between individuals but instead establishing its own will under color of forms of law.

Locke, who believed these violations of trust had all been committed by the English king, Charles II, during 1679–1683, was probably composing these arguments in the midst of plans for armed resistance against the king. By late 1681 Charles was ruling without Parliament and

JOHN LOCKE

had prevented parliamentary attempts to exclude his brother James, Duke of York, from the succession: Many parliamentarians held that James, because he was a Roman Catholic, would not protect the Protestant religion and the liberties and property of Englishmen. Charles had then instigated trials and executions of parliamentary supporters by questionable legal means, though using the forms of law.

In 1681 Charles attempted to have the Earl of Shaftesbury, Locke's patron, indicted for treason, but a Middlesex (London) Grand Jury refused. The Crown then forced surrender of various charters and franchises and gained control of the appointment of grand juries. Shaftesbury and others planned armed resistance in 1682–1683, and perhaps earlier. It did not materialize, and Locke fled into exile in Holland. After Charles's death, the Duke of York succeeded his brother in 1685, as James II.

In 1688–1689 William of Orange and his wife, Mary (daughter of James), gained the English throne after leading an invasion against James that was supported by much of the English political nation. Locke's *Two Treatises* were largely ignored as immoderately radical when they were first published as an interpretation of this "revolution." Locke's contemporaries generally agreed that James had "abdicated" in an essentially unchanged "ancient constitution," not that the government had been dissolved and reconstituted in a way that involved Lockeian natural rights of resistance.

Locke's ideas, however, circulated in England, the Netherlands, and the American colonies. In the late eighteenth century some of his arguments became important to justify American resistance to the "tyranny" of the British Crown. Thomas Jefferson, author of the Declaration of Independence (1776), cited Locke's work as among the books expressing the sentiments that were harmonized in the declaration.

See also *William of Orange (King William III of England)*.

JOHN MARSHALL

BIBLIOGRAPHY

Ashcraft, Richard. *Revolutionary Politics and Locke's Two Treatises of Government.* Princeton, N.J.: Princeton University Press, 1986.

Dunn, John. *The Political Thought of John Locke.* Cambridge: Cambridge University Press, 1969.

Goldie, Mark A., ed. *Two Treatises of Government by John Locke.* New York: Everyman, 1993.

Marshall, John W. *John Locke: Resistance, Religion, and Responsibility.* Cambridge: Cambridge University Press, 1994.

Wootton, David, ed. *Locke: Political Writings.* New York: Penguin, 1993.

FRANÇOIS-DOMINIQUE TOUSSAINT L'OUVERTURE

L'Ouverture, originally known as Toussaint Bréda, was born a slave in 1743, or 1746 depending on the source, on the Bréda plantation (hence his original name) in the north of the French colony of Saint-Domingue (present-day Haiti). He died imprisoned at Fort de Joux, near Paris, France, in April 1803, where he had been sent after his capture in Saint-Domingue by Gen. Victor Emmanuel Leclerc in June 1802.

FRANÇOIS-DOMINIQUE TOUSSAINT L'OUVERTURE

L'Ouverture belonged to that relatively privileged group of slaves whose occupations distinguished them from field hands. In addition to receiving a rudimentary education in French and Latin, he initially took care of flocks and herds, then became a coachman to the plantation's overseer, and ultimately a manager of all the livestock on the plantation.

L'Ouverture was not among the original leaders of the slave revolution that erupted in August 1791. Around November 1791, however, he joined the rebellious slaves who had defected to the Spanish army in neighboring Spanish San Domingo, which, along with the English, was fighting the French in Saint-Domingue. L'Ouverture never intended to remain in the Spanish army. He agreed to join the French army to help it expel the Spanish and English from Saint-Domingue only after the French government decreed the emancipation of the slaves in 1794. He took with him a force of 4,000 experienced fighters, all former slaves, and was promoted to the rank of brigadier general.

By mid-1800 L'Ouverture and his army of ex-slaves had emerged as the dominant force in Saint-Domingue. Once he consolidated his power, L'Ouverture proceeded to reorganize the colony without declaring its independence from France. This would prove to be his greatest mistake. L'Ouverture believed in self-government for Saint-Domingue, but he wanted it to remain a French possession and the former slaves to become French citizens because he did not believe that the colony could prosper without maintaining its economic, political, and cultural ties with France. Therefore, L'Ouverture sought to preserve the plantation system established by the French in the seventeenth century, and he encouraged the former slave-owning planter class to remain in the colony, to invest in their plantations, and to employ their former slaves as wage-laborers.

L'Ouverture's solution was 146 years too early. The status he sought for Saint-Domingue in 1800 was implemented by the remaining French Caribbean colonies of Guadeloupe, French Guiana, and Martinique in 1946, when their General Councils voted to become overseas departments of France. But in 1800 all major social interests in Saint-Domingue opposed L'Ouverture's policies for different reasons, and they sought to undermine him. Consequently, when Napoleon Bonaparte sent a military force to recapture the colony and reimpose slavery in 1802, L'Ouverture's most trusted general officers abandoned him and allowed General Leclerc to capture and deport him. Jean-Jacques Dessalines then took over the leadership of the revolutionary forces and continued the war that won Haiti its independence in January 1804.

ALEX DUPUY

BIBLIOGRAPHY

Dupuy, Alex. *Haiti in the World Economy: Class, Race, and Underdevelopment since 1700.* Boulder, Colo.: Westview Press, 1989.

James, C. L. R. *The Black Jacobins: Toussaint L'Ouverture and the San Domingo Revolution.* New York: Vintage Books, 1963.

Pluchon, Pierre. *Toussaint Louverture: de l'esclavage au pouvoir.* Paris: Éditions de l'École; Port-au-Prince: Éditions Caraïbes, 1979.

Schoelcher, Victor. *Vie de Toussaint-Louverture.* Deuxième Édition. Paris: Paul Ollendorff, 1889.

PATRICE LUMUMBA

Lumumba (1925–1961) was a leading Congolese nationalist at the time of independence and, through his assassination, a martyr to African liberation. He enjoyed only the briefest moment on the political stage in the Congo, but the flamboyant aggressiveness of his nationalist commitment, and the international complicities in his overthrow and assassination, made his short life a symbol of the struggle for African liberation. (The Congo was renamed Zaire in 1971 and became the Democratic Republic of the Congo in 1997.) In his martyrdom, he became a figure much larger than life.

He was born in a small village in east central Congo. After checkered experiences in mission schools, where he reached the secondary level, he became a postal clerk in Stanleyville (now Kisangani). By the early 1950s he was making a mark as an organizer and leader in the welter of urban associations, which engaged the energies of the emerging elite. He also attracted Belgian notice as a talented and able young subject; he had two audiences with King Baudouin during the king's 1955 tour of the colony.

Nationalism, virtually absent in Congo until 1956, spread rapidly in the years following. Lumumba, who moved to the capital city of Leopoldville (now Kinshasa) in 1957 as sales agent for a brewery, emerged as the leader of a major political party, the Congolese National Movement (MNC). In 1959 the party split, and Lumumba retained control of the larger faction, now renamed MNC-Lumumba. At the end of 1958 he attended a pan-African conference in Accra, Ghana, where he came into contact with such leading African nationalists as Kwame Nkrumah and Ahmed Sekou Touré. He rapidly absorbed the doctrine of radical anticolonial nationalism, dedicated to a unitary, centralized, strong state.

PATRICE LUMUMBA (LEFT), ARRIVING IN WASHINGTON, D.C., FOR TALKS WITH U.S. AND WORLD BANK OFFICIALS, IS MET BY U.S. SECRETARY OF STATE CHRISTIAN A. HERTER, JULY 28, 1960.

Belgium in January 1960 agreed to immediate independence for its colony; a short but intense process of extending party mobilization from the towns into the countryside followed. Lumumba, fluent in several Congolese languages, proved a superb tribune. In the elections of May 1960, his party and its allies, though far from achieving a parliamentary majority, demonstrated more widespread national support than any other party. Lumumba became prime minister.

Impulsive and intolerant of opposition, he quickly found himself embattled. Within a fortnight of independence, the army mutinied against its Belgian officers; the Belgian functionaries who occupied nearly all the top government posts fled; the richest province, Katanga, seceded; and the country became the cockpit of international influences and cold war rivalry.

Lumumba's conflict with his political rival, President Joseph Kasavubu, deepened, and Western powers became increasingly distrustful of what they saw as Lumumba's erratic behavior and disposition to seek Soviet support. On September 5, 1960, Lumumba was ousted from office with Western support, and soon thereafter he was arrested. Even in prison he was feared by the West, and the American Central Intelligence Agency in fall 1960 plotted his assassination. Its schemes failed, but in January 1961 Lumumba was transferred to the secessionist province of Katanga and at once assassinated.

A huge international wave of indignation followed. The memory of Lumumba served as a mobilizing symbol in a rebellion that swept the country in 1964–1965. Throughout Africa the name Lumumba remains an evocative symbol, representing the dream of total African liberation.

See also *Nkrumah, Kwame*.

CRAWFORD YOUNG

BIBLIOGRAPHY

Kanza, Thomas. *Conflict in the Congo: The Rise and Fall of Lumumba*. London: Rex Collings, 1978.

Lumumba, Patrice. *Le Congo terre d'avenir est-il menacé*. Brussels: Office de Publicité, 1961.

van Lierde, Jean. *La pensée politique de Patrice Lumumba*. Paris: Présence Africaine, 1963.

Willame, Jean-Claude. *Patrice Lumumba: la crise congolaise revisitée*. Paris: Karthala, 1990.

Young, Crawford. *Politics in the Congo*. Princeton, N.J.: Princeton University Press, 1965

MARTIN LUTHER

The leading figure in the Protestant Reformation in Germany, Luther (1489–1546) was the founding theologian of the Lutheran confession and, indirectly, of all forms of Protestant religion. Born into a prosperous family at Eisleben in Thuringia, he attended the University of Erfurt, entered the Order of the Augustinian Hermits there, and became professor of theology in the University of Wittenberg in Saxony. After 1517 he became antagonistic toward local church authorities, the papacy at Rome, and the Holy Roman Empire. Protected by the electors of Saxony, Luther presided over the defining of German Protestantism and influenced, through the unprecedented explosion of his works in print, movements against Rome in Germany and in other countries of transalpine Europe.

Luther's relationship to political revolution is twofold. In the first place, he encouraged the German princes to revolt against the Catholic Church's authority *(Address to the Christian Nobility,* 1520) and stimulated Christian individuals to take the interpretation of the Bible and the organization of congregations into their own hands. He nonetheless decided even before the Peasant War (1524–1526) that Christians must obey the legitimate temporal ruler *(On Temporal Authority,* 1523), and in 1525 he condemned the rebels for appealing to religion to justify their demands. He never admitted an individual's right to resist authority, and in 1530 he deferred to the

MARTIN LUTHER

jurists the question of the prince's right to resist the emperor. It is widely held, and not only by Marxist historians, that Luther, having early encouraged private judgment and spontaneous church organization, had turned against them (and, some would say, against the common people) by the mid-1520s. In the German Democratic Republic he was long officially regarded as a traitor to the cause of revolution.

Second, Luther has long been regarded as a deeply conservative force for political passivity in the German-speaking world. The definitive form of this charge was framed by the theologian Ernst Troeltsch (1865–1923), who considered Luther's social and political thinking to have been trapped in the conservative, aristocratic, feudal world of Saxony. In the twentieth century Luther has been portrayed as one of the major counterrevolutionary figures in German history, an image Thomas Mann, Germany's best-known twentieth-century author, did much to encourage. Probably, his counterrevolutionary image owes a great deal more to Allied propaganda in the two world wars, which portrayed the reformer as the source of German authoritarianism, than it does to Luther's actual influence in German history. It is worth mentioning that his movement was successful, in the sense that it came to dominate the religious life, in only about one-third of the Holy Roman Empire, and also that Lutheranism produced its own versions of apocalypticism as well as the basic elements of the Protestant resistance theory, chiefly that subordinate magistrates—but not individuals—may resist a ruler whose commands contradict God's laws. The Prussian Lutheran philosopher Johann Gottlieb Fichte (1762–1814) cited Luther and Jesus as patron saints of revolution.

THOMAS BRADY JR.

BIBLIOGRAPHY

Cargill Thompson, W. D. J. *The Political Thought of Martin Luther.* Totowa, N.J.: Barnes and Noble, 1984.

Troeltsch, Ernst. *Protestantism and Progress: A Historical Study of the Relation of Protestantism to the Modern World.* 2d ed. Boston: Beacon Press, 1958. (1st ed., 1912)

Wolgast, Eike. *Die Wittenberger Theologie und die Politik der evangelischen Stände.* Gütersloh: Gerd Mohn Verlag, 1977.

ROSA LUXEMBURG

Luxemburg (1871–1919), a Polish-born German revolutionary leader, advocated a militantly libertarian Marxism opposed to both bureaucratic reformism and communist authoritarianism. Luxemburg based her conception of democracy on a refusal to identify freedom with any set of institutions and a concern with furthering the self-administrative capacities of working people. Thus her influence has largely been confined to movements and thinkers critical of both the socialist and communist mainstream.

Born in Russian Poland, Luxemburg became involved in antitsarist politics as a teenager. Forced into exile, she entered the University of Zurich, where in 1898 she completed a dissertation on the industrial development of Poland. The internationalism evident in this work became her trademark.

Luxemburg feared that nationalism would divide workers, foster militarism, generate class compromise, and threaten the values of socialist democracy. Her most important work, *The Accumulation of Capital* (1913), attempts to demonstrate how capitalism generates militarism, nationalism, and imperialism. Because of these views, she remained a pacifist during World War I, spending much of the war in prison.

Luxemburg gained notoriety with her contribution to the revisionism debate. The chief advocate of revisionism, Eduard Bernstein, sought to replace the revolutionary ideology of the labor

ROSA LUXEMBURG

movement with evolutionary reform. He aimed to substitute a politics of class compromise for visions of a future capitalist collapse. Luxemburg, in *Social Reform or Revolution* (1899), insisted that reform is limited, that a systemic breakdown is unavoidable, and that a policy of class compromise will only empower party bureaucrats.

Luxemburg's *Organizational Questions of Social Democracy* (1904), in the same vein, criticized Vladimir Ilyich Lenin's concept of the "vanguard party." During the following year she participated in the Russian revolution of 1905. The experience inspired perhaps her finest theoretical work. *Mass Strike, Party, and Trade Unions* (1906) emphasized the spontaneity of revolutionary uprisings and the ability of the working class to rule society in a democratic fashion. The pamphlet anticipates her most famous work, *The Russian Revolution,* written in 1918, while she was in jail. In this work Luxemburg criticized Lenin's dictatorship by claiming that political democracy with full civil rights must serve as the precondition for socialism.

When Luxemburg was released from prison in 1918, proletarian uprisings were sweeping Europe. She became president of the new German Communist Party and participated in the attempt to bring a new regime of soviets, or workers' councils, into being. In 1919 she was murdered by the right-wing militia employed by the first government of the Weimar Republic.

See also *Marx, Karl, and Friedrich Engels.*

STEPHEN ERIC BRONNER

BIBLIOGRAPHY

Bronner, Stephen Eric. *Rosa Luxemburg: A Revolutionary for Our Times.* University Park: Pennsylvania State University Press, 1997.

Frolich, Paul. *Rosa Luxemburg: Her Life and Work.* Translated by Johanna Hoornweg. New York: Monthly Review Press, 1972.

Nettl, J. P. *Rosa Luxemburg.* 2 vols. New York: Oxford University Press, 1966.

Waters, Mary-Alice, ed. *Rosa Luxemburg Speaks.* New York: Pathfinder, 1970.

JAMES MADISON

Madison (1751–1836), planter, writer, and political leader, participated in the American revolutionary and nation-building movement from his resistance to the Townshend Acts in 1769 to his politically active retirement in the 1830s. As a member of Virginia revolutionary, constitutional, and legislative assemblies, as a member of the Continental Congress, the Constitutional Convention of 1787, and the Federal House of Representatives, as secretary of state and president, and as sage and public affairs adviser in twenty years of retirement, he took part in every phase of the long American revolutions in loyalty, purpose, and character that extended throughout his lifetime.

As a schoolboy in the 1760s Madison seems to have had access to such civic republican, liberal, revolution-sustaining works as those of Cicero, Joseph Addison, Montesquieu, and John Locke, doubtless along with early revolutionary pamphlets of John Dickinson, Richard Bland, and others. We know, too, that his father corresponded about and took part in the boycotts of and resistances to the Stamp Act (1765), the Townshend duties, and other British measures. Then, during his years at the College of New Jersey in Princeton, 1769–1772, Madison studied in a hotbed of radical Whiggery presided over by a fervent opponent of "lordly domination and sacerdotal tyranny," Presbyterian John Witherspoon (later a signer of the Declaration of Independence). Reading more Locke as well as

John Trenchard and Thomas Gordon, John Milton, Algernon Sidney, Adam Ferguson, and other Whiggish writers, participating in student protests against the Townshend duties, and then listening to graduation orations by his classmates on such subjects as "Omnes Homines, Jura Naturae, liberti sunt" (all men, under natural law, are free), Madison was imbued with revolutionary ideals long before 1776.

His participation in revolutionary activity began formally when at age twenty-three, in December 1774, he was elected to the Orange County, Virginia, Committee of Safety, of which his father was chair. He practiced marksmanship and took part in some militia forays in 1775, but his sickliness then and later kept him from entering the army. Instead, he mustered local soldiers, collected arms and supplies, and harassed Tories—he gloated that "one Scotch parson. . . [was] ducked in a coat of tar and surplice of feathers. . . [for] his insolence."

Elected at age twenty-five to the Virginia Convention of 1776 that voted for independence and drafted a new, republican constitution for the state, Madison wrote the clause that declared that "all men are equally entitled to the free exercise of religion, according to the dictates of conscience," language substituted for the more invidious concept of "fullest toleration" in matters of religion. In this and other extensions of freedoms and civil rights, Madison remained a front-running revolutionary all his life. Service in the leg-

JAMES MADISON

islative session of 1776 that undertook Jefferson's "republicanizing" of the laws of Virginia began the fifty-year-long collaboration of the two men in fashioning the meaning of the American Revolution. Membership on the Virginia Council of State, 1777–1779, where he took day-to-day part in sustaining Virginia's war effort, completed his revolutionary activity in the state.

Elected to the Continental Congress in 1780, he began more than three years of steady service there doing all he could to support Washington's army, rescue disastrously inflationary finances, defend the French alliance, and otherwise bring the Revolutionary War to the successful conclusion secured by the Treaty of Paris in 1783, which Madison voted to ratify. Independence, though, for Madison was not the end, but the beginning of the revolution. He worked to further revise the laws of Virginia, 1784–1786, but paid greatest attention to strengthening and making more republican the union of the states. As chief proposer of the Federal Convention of 1787, as a leading advocate there of measures to strengthen the national government, as explainer

of the new Constitution in the *Federalist Papers,* and as its profound and stalwart defender at the Virginia ratifying convention of 1788, Madison more than any other person defined the frame, nature, and future of American revolutionary government. His service as one of President Washington's chief advisers and as a member of the Federal Congress, 1789–1797, completed his primary revolutionary career begun a quarter-century earlier. He had no career other than revolutionary and nation-builder.

In sixteen years as secretary of state and president, 1801–1817, Madison worked out what he saw as the foreign policy implications of the American Revolution and the domestic postures in government appropriate to it. He supported and sympathized with the ideals of the French Revolution ("republics should draw near to each other," he thought), resisted unlawful depredations (mainly by Great Britain) on American high seas commerce, and led the nation in 1812 into what he saw as a "Second War for American Independence," at once defeating Britain's renewed attempt to dominate the United States and assuring republican survival. For Madison, victory in the War of 1812 completed the American Revolution.

RALPH KETCHAM

BIBLIOGRAPHY

Hutchinson, William T., et al., eds. *The Papers of James Madison.* Chicago: University of Chicago Press; and Charlottesville: University Press of Virginia, 1962. Three series, 23 vols. to date.

Brant, Irving. *James Madison, the Virginia Revolutionist.* Indianapolis, Ind.: Bobbs Merrill, 1941.

Ketcham, Ralph. *James Madison: A Biography.* New York: Macmillan, 1971; Charlottesville: University Press of Virginia, 1991.

Miller, William Lee. *The Business of May Next: James Madison and the Founding.* Charlottesville, Va.: University Press of Virginia, 1992.

NELSON ROLIHLAHLA MANDELA

Mandela (1918–) is the president of South Africa and the internationally venerated voice of all South Africans. As a young leader of the African National Congress, Mandela, together with Walter Sisulu and Oliver Tambo, founded the ANC Youth League (ANCYL) in 1944. In 1948 he was named its national secretary, and in 1950 its president. They radicalized the ANCYL and later the ANC itself, moving it from an essentially bourgeois reformist body to one aggressively seeking sociopolitical revolution.

In the 1950s Mandela was arrested and convicted under the Suppression of Communism Act and was banned for nine years, yet he continued his work. He developed the "M Plan" (named after him), by which the ANC branches prepared for underground activity. Arrested again in 1956 for high treason, he was acquitted more than four years later.

In March 1960, panicky police fired on demonstrators at a police station in a township south of Johannesburg, killing sixty-nine people. After the Sharpeville massacre, the ANC and the Pan-Africanist Congress were outlawed, and during the subsequent state of emergency Mandela was detained without charge, although he was allowed to practice law in Johannesburg on weekends. In March 1961, after his acquittal in the treason trial, he defied his banning order and went underground, remaining an active ANC organizer and fugitive for seventeen

months. During that time he helped organize Umkhonto we Sizwe (March 1961), the ANC's military wing, and served as its commander in chief from December 1961.

Mandela fled South Africa, received guerrilla training in Algeria, and traveled throughout Africa and to London. On his return he was captured in August 1962 and sentenced to five years' imprisonment. He was tried again with seven other ANC leaders in the Rivonia trial of 1963–1964. Mandela's four-hour statement from the dock received worldwide publicity. All eight defendants were sentenced to life imprisonment, beginning in 1964, at the notorious Robben Island prison. In 1982 Mandela was transferred to Pollsmoor prison outside of Cape Town, and in 1988 to Victor Verster prison.

From July 1986 onward, Mandela met government representatives secretly and eventually met with Presidents P. W. Botha (July 1989) and F. W. de Klerk (December 1989). He also met with senior members of various antiapartheid groups in his final months in prison. His position on the issues for negotiation was straightforward. Mandela demanded his and others' unconditional release, amnesty for returning exiles, the legalization of the ANC and other resistance groups, and the commencement of a process of negotiations leading to a transfer of power. Upon his dramatic release from prison on February 11, 1990, Mandela traveled to Zambia to meet the ANC executive committee in exile and to Sweden to

Newly elected president Nelson Mandela addresses the crowd from a balcony of the town hall in 1994.

meet ANC president Tambo. Mandela was appointed the ANC's deputy president and served in that capacity until Tambo's death in 1993.

The discussions about the transfer of power, which began with the government in May 1990, culminated with the general elections of April 1994, in which the ANC carried 62 percent of the vote. The resulting Government of National Unity included the ANC, the National Party, and the Inkatha Freedom Party. These three parties also hammered out the outlines of a constitution. On May 9, 1994, Mandela was elected by the National Assembly unopposed as president.

In 1993 Mandela shared the Nobel Peace Prize with de Klerk. Mandela's unchallenged leadership comes by virtue of his personal qualities, particularly his energy, integrity, negotiating skills, dignity, and courtesy. He is a superb strategist and tactician. Mandela is respected for his unbending opposition to minority rule and his loyalty to ANC principles and discipline, but he is not especially at home with ideas. His leanings toward reconciliation with the whites, a multicultural, ecumenical "rainbow" nation, rights for all, respect for tradition and personal loyalty, and a flexible approach to economic development provide the nation with a model of tolerant, mature leadership. He has quietly abandoned the ANC's earlier attraction to socialism and nationalization and now seems inclined toward a social democratic approach to "unbundling" large corporations and to attracting foreign investments and creating economic opportunities for all. Thus Mandela's revolutionary appeal as president is moderated by his image as a dignified, wise, and steadfast leader, one prepared to compromise only on strategy and tactics, not principle. Mandela's activist reputation had been forged during the early resistance years. His twenty-seven years out of the limelight allowed the metamorphosis to occur and be accepted by the world.

See also *Biko, Stephen.*

KENNETH W. GRUNDY

BIBLIOGRAPHY

Benson, Mary. *Nelson Mandela: The Man and the Movement.* Harmondsworth: Penguin, 1994.

Johns, Sheridan, and R. Hunt Davis Jr., eds. *Mandela, Tambo and the African National Congress: The Struggle against Apartheid, 1948–1990.* New York: Oxford University Press, 1991.

Lewis, Anthony. "Mandela the Pol." *New York Times Magazine.* (March 23, 1997): 40–79.

Mandela, Nelson. *The Struggle Is My Life: His Speeches and His Writings.* London: International Defence and Aid, 1990.

———. *Long Walk to Freedom: The Autobiography of Nelson Mandela.* Boston: Little, Brown, 1994.

MAO ZEDONG

ao Zedong (1893–1976) was arguably the most outstanding revolutionary figure of the twentieth century. Indeed, his name has become the universally recognized label for radical revolutionary extremism, as in *Maoism* and *Maoist*. He was the embodiment of the Chinese communist revolution. His military skills brought the party to power in 1949. His passion for ideological purity and revolutionary commitment stirred the Chinese people to make great sacrifices. His policies advanced but also seriously set back China's progress. Mao himself believed that he rightfully belonged in the apostolic succession of communism's great leaders as the next in line after Marx, Engels, Lenin, and Stalin. The Chinese people treated his "Thoughts" as sacred words, and his *Little Red Book* of quotations as a guide for all manner of actions. His rule made China probably among the most ideologically saturated and politically disciplined societies in world history.

Mao was born in the small town of Shaoshan in Hunan Province, where his father was a suc-

MAO ZEDONG ADDRESSES A GROUP OF HIS FOLLOWERS AT THE COMMUNIST BASE IN YAN'AN.

cessful farmer and landlord. At the age of sixteen he left home in search of more education, and subsequently attended the First Teacher's Training School in the provincial capital of Changsha. When his professor moved to Peking University, Mao went with him and became an assistant librarian. It was there during the excitement of the May Fourth Movement of 1919 that Mao became a Marxist.

Mao was one of a small band of student-intellectuals who founded the Chinese Communist Party in Shanghai in 1921. Whereas others went on to France or Russia to learn more about revolutionary work, Mao remained in China, first working as a union organizer and then most successfully as a guerrilla leader. Driven into the mountains of Jiangxi Province by the encircling Nationalist armies of Chiang Kai-shek, Mao built up a military force that would in time make the Long March up to Yan'an. There, Mao transformed the Chinese Communist Party from a leftist intellectual movement into a disciplined Leninist party. When the Japanese army began conquering China in 1937, Mao's guerrilla fighters expanded the communists' political power base into the territories occupied by Japan.

After the defeat of Japan, the communists mounted their successful campaign against the far stronger Nationalist forces under Chiang Kai-shek. Mao's dependence on military force, codified by his dictum that "Power grows out of the barrel of the gun," meant that the Chinese revolution depended on rural peasants, who made up the guerrilla armies, and not the orthodox Marxist revolutionary base of urban workers.

On October 1, 1949, Mao proclaimed the establishment of the People's Republic of China from the reviewing stand in Tiananmen Square.

The immediate task of the party was to revive the economy and indoctrinate the entire population with communist ideology. Just as he had done in relying on peasants rather than workers to gain victory, Mao did not follow orthodox Marxism in meeting these new challenges. Mao made class distinctions in China depend, not on objective economic criteria, but on people's subjective orientations and thoughts.

During the first years of Mao's rule the Chinese communists relied heavily on economic assistance from their "big brother," the Soviet Union. The Moscow–Beijing alliance became even more intense after China entered the Korean War and came to view the United States as its mortal enemy. However, strains in relations with Moscow began to surface after Stalin's death. Mao was critical of Stalin's successors and felt that he should become the acknowledged leader of the world communist movement.

By 1958 Mao's impatience to make China a modern power drove him to some serious policy mistakes. Although the Chinese economy was growing at a respectable rate in the early 1950s, Mao decided to mobilize the entire country in a great effort to increase output, which became the disastrous campaign known as the Great Leap Forward. The focus was on rapid collectivization in the countryside, where the existing cooperatives were consolidated into large communes run like huge factories. Agricultural decisions were made by party officials and not by knowledgeable farmers. People were also encouraged to operate small "backyard furnaces" to increase steel production, diverting labor and resources from other necessary economic pursuits. The end result was the worst famine in known history, and the deaths of 25 to 40 million Chinese.

By 1961 Mao had to accept the failure of the

Great Leap, and for a brief period he pulled back from day-to-day involvement in government. However, as the Chinese economy recovered, Mao became increasingly concerned about the loss of revolutionary fervor and the danger of revisionism, that is, a return to bourgeois thinking and practices. He was convinced that the Soviet Union had become a revisionist state. In 1965, to revive the people's revolutionary spirit and regain full control of the party, Mao launched the Great Proletarian Cultural Revolution. This was another disastrous campaign, which tore the party apart, closed schools and universities, disrupted government administration, set back all forms of science and technology, and eventually sent a whole generation of young people to the countryside to "learn" the presumed "revolutionary spirit" of the peasants. For much of the world it seemed as though China had gone mad.

Although the country had by 1969 reached a perilous state, it took the shock of a border conflict with Soviet troops to end the excesses of the Cultural Revolution. The danger of war with the Soviet Union now occupied the attention of Chairman Mao, and he was quick to pick up on President Richard Nixon's offer of better relations with the United States. During the last years of his rule, Mao had to accept the idea of a gradual opening to the outside world, although he still insisted on upholding his vision of a China totally under the control of an all-powerful Communist Party. Until his death Mao still believed that China's development called for ideological dedication, national self-reliance, economic autarky, and the intellectual leadership of ordinary workers and peasants.

Mao's successor, Deng Xiaoping, succeeded in putting China on the path of rapid economic growth and fuller integration with the world economy. With the hindsight of the post–Mao era, most Chinese came to accept that Mao's leadership had been seriously flawed, especially in the economic realm. However, in spite of his manifest failures, Mao also had many notable achievements. He unquestionably consolidated the unity of China as a modern nation; he broke down the iron grip of traditional thinking and practices that had held Chinese progress back; even his call for China's youth to challenge authority during the Cultural Revolution had the quite unintended effect of making a generation of Chinese more skeptical of their government and more open to new ideas. Thus, although no longer worshipped by the Chinese people as a god-figure, Mao is still seen in China as a great revolutionary hero.

See also *Chiang Kai-shek.*

LUCIAN W. PYE

BIBLIOGRAPHY

Karnow, Stanley. *Mao on China: A Legacy of Turmoil.* New York: Penguin Books, 1990.

Li, Zhisui. *The Private Life of Chairman Mao.* London: Chatto and Windus, 1994.

Pye, Lucian W. *Mao Tse-tung: The Man in the Leader.* New York: Basic Books, 1976.

Salisbury, Harrison E. *The New Emperors: China in the Era of Mao and Deng.* Boston: Little, Brown, 1992.

Schram, Stuart R. *The Political Thought of Mao Tse-tung.* New York: Praeger, 1969.

———. *Chairman Mao Talks to the People: Talks and Letters, 1961–71.* New York: Pantheon, 1974.

Terrill, Ross. *Mao: A Biography.* Stanford: Stanford University Press, 1998.

Wilson, Dick. *Mao Tse-tung in the Scales of History.* New York: Cambridge University Press, 1977.

Jean-Paul Marat

Between 1789 and 1793 Marat (1743–1793) was the most notorious of French revolutionary journalists. His assassination, commemorated by Jacques-Louis David in a moving portrait of the suffering hero, made him a martyr to the revolutionary republican cause.

Born a Prussian subject at Boudry near Neuchâtel into a family of modest means, Marat left school at sixteen to spend six years in France, where he became interested in medicine. From 1765 to 1776 he lived in England. Here his medical expertise was accepted, making him enough money to buy a doctorate. He also began to write

works of speculative philosophy and in 1774 produced *The Chains of Slavery,* in which he denounced government as a violent usurpation against which insurrection was a legitimate recourse. (Written in English, the book became well known only when he published a French translation in 1792.) Back in France by 1777, Marat lived from medicine and sought to make his name as a writer on science. Rejection of his discoveries by the Academy of Sciences left him convinced that he was a victim of a conspiracy of envious but well-connected mediocrities.

During the political excitement of the spring of 1789 Marat wrote a number of unmemorable pamphlets, but in September he found his vocation when he began to publish a regular newspaper of comment. After the first few issues he called it *The People's Friend,* a title by which he soon became known himself. Though not an outright republican until the fall of the monarchy in 1792, Marat was a consistent populist. The people, he claimed, were forever being duped and betrayed by those in power. Their salvation lay either in choosing a self-

A period etching (1793) shows Jean-Paul Marat and others celebrating his acquittal by the Revolutionary Tribunal.

less dictator or in massacre of the guilty. On several occasions he was forced into hiding or fled abroad after inciting his readers to kill public officials or deputies. When suspected counterrevolutionaries were massacred in September 1792, Marat was widely blamed, and he reveled in the fact.

Marat was popular enough in Paris to win election to the Convention in the fall of 1792, where he voted for the king's death and denounced a number of fellow deputies as counterrevolutionaries. Prosecuted in the newly established Revolutionary Tribunal for his denunciations in the Convention, he was triumphantly acquitted and had the satisfaction six weeks later of seeing those he had denounced purged from the Convention under popular pressure (June 2, 1793). But by now he was seriously ill with a skin disease for which the only relief came from constant hot baths. He was in his bath when the royalist Charlotte Corday stabbed him to death on July 13, 1793.

The government capitalized on the genuine popular grief in Paris to make Marat's memory into a political cult. He became a sort of patron saint for the policy of Terror, which dominated the twelve months after his death. His cult culminated in September 1794 with the installation of his remains in the Pantheon, but after the retreat from Terror they were removed in February 1795. Since then his memory has never been entirely rehabilitated, and scholarly research has largely confirmed his enemies' charges of prerevolutionary charlatanism. Left-wing historians, however, stress his pioneering commitment to popular democracy.

WILLIAM DOYLE

BIBLIOGRAPHY

Gottschalk, Louis R. *Jean Paul Marat. A Study in Radicalism.* New York: Greenberg, 1927.
Hampson, Norman. *Will and Circumstance. Montesquieu, Rousseau and the French Revolution.* London: Duckworth, 1983.

JOSÉ MARTÍ

In 1953, following an abortive attack on the Moncada garrison in Santiago, Cuba, Fidel Castro announced that the inspiration for his uprising was José Martí (1853–1895), a poet-revolutionary who had been killed nearly sixty years earlier. Martí, a hero of the Cuban fight against Spanish colonial rule, continues to be a symbol for all Cubans, regardless of their political ideology. In Havana he is particularly revered, with his bust featured in front of every school; the national library, revolutionary square, and Havana's major airport are named after him, his picture appears on one-peso bills, and President Castro has often cited his influence.

Martí was born of lower-middle-class Spanish parents in Havana. His father was a member of the occupying military forces, determined to prevent Cuba from securing independence, as mainland Latin America had done several decades earlier. Martí was educated by a well-known poet and supporter of Cuban independence, Rafael Maria de Mendive. Throughout his adult life, Martí would struggle for Cuban independence. Indeed, from the age of sixteen, his life revolved around the goal of winning political freedom for his country, and he paid dearly for his revolutionary vocation: he was jailed for treason by the Spanish authorities from 1869 to 1871, deported in 1871, returned to Cuba in 1878, was deported again in 1879, saw his family life fall apart, and traveled feverishly among groups of Cuban exiles in the United States to

JOSÉ MARTÍ

organize a rebellion against Spain. On May 19, 1895, he was shot by Spanish forces, just a month after returning to Cuba to lead the revolution.

Martí is important for several reasons. First, he was the leader of the independence struggle of Cuba, which would win political liberation from Spain in 1898. Second, he was a superb writer. Although he dabbled in a variety of literary genres, he was best known for his poetry and journalism, both of which were internationally recognized in the 1880s. If his fame had not rested upon his political activities, he would have been remembered as one of the leading Spanish American men of letters of the nineteenth century. Third, Martí was a superb political thinker and organizer, uniting diverse Cuban exile groups living in the United States in a movement to overthrow Spanish control of the island.

Debates have arisen in Miami and Havana about the nature of Martí's political thought. For some, his work was inspired by socialist goals; others have seen him as a classical liberal; and a minority have emphasized his adventurism. It is clear, however, that Martí was a radical and an anti-imperialist (he denounced the Spanish, French, and British Empires). He was also extremely suspicious of U.S. goals in Latin America, and particularly in Cuba, and tried to alert the people of what he called "Nuestra (Our) América" about the nature of Washington's interests in Latin America. Martí was also a revolutionary, who struggled all his adult life to win independence of his country from Spain and introduce a variety of radical sociopolitical policies in Cuba.

Martí will be remembered for his progressive political thought and his superb literature (his *Complete Works* consist of some twenty-seven hefty volumes). A man of action who paid the ultimate price for his political goals, he espoused a moral approach to politics. It was necessary to educate Cubans about the need to sacrifice everything for the country and to inculcate in them a sense of duty, he believed. His untimely death at the hands of Spanish marksmen denied him the opportunity to introduce his well-developed political ideas.

JOHN KIRK

BIBLIOGRAPHY

Fernández Retamar, Roberto. *Lectura de Martí*. Mexico: Editorial Nuestro Tiempo, 1972.

González, Manuel Pedro. *José Martí, Epic Chronicler of the U.S. in the Eighties*. Chapel Hill: University of North Carolina Press, 1953.

Kirk, John M. *José Martí, Mentor of the Cuban Nation*. Gainesville: University Press of Florida, 1983.

Mañach, Jorge. *Martí Apostle of Freedom*. New York: Devin-Adan, 1950.

Martínez Estrada, Ezequiel. *Martí revolucionario*. Havana: Casa de las Americas, 1967.

KARL MARX AND FRIEDRICH ENGELS

The ideas of Marx (1818–1883) and Engels (1820–1895) on revolution are a direct consequence of their general materialist views on historical development, that is, that the development of society is determined by changes in its economic basis, in the tools and implements that people have at their disposal at any given time (the forces of production, in Marx's terminology), and the corresponding way in which people organize themselves to make use of their tools (the relations of production). They wrote: "At a certain stage of their development the material forces of production in society come into conflict with the existing relations of production, or—what is but a legal expression for the same thing—with the property relations within which they had been at work before. From forms of development of the forces of production these relations turn into their fetters. Then comes the period of social revolution." Thus Marx could call the revolution "the driving force of history," and all of his and Engels's studies in other fields were devoted to uncovering the springs of that driving force.

The most important characteristic of the next revolution was that it would be social and not merely political: it would not only proclaim abstract rights such as freedom of the press, which in fact only a few could enjoy, but achieve a general emancipation by penetrating to the real life of humanity—socioeconomic life. The next revolution would be the first to involve the whole of society:

> All previous historical movements were movements of minorities, or in the interest of minorities. The proletarian movement is the self-conscious, independent movement of the immense majority, in the interests of the immense majority. The proletariat, the lowest stratum of our present society, cannot stir, cannot raise itself up, without the whole superincumbent strata of official society being exploded into the air.

Thus the radicalism of the revolution depended on the class that was carrying it out: the proletariat could represent the interests of society as a whole, a society in which class antagonisms were sharpened and simplified to an extent that permitted their abolition. Marx returned to this distinction between the political and the social in his discussion of the Paris Commune (1871), which he claimed was "the political form of social emancipation."

Because they were no prophets, Marx and Engels did not go into great detail concerning the exact nature and circumstances of the revolution they believed to be imminent. They did, however, say something about when a revolution might occur, where it would break out, and whether it would be violent.

Concerning the conditions necessary to produce a successful revolution, Marx and Engels were more or less sanguine depending on the historical situation in which they found themselves. Their expectations were strongest during

Karl Marx

Friedrich Engels

the 1848 revolutions and faded gradually thereafter, except for a brief renascence during the Paris Commune.

Linked to the necessary conditions was the question of where the revolution would break out first. The materialist view of history of Marx and Engels seemed to indicate that the most advanced industrial countries were most ripe for revolution. Yet they realized that European revolutions were becoming more dependent on the general world situation. In a letter to Engels in 1859 Marx mentioned the opening up of California, Australia, and the Far East and continued: "Revolution is imminent on the Continent and will also immediately assume a socialist character. Can it avoid being crushed in this small corner, because the movement of bourgeois society is in the ascendant over much

larger areas of the earth?" But Marx also thought that in some underdeveloped countries (for example, Germany) a bourgeois revolution could spark a subsequent proletarian revolution. Later in his life Marx came to believe that Russia might prove the starting-point of the revolution, which "begins this time in the East, hitherto the invulnerable bulwark and reinforcement of the counterrevolution." Of Russia he said a year before his death: "If the Russian revolution becomes the signal for a proletarian revolution in the West, so that both complete each other, then the present Russian system of community ownership of land could serve as the starting point for a communist development."

Marx was certainly well aware of the importance of colonial exploitation for hastening the coming revolution. After describing the influence of English industry on India, he outlined the prospects that colonialism afforded for a worldwide revolution: Colonial exploitation has globalized the world, but only egalitarian social revolution will enable all of humanity to enjoy the fruits of this globalization.

One of the reasons why Marx and Engels did not think that violent revolution would automatically occur in the most advanced countries was that in some of the advanced countries communism could come about by peaceful means. In 1872 Marx spoke of his belief in the possibility of a peaceful revolution in America, England, and Holland. He took the same line in 1879 when he wrote:

> A historical development can only remain "peaceful" so long as it is not opposed by the violence of those who wield power in society at that time. If in England or the United States, for example, the working class were to gain a majority in Parliament or Congress, then it could by legal means set aside the laws and structures that stood in its way.

Were the proletariat to gain a voting majority, Marx continued, any violence would come from the other side. However, in 1871 he blamed the Paris Commune for not being willing to start a civil war, and declared at the Congress of the International in the same year: "We must make clear to the governments, we know that you are the armed power that is directed against the proletariat; we will proceed against you by peaceful means where that is possible and with arms when it is necessary." But however much both Marx and Engels may have thought that force was sometimes the midwife of revolution, they never (except briefly in 1848 and under tsarist conditions in Russia) approved of the use of revolutionary terror. They strongly criticized the use

of terror by the Jacobins in the French Revolution; its use was for Marx and Engels a sign of the weakness and immaturity of that revolution, which had tried to impose by sheer force what was not yet inherent in society. Marx believed that a revolution, if the socioeconomic conditions are not appropriate, inevitably leads to a reign of terror during which the revolutionary powers attempt to reorganize society from above.

Physical force, however, as opposed to terror, was to Marx and Engels a perfectly acceptable revolutionary weapon provided that the economic, social, and political conditions were such as to make its use successful. In their view the form of government that would follow a successful revolution was a "dictatorship of the proletariat." The expression was seldom used by Marx, and never in documents for publication, though Engels did later cite the Paris Commune as a good example. In a letter to his friend Joseph Weydemeyer Marx claims as one of his contributions to socialist theory the idea that "the class struggle necessarily leads to the dictatorship of the proletariat; that this dictatorship itself is only a transitional stage toward the abolition of all classes." And in the *Critique of the Gotha Program* Marx wrote that when capitalist society was being transformed into communist society, there would be "a political transition period during which the state can be nothing but the revolutionary dictatorship of the proletariat." It should be noted that the word *dictatorship* did not have quite the same connotation for Marx and Engels that it does for us. They associated it principally with the Roman office of *dictatura,* where all power was legally concentrated in the hands of a single man during a limited period in a time of crisis. Although Marx and Engels seldom discuss the measures that such a government would enact, the fullest account is the ten-point program outlined in the *Communist Manifesto,* which is in many respects a fairly moderate program.

It was also Marx's view that a successful revolution—at least in the long run—was impossible if confined to one country. In *The Class Struggles in France* Marx criticized the leaders of the French proletariat for thinking that they could consummate a proletarian revolution within a France surrounded by bourgeois nations. But Marx believed equally that the degree of working-class organization necessary to produce an international revolution could only be achieved by building up working-class parties within existing nations. Marx was strongly in favor of the unification of Germany and Italy and of the resurgence of Polish nationalism.

Engels survived Marx by thirteen years, and toward the end of his life the growing electoral success of the Social Democrats in Germany led him to stress the evolutionary rather than the revolutionary side of Marxism and to declare the tactics of 1848 to be outmoded in every respect. This view is encapsulated in the preface to a reprint of Marx's *Class Struggles in France,* written by Engels in 1895 shortly before he died, where he portrays the growth of social democracy as a natural, organic process that could be endangered by revolutionary hotheads.

DAVID MCLELLAN

BIBLIOGRAPHY

Berlin, Isaiah. *Karl Marx.* 3d ed. Oxford: Oxford University Press, 1963.

Draper, Hal. *Karl Marx's Theory of Revolution.* New York: Monthly Review Press, 1986.

Hunt, Richard. *The Political Ideas of Marx and Engels.* Pittsburgh: University of Pittsburgh Press, 1974.

Marx, Karl. *Selected Writings.* Edited by David McLellan. Oxford: Oxford University Press, 1977.

Tucker, Robert. *The Marxian Revolutionary Idea.* New York: Norton, 1970.

RIGOBERTA MENCHÚ TUM

RIGOBERTA MENCHÚ TUM SMILES AFTER LEARNING SHE HAS BEEN AWARDED THE NOBEL PEACE PRIZE, OCTOBER 16, 1992.

Menchú's name has become synonymous with the fight for economic justice, human rights, and democracy in Guatemala. As a Nobel laureate, she has also become a spokersperson and activist for indigenous peoples throughout the world.

Menchú (1959–) was born in the village of Chimel, El Quiché, Guatemala, and grew up in a context of extreme poverty, inequitable land distribution, inhuman labor conditions, and repressive authoritarian rule. These pervasive socioeconomic conditions, shared by the majority indigenous population, gave rise in the 1960s and 1970s to popular movements, revolutionary organizations, and civil war.

Menchú and her family played an active role in popular movement organizing in the 1970s. Her father, Vicente Menchú, a prominent Mayan peasant and catechist leader, cofounded the Committee for Peasant Unity (CUC). The CUC mobilized indigenous and nonindigenous peasants throughout the countryside and soon became one of the country's most significant legal opposition movements. Rigoberta Menchú officially joined the CUC in 1979, at a time of heightening civil war that resulted in an estimated 100,000–140,000 killed, 40,000 disappeared, 440 villages razed, and 1,000,000 internal and external refugees.

Following the political assassination of her brother, mother, and father, Menchú went into political exile in Mexico in 1981. There she joined the exile community in its international campaign to denounce atrocities committed by the Guatemalan government and to garner support for the popular movements. As a member of the CUC and of the Unitary Representation of the Guatemalan Opposition (RUOG), she repeatedly traveled to the United States and Europe and demonstrated her capacity to generate support from audiences moved by her experiences. With backing from the exile community, she collaborated in 1982 with Elisabeth Burgos-Debray to produce her testimonial, *I, Rigoberta Menchú: An Indian Woman in Guatemala*. The book was awarded the Casa de las Américas prize for the best testimonial work in 1983. With the book's publication, Menchú gained international recognition and a platform to denounce the Guatemalan government's repression. She simultaneously gained a more prominent voice in the United Nations, where she had been participating regularly at the UN Subcommittee for Ethnic Issues.

Menchú's work, however, was not widely known within Guatemala until 1988, when she returned for a meeting with the National Reconciliation Committee. Upon arrival, the government arrested her and another RUOG member. Protests mounted, newspapers wrote front-page articles, and television stations prepared interviews. The military's actions and her powerful comments following the arrest catapulted her to center stage. Within Guatemala, she subsequently became a symbol and interlocutor of the Guatemalan opposition movement—speaking for peasant, labor, indigenous, and women's organizations.

Menchú received the Nobel Peace Prize in 1992. With the prize money, Menchú founded the Rigoberta Menchú Tum Foundation. The foundation supports education, health, and human rights projects and has played an active role in the return and resettlement of Guatemalan refugees. Menchú has since returned to Guatemala to live and has played a prominent role in defending democratic institutions and promoting the peace accords, which were signed in December 1996 by the government and the revolutionary forces.

She continues to maintain a high international profile and participates in various UN- and indigenous-sponsored conferences. In 1993 she was the UN goodwill ambassador for the International Year of Indigenous Peoples, and, among other things, she is currently a promoter for the UN's Decade of Indigenous Peoples.

DEBORAH J. YASHAR

BIBLIOGRAPHY

Arias, Arturo. "From Peasant to National Symbol." In *Teaching and Testimony: Rigoberta Menchú and the North American Classroom*. Edited by Allen Carey-Webb and Stephen Benz. Albany: State University of New York Press, 1996.

Brittin, Alice. "Close Encounters of the Third World Kind: Rigoberta Menchú and Elisabeth Burgos's *Me llamo Rigoberta Menchú.*" *Latin American Perspectives* 22 (fall 1992): 100–115.

Carmack, R. ed. *Harvest of Violence.* Norman: University of Oklahoma Press, 1988.

Menchú, Rigoberta. *I, Rigoberta Menchú: An Indian Woman in Guatemala.* Edited and introduced by Elisabeth Burgos-Debray. Translated by Ann Wright. London: 1984. First published as *Me llamo Rigoberta Menchú y así me nació la conciencia.*

Menchú, Rigoberta, y Comité de Unidad Campesina. *Trenzando el futuro: luchas campesinas en la historia receinte de Guatemala.* Guatemala City: Tercera Prensa, 1992.

MOHAMMAD MOSADDEQ

Mosaddeq (1882–1967), liberal, democrat, parliamentarian, and prime minister, was a leader in the struggle for Iranian democracy and national sovereignty, known as the Popular Movement of Iran. His father was a notable and a high state official, his mother, a first cousin of the reigning monarch.

He became active—as a vice president of the Society for Humanity—in the Constitutional Revolution of 1905, and in 1906 he was elected to the first Majlis, but Mosaddeq was not summoned because he did not meet the minimum age qualification. Between 1909 and 1914 he studied in Paris and Switzerland, and he obtained his doctorate in law from the University of Neuchâtel, being the first Iranian to obtain such a degree from a European institution. On return, he taught at Tehran's School of Law and Politics and became deputy minister of finance.

In 1919 he went back to Switzerland and became so depressed by the news of the 1919 Anglo-Iranian agreement that he decided to become a Swiss citizen. The agreement had been almost universally interpreted as turning Iran into a British protectorate. But the climate in Iran quickly changed, and Mossadeq was named minister of justice in the new cabinet, though he ended up as the governor general of Fars. While in that post he opposed the 1921 coup by Reza Khan and Sayyed Zia, and he had to go into hiding until the fall of Zia's cabinet three months later.

In the next two years Mosaddeq served in various cabinets as finance minister, governor general of Azerbaijan, and foreign minister, but when in 1923 Reza Khan became prime minister, Mossadeq became a Majlis deputy, where he joined the "independents" who sometimes voted with the government and sometimes with the opposition. In 1925 he was one of five deputies to reject openly the change of dynasty in favor of Reza Shah, saying in a most effective speech that it would result in dictatorship.

MOHAMMAD MOSADDEQ

He withdrew from politics after 1928. Then in 1940 he was imprisoned without charge. A year later he was allowed to return to his farm under house arrest. Reza Shah abdicated in 1941—in the wake of the Allied invasion of Iran—and in 1943 Mosaddeq again became a Majlis deputy, where he campaigned for democracy and clean government. But he was most effective in his opposition to the Soviet demand for an oil concession. He also passed a bill prohibiting the grant of any foreign oil concession without prior Majlis approval.

In 1949 Mosaddeq founded the Popular (commonly known as "National") Front, and after an intense parliamentary struggle he managed to nationalize Iranian oil shortly before becoming prime minister in May 1951. The Tudeh (communist) Party saw Mossadeq as an agent of American imperialism, and his insistence that the shah reign, not rule, angered the shah and worried the religious establishment that the country would go communist. The American government became convinced of the same danger.

Mosaddeq's government was overthrown in an August 1953 coup in which his domestic opposition (including a splinter group of the Popular Front) was financed and organized by the American and British governments. He was put in solitary confinement for three years after a military trial, and afterward he was banished to his farm without further legal proceedings.

His last involvement in politics was between 1963 and 1965. Upon the failure of the second Popular Front, which he had had no hand in forming or leading, Mossadeq organized via secret correspondence the third Popular Front. This front was very short lived because of the regime's onslaught against it.

Mosaddeq died in March 1967 and was mourned by most of the politically aware public as a symbol of the struggle for democracy within their country and for its full sovereignty and independence.

HOMA KATOUZIAN

BIBLIOGRAPHY

Abrahamian, Eravand. *Iran between Two Revolutions.* Princeton, N.J.: Princeton University Press, 1982.

Azimi, Fakhr al-Din. "The Reconciliation of Politics and Ethics, Nationalism and Democracy: An Overview of the Political Career of Dr. Muhammad Musaddiq." In *Musaddiq, Iranian Nationalism and Oil.* Edited by James A. Bill and William Roger Louis. London: I. B. Tauris, 1988.

Katouzian, Homa. *Musaddiq and the Struggle for Power in Iran.* London: I. B. Tauris, 1990.

Keddie, Nikki. *Roots of Revolution.* New Haven, Conn.: Yale University Press, 1981.

Musaddiq, Mohammad. *Musaddiq's Memoirs.* Edited and introduced by Homa Katouzian. Translated by S. H. Amin and Homa Katouzian. London: Jebhe, 1988.

ROBERT GABRIEL MUGABE

Mugabe (1924–), Zimbabwean nationalist and political leader, was considered the most committed of his fellow revolutionaries to scientific socialist ideology, but he was also a pragmatist. He believed in a one-party Marxist state but promised to introduce it only if it had the people's support. He envisaged a gradual state takeover of all land, private investment, and banks.

ROBERT GABRIEL MUGABE

He was born in Kutama, Rhodesia (now Zimbabwe), some eighty miles west of the capital, Salisbury (now Harare). He received a Jesuit education. After teaching primary school, he won a scholarship to the University of Fort Hare in South Africa, where he obtained a B.A. in 1951. Mugabe then taught in Rhodesia, Northern Rhodesia, and Ghana.

In 1960 he returned from Ghana and began his political career in the National Democratic Party. Joining those who broke from Joshua Nkomo and the Zimbabwe African People's Union (ZAPU) to form the Zimbabwe African National Union (ZANU), he became secretary general, and Ndabaningi Sithole became president.

Mugabe was among the nationalist leaders imprisoned in 1964 by the white regime of Ian Smith. While in prison, Mugabe obtained a law degree and a B.A. (administration) through the University of London. Imprisoned ZANU central committee members removed Sithole as president of the party in 1970 because he had renounced the armed struggle while on trial for his alleged attempt to assassinate Prime Minister Smith, and they installed Mugabe as leader.

In November 1974 Mugabe was released from prison to represent ZANU at unity talks among the nationalists in Lusaka, Zambia. But the front-line states refused to recognize his leadership over Sithole's. In March 1975 ZANU was thrown into turmoil by the assassination in

Zambia of ZANU's acting president, Herbert Chitepo. The Zambian government jailed ZANU's military and political leaders, whom it blamed for Chitepo's death. Sent to fill the vacuum in political leadership, Mugabe and Edgar Tekere clandestinely crossed into Mozambique in April 1975.

Fearing that Mugabe did not control the guerrillas in Mozambique, President Samora Machel restricted the two men to Quelimane, away from the guerrilla camps. In September 1975 imprisoned members of ZANU's War Council made it known that they wanted Mugabe to replace Sithole. Commanders at Mgagao, the most important camp in Tanzania, signed a declaration, later accepted at other camps, that Mugabe was the only political leader they would accept. Mugabe represented ZANU at British-sponsored settlement talks in Geneva. On his return to Mozambique, leaders who had controlled the war effort from late 1975 and who opposed his leadership were imprisoned. Mugabe was formally elected president and commander-in-chief at ZANU's September 1977 congress in Chimoio, Mozambique. Mugabe's remaining opponents on the ZANU central committee were imprisoned in Mozambique in 1978. Mugabe thus established his leadership of ZANU late in the struggle for independence.

Mugabe's reign as prime minister (1980–1987) and as president (1988–) has been marked by the consolidation of the renamed ZANU-PF's power. Mugabe presided over a vicious campaign against a small band once loyal to ZAPU. The conflict ended only in December 1987 when ZAPU agreed to merge with the ruling party. In practice, ZANU-PF enjoys the advantages of a one-party system, and its radical-ism—it abandoned Marxism–Leninism in 1991—has been chiefly rhetorical. Mugabe is confronting unprecedented criticism for the rapidly deteriorating economy, and many are calling for him to step down.

NORMA KRIGER

BIBLIOGRAPHY

Mugabe, Robert Gabriel. *Our War of Liberation. Speeches, Articles, Interviews 1976–1979.* Gweru, Zimbabwe: Mambo Press, 1983.

Rake, Alan. "Man Behind the Mask: Robert Mugabe." In *100 Great Africans,* edited by Alan Rake, 408–412. Metuchen, N.J.: Scarecrow Press, 1994.

Smith, David, and Colin Simpson, with Ian Davies. *Mugabe.* Salisbury, Zimbabwe: Sphere, 1981.

BENITO MUSSOLINI

Mussolini (1883–1945) was one of the great revolutionary figures of the twentieth century, but he is rarely recognized as such because his foreign policies led Italy to ruinous defeat and his revolutionary ideals were fatally compromised by his alliance with conservative interests in Italy. His goal was to end free-market capitalism, parliamentary democracy, and bourgeois values in order to replace them with a tightly controlled, state-run economy, a totalitarian (he was the first to use this term) dictatorship, and a new set of heroic values. His new form of social organization, corporatism, was supposed to end the class conflict and alienation that marked the modern industrial world.

His ideas were much admired and inspired revolutionaries from South America to East Asia. Among those he influenced was Juan Domingo Perón of Argentina. The Iron Guard in Romania, a nationalist and antidemocratic organization founded in 1924, also took many of its ideas from Mussolini, as did the Thai generals who came to power in 1932. The combination of nationalism and corporatism was appealing, as well, to the Falange in Spain and to Francisco Franco, who came to power in 1939 in the wake of the Spanish Civil War. The idea of a centrally coordinated economy and society survived Mussolini and in a milder form led to many of the reforms made throughout western Europe after World War II.

Mussolini's bombastic style also inspired Adolf Hitler, who always thought of Mussolini as a kind of spiritual father figure. Mussolini saw Italy as being in the vanguard of the poorer, developing nations, those he called "proletarian," in the struggle against the established great powers, which he called "plutocratic." This world view was also admired in the 1920s and 1930s by the leaders of non-Western nations, and many of the anti-Western leaders of newly independent states after World War II adopted his style, rhetoric, and belief in militant, aggressive nationalism.

Born into a fervently socialist family, Mussolini became a leading socialist himself and a prominent journalist. He broke with socialists during World War I, when he turned to extreme nationalism, and after the war he organized disgruntled veterans into a militaristic, violent revolutionary movement that came to be called "fascism." (This, also, was a term that he originated.) In the chaos and disillusionment that enveloped Italy after the war, he offered a promise of order and renewed grandeur. Conservative forces, including leading intellectuals, businessmen, and the king of Italy, turned to him as a savior and conferred executive power on him in 1922. He established a police state and had some of his key opponents murdered or imprisoned, though compared with his contemporaries, Hitler and Joseph Stalin, his rule was fairly mild. In order to keep his conservative and business allies, he had to tone down the revolutionary side of his program, so that corporatism

BENITO MUSSOLINI (FAR RIGHT) INSPIRED ADOLF HITLER (FAR LEFT), WHO VISITED MUSSOLINI IN VENICE IN JUNE 1934, LESS THAN A YEAR AFTER COMING TO POWER IN GERMANY.

became, in effect, little more than a way of repressing unions. To make up for this, he turned increasingly to foreign adventures.

Mussolini used the Italian army to establish control over the rebellious colony of Libya, in North Africa, from 1923 to 1931. In the process, he killed close to half its population. In 1935 he shocked world opinion by invading Ethiopia and using modern weapons, including poison gas, to subdue this technologically backward African country. In 1936 he sent an Italian army to Spain to help the rebellious fascist General Franco.

When World War II began, Il Duce ("the leader," as he liked to be called) remained neutral until 1940, when he saw that Hitler was defeating France. Then he joined the Germans. He invaded Greece, and then British-held Egypt, but in both instances his armies were routed and saved only by massive German intervention. As the war turned against Germany, and Italy was invaded by the Americans and British in 1943, he was overthrown by the Fascist Party and imprisoned. Mussolini was rescued by commandos sent by Hitler, who set him up as leader of a puppet Italian fascist state in northern Italy. In 1945, with the Germans on the verge of surrender, he was captured by Italian communist resistance fighters as he was trying to flee to Switzerland. He and his mistress were shot, and their bodies were hung up for public viewing in the streets of Milan.

See also *Hitler, Adolf.*

DANIEL CHIROT

BIBLIOGRAPHY

Mack Smith, Dennis. *Mussolini.* New York: Vintage, 1983.

Sternhell, Zeev. *The Birth of Fascist Ideology.* Princeton, N.J.: Princeton University Press, 1994.

GAMAL ABDEL NASSER

Popularly known as the first Egyptian to rule his country since the pharaohs, Nasser (1918–1970) led the Free Officers coup of July 23, 1952, which toppled a discredited monarchy, secured full independence from Great Britain, instituted sweeping social reforms, and defined an era in the Arab world. The son of a junior postal official, Nasser grew up in the tumultuous aftermath of the 1919 rebellion against British rule. In secondary school he participated in anti-British demonstrations, once receiving a slight bullet wound. He enrolled in the Military Academy in 1937, a year after the officer corps was opened to middle-class sons, and soon became involved in secret nationalist activities. The core of the Free Officers movement coalesced within cells organized by the Muslim Brotherhood in 1943–1944; movement leaders later determined to maintain their independence from all civilian forces. During the 1948 Palestine war, Nasser and his comrades resolved upon military intervention

GAMAL ABDEL NASSER IS GREETED BY A CHEERING CROWD UPON HIS RETURN TO CAIRO FROM ALEXANDRIA, WHERE HE ANNOUNCED THAT HE HAD NATIONALIZED THE SUEZ CANAL.

within Egypt to enforce political reform, then acted in July 1952, well ahead of their schedule, when they feared arrest.

Initially a reform movement led by a joint command of junior officers, the Free Officers consolidated power over a two-year period, abrogating the existing constitution, abolishing political parties, outlawing radical movements, and proclaiming a republic. Nasser increasingly assumed individual power. After an attempt on his life in October 1954, reputedly organized by the Muslim Brotherhood, the regime eliminated its greatest internal threat. Elected president in January 1956, Nasser governed virtually uncontested until his death.

In 1955 escalating tensions on the Egyptian-Israeli border, Egyptian support for nonalignment and Afro-Asian liberation struggles, and the purchase of Eastern Bloc arms put Egypt on a collision course with the West. Nationalization of the Suez Canal in July 1956 precipitated the Suez War in October against British-French-Israeli forces. Egyptian troops and civilians suffered grave setbacks, but the "tripartite" invasion stalled in the face of Soviet and American opposition, and Nasser emerged triumphant throughout the region.

Nasser's multiple legacies remain controversial. Nasserism comprised a variety of sociopolitical elements: authoritarian single-party rule; land and health reform; public education; nationalization of heavy industry, finance, mass media, and the arts; and pan-Arabism. In the late 1950s the regime espoused a radical program of Arab socialism, which was formally proclaimed in the 1962 National Charter. In 1965 Egyptian communists, many imprisoned for over a decade, agreed to dissolve their organizations and join Nasser's mass party, the Arab Socialist Union. Nasserist foreign policy led Egypt into an ill-fated union with Syria (1958–1961), debilitating involvement in the Yemeni civil war (1962–1968), and, finally, the crushing defeat of the June 1967 Arab-Israeli war. The financial cost of foreign involvement undercut many of Nasser's domestic reforms.

In his last years Nasser struggled to rebuild a shattered country, materially and morally, and to unite a divided Arab world. He died of heart failure on September 28, 1970, after negotiating a cease-fire between Jordanian troops and Palestinian guerrillas: perhaps his greatest diplomatic achievement. Nasser's sudden death stunned Egyptians, who mourned openly in the streets. But his successor, Anwar al-Sadat, downplayed his achievements, highlighting Nasser's authoritarian rule and corrupt associates. In recent years Egyptians increasingly recall Nasser as a populist hero, and the Nasser era as one of national pride and unity, aspirations for social justice, and a golden age of cultural production.

JOEL GORDON

BIBLIOGRAPHY

Gordon, Joel. *Nasser's Blessed Movement: Egypt's Free Officers and the July Revolution.* 2d ed. Cairo: American University in Cairo Press, 1996.

Lacouture, Jean. *Nasser.* New York: Knopf, 1973.

Magid Farid, Abdel. *Nasser: The Final Years.* Reading, U.K.: Ithaca Press, 1994.

Nasser, Gamal Abdel. *Egypt's Liberation.* Washington, D.C.: Public Affairs Press, 1955.

JAWAHARLAL NEHRU

JAWAHARLAL NEHRU

Nehru (1889–1964), India's first prime minister, was born in Allahabad, the only son of Kashmiri Brahman Pandit Motilal Nehru, an upper caste Brahman from Kashmir and one of the wealthiest lawyers in India. Motilal enrolled Jawaharlal at the prestigious boarding school, Harrow, in 1905, and "Master Joe" went from there to Trinity College at Cambridge, in 1907. After graduating from Cambridge, Nehru studied law at London's Inner Temple. He hoped to remain in London, but his father was eager to bring him home to his legal practice after Jawaharlal was admitted to the bar in 1912. Motilal also found a suitable Kashmiri bride for his son and arranged Nehru's marriage to young Kamala Kaul in Delhi in 1916. Their only child, Indira, was born the following year.

Young Nehru was as bored by the provincialism of Allahabad as he was by family life and his uneducated child bride. He had heard Sinn Fein revolutionary thunder in Dublin and was attracted to George Bernard Shaw's Fabian socialist rhetoric at Cambridge, but it was Mahatma Gandhi's revolutionary *satyagraha* ("hold fast to the truth") movement that changed his life, transforming him into an ardent Indian nationalist revolutionary. Thanks to Gandhi, Nehru discovered India's peasant village poverty and became a passionately brilliant opponent of British paternalistic imperial rule in the aftermath of World War I. He was first imprisoned in 1921; between 1921 and the end of World War II, Nehru was locked behind British Indian bars for almost nine years, during which time he wrote his autobiography and *Discovery of India*.

In 1927 Nehru returned to Europe and visited Moscow for the tenth anniversary of the Russian Revolution. He became an ardent admirer of the Soviet Union, especially its state planning, which he tried to adopt for India. From this time forward he remained an intellectual Marxist-Leninist, though he did not join the Communist Party. Despite growing ideological differences with Gandhi, Nehru never broke with him, remaining his heir to leadership of India's National Congress Party. Nehru's socialist predisposition attracted Britain's Labour Party leadership, and Prime Minister Clement Attlee's viceroy, Lord Mountbatten, invited him to serve as the Dominion of India's first prime minister in 1947. Mountbatten became governor general. Nehru remained prime minister for seventeen years, from mid-August 1947 until his death on May 27, 1964. His popularity was second only to Gandhi's, and he led their Congress Party to victory in every election, enjoying more power over democratic India than any Mughal emperor or British viceroy.

Nehru's nonaligned foreign policy helped win substantial foreign economic support for India's five-year plans, over which he personally presided. He aspired to lead a pan-Asian–African Third World as a counter to cold war superpower confrontation, but he failed to win either Chinese or Pakistani support for that movement. Nehru's excessive faith in socialism and the Soviet Union ultimately weakened India's eco-nomic development. His inability to work with Mohammad Ali Jinnah proved a fatal blow to Hindu-Muslim cooperation before British India's partition and to Indo-Pakistani cooperation after it. His domestic policy of secular and democratic ideals, however, helped liberate India's ancient polity from many of its caste-related prejudices and deep-rooted authoritarian weaknesses. Despite his revolutionary socialist rhetoric, Nehru groomed his daughter Indira to inherit his premier power, thus founding a "democratic" dynasty.

See also *Gandhi, Mahatma; Jinnah, Mohammad Ali.*

STANLEY WOLPERT

BIBLIOGRAPHY

Brecher, Michael. *Nehru: A Political Biography.* London: Oxford University Press, 1959.

Nanda, B. R. *The Nehrus: Motilal and Jawaharlal.* New York: John Day, 1963.

Nehru, Jawaharlal. *Toward Freedom.* New York: John Day, 1941.

Sar Desai, D. R., and Anand Mohan, eds. *The Legacy of Nehru: A Centennial Assessment.* Springfield, Mass.: Nataraj Books, 1992.

Wolpert, Stanley. *Nehru: A Tryst With Destiny.* New York: Oxford University Press, 1996.

KWAME NKRUMAH

Nkrumah (1909–1972) led Ghana to become in 1957 the first black African colony to win independence and was the foremost Pan-African leader of his era. He was Ghana's first prime minister (1951–1957, 1957–1960) and president (1960–1966).

Born of poor parents in rural Ghana, Nkrumah was an exceptional student and was educated as a teacher at Achimota Teachers College. After teaching briefly, Nkrumah went to the United States (1935–1945), where he successfully pursued a university education. He engaged in African nationalist organizing in England from 1945 to 1947, when he was invited home to be secretary to Ghana's new, bourgeois-led nationalist movement.

By 1949 Nkrumah had organized a more radical populist Convention People's Party (CPP), whose militant protests and strikes demanding independence forced the British to accelerate constitutional reforms. The CPP drew heavily for its activists and leaders on commoners in the traditional order, many of whom were elementary school graduates or teachers whose rising aspirations and nationalism Nkrumah articulated and embodied. The CPP became the dominant nationalist movement, winning repeated elections and independence in 1957, with Nkrumah as prime minister. Nkrumah's leadership was highly charismatic and populist. It was also autocratic after 1959, when a one-party system was consolidated. Nkrumah's personal authority dominated. More positively, Nkrumah was crucial to the CPP's role in integrating a multiethnic society and creating a Ghanaian national, rather than ethnic, identity.

Nkrumah was the architect in 1959–1966 of a serious, if unsuccessful, state socialist effort to restructure the Ghanaian economy through industrialization and agricultural mechanization. Despite many failures, Nkrumah's program was the only sustained effort in Ghana up through the 1990s. Nkrumah personally pushed con-

KWAME NKRUMAH

struction of the massive Volta Dam and electrification project and the associated alumina operation. Nkrumah's government was overthrown by military coup in 1966. He spent his last years in exile in Guinea. Nkrumah's life was politics. He married late, an Egyptian, Fathia, and had three children by her and a son by a prior relationship.

Despite criticism of Nkrumah's dictatorship and CPP corruption, the Nkrumah/CPP legacy became an enduring political tradition in Ghana owing to successful policies in education and employment, the populist egalitarian ethos, economic nationalism, and the CPP's extensive organization. Nkrumahist/CPP-based parties reappeared as one of two dominant political orientations for voters in subsequent democratic regimes.

One of Nkrumah's most lasting contributions was his powerful commitment to pan-African unity among Africa's new, weak states, so that Africa could escape imperial domination, develop bargaining power with multinational corporations, and prevent great power interventions. Nkrumah was insistent on the need for continental political union, which proved unrealistic. Nkrumah devoted enormous resources to push-

ing for African unity, from his student days on, at the level of governments and of political parties. Nkrumah's efforts involved both personal ambition and genuine ideals for Africa. He provided intellectual and political support for African unity efforts, with some major impacts: he made the intellectual case for unified policies and strategies to overcome structural dependence; he organized many Pan-African conferences and several political unions, forcing Africa's reluctant states to concede at least to creating the Organization of African Unity in 1963; and he successfully delegitimated great power interventions through forceful Pan-African diplomacy against such intrusions in Africa.

JON KRAUS

BIBLIOGRAPHY

Apter, David. *Ghana in Transition*. 2d ed. rev. Princeton, N.J.: Princeton University Press, 1972.

Arhin, Kwame, ed. *The Life and Times of Kwame Nkrumah*. Accra: Sedco Publishing, 1991.

Davidson, Basil. *Black Star: A View of the Life and Times of Kwame Nkrumah*. New York: Praeger, 1973.

Nkrumah, Kwame. *The Autobiography of Kwame Nkrumah*. London: Thomas Nelson, 1957.

Thompson, Scott. *Ghana's Foreign Policy, 1957–1966*. Princeton, N.J.: Princeton University Press, 1969.

JULIUS KAMBARAGE NYERERE

Nyerere (1922–) was an anticolonial African nationalist who after World War II sought the independence of Tanganyika, which was at the time a United Nations trusteeship under British administration. In pursuit of self-government and independence, Nyerere helped form the Tanganyika African National Union on July 7, 1954. The movement was successful, and the country became independent on December 9, 1961, with Nyerere as prime minister. Nyerere became president on December 9, 1962.

Linked to Nyerere's nationalism was his pan-Africanism, a commitment to the pursuit of African unity. Sometimes he put his pan-Africanism ahead of his nationalism, as when in 1960 he offered to delay Tanganyika's independence if this would help achieve the creation of an East African federation of Tanganyika, Kenya, and Uganda. In the end there was not enough political will in the other two countries to achieve such a union. On the other hand, Nyerere's Tanganyika did form a union with Zanzibar, in 1964, to form the United Republic of Tanzania. This remains the only case in Africa of previously sovereign states uniting into a new country.

Tanganyika played host to other major Pan-African activities. It became a frontline state for the liberation of Mozambique and Angola from Portuguese rule, and Rhodesia and South Africa from white minority government. Tanganyika established major training camps for southern African liberation fighters.

Nyerere's credentials as official host to liberation movements were put into question in 1964 when he was forced to invite British troops to put down a mutiny of his own army. More radical African heads of state, like Ghana's Kwame Nkrumah, regarded Nyerere's use of British troops as "neocolonial." Nyerere defended himself and continued his liberation role, successfully most of the time.

Domestically, Nyerere inaugurated three areas of reform—a political system based on the principle of the one-party state; an economic system based on an African approach to socialism (what he called *ujamaa,* or familyhood); and a cultural policy based on the Swahili language.

The cultural policy was the earliest and the most durable. Tanganyika (and later Tanzania) became one of the few African countries to use an indigenous language in parliament and as the primary language of national business. Kiswahili was promoted increasingly in politics, administration, education, and the media. It became a major instrument of nation-building, and nation-building became the most lasting of Nyerere's legacies.

Nyerere's one-party state produced good political theory but bad political practice. The theory that the one-party state could be as democratic as the multiparty system and was more culturally suited to Africa was intellectual-

JULIUS KAMBARAGE NYERERE

ly stimulating, but it failed the test in practice. Tanzania became a multiparty state not long after Nyerere left office. He personally accepted the transition to multiparty rule.

The economic experiment of *ujamaa,* which was launched dramatically by the Arusha Declaration on Socialism and Self-Reliance in 1967, captured the imagination of millions of reform-minded Africans. It was also greatly admired by Western liberals, intellectuals, and some governments. By 1987, however, disenchantment with *ujamaa* was widespread. Far from being self-reliant, Tanzania was more dependent on foreign aid than ever. And *ujamaa* had left the country poorer than it might otherwise have been. Liberalization, privatization, and marketization were not far behind.

Nyerere's regional East African legacy is also mixed. Although he was once committed to creating an East African federation, his socialist ideals clashed with his East African ideals. As he struggled to create socialism in his own country, he had to create barriers against free movement of capital, labor, and resources in and out of Kenya and Uganda. Socialist planning in one country proved to be incompatible with an open-door, pan-East-African policy.

Nyerere was raised as a Roman Catholic. Some believe that his recognition of the secessionist Biafra in 1968 was a form of solidarity with fellow Catholics, the Igbos, against a federal Nigeria which was potentially dominated by Muslims. Less convincing is the assertion that Nyerere's military intervention in Uganda in 1979 was motivated by a sectarian calculation to defend a mainly Christian Uganda from the Muslim dictator Idi Amin. In reality, Nyerere might have been motivated by a wider sense of humanitarianism and universal ethics. He was also defending Tanzania from Idi Amin's territorial appetite.

See also *Nkrumah, Kwame.*

ALI A. MAZRUI

BIBLIOGRAPHY

Nyerere, Julius Kambarage. *Freedom and Development: Uhuru na Maerdeleo* Oxford: Oxford University Press, 1973.

———. *Freedom and Socialism: Uhuru na Ujamaa.* Oxford: Oxford University Press, 1969.

———. *Freedom and Unity: Uhuru na Umoja.* Oxford: Oxford University Press, 1969.

———. *Ujamaa: Essays on Socialism.* Oxford: Oxford University Press, 1968.

GEORGE ORWELL

O rwell (1903–1951) attempted, in his writing, to confront the paradox of socialist revolution: that a successful socialist revolution could only grow out of a politically conscious proletariat and that a politically conscious proletariat could only grow out of a successful socialist revolution. A believer in the innate virtue of the proletariat, Orwell was led by his experience to conclude that these virtues would be undermined by the very process of revolution. Orwell was born Eric Arthur Blair in Motihari, Bengal, the son of an Indian civil servant. He joined the Imperial Police in 1922, serving in Burma. Almost from the beginning Orwell hated his work and left the service upon his return to Britain on leave in 1927.

While in Burma Orwell had worked on a novel, *Burmese Days* (1935), and also developed an ideology based upon the nexus of imperialism. Orwell came to see the inevitably corrupting nature of power, and his subsequent association of power with capital turned him into a socialist. He spent a period of time on a commission from the Left Book Club, living with working-class families in the north of England, and subsequently published these experiences in *Road to Wigan Pier* (1937), in which he extolled the values of ordinary workers and contrasted these with the self-seeking and patronizing values of middle-class socialists and communists. Orwell went to Spain in 1936; joined one of the

GEORGE ORWELL

pro-Republican militias, POUM (the Marxist Workers Party), which had Trotskyist affiliations; and fought on the front. He came to believe that the Republican forces had been betrayed by the USSR and its communist allies. As a consequence of his service in Spain, Orwell redefined his socialism, becoming profoundly anti-Soviet. He published a record of his war experiences, *Homage to Catalonia* (1938), which did even less to endear him to the orthodox left than his previous work.

As a writer Orwell spent a great deal of time living with and writing about the working class in Britain, and he became a champion of what he took to be working-class socialism. Nonideological—maybe anti-ideological—and certainly anti-intellectual, Orwell emphasized the importance of common decency; institutions should reflect structures that enable ordinary people to participate in their decisions. He saw the USSR as embodying the opposite set of values and wrote a devastating critique of the Russian Revolution and its consequences in the form of a fable, *Animal Farm* (1945), and a bitter, even bilious, characterization of life in a centralized, technocratic—and socialist—state, *Nineteen Eighty-Four* (1949).

Orwell could claim to have been a man of action. He craved for the "barricades to go up" and for the workers to confront their "natural enemy" the police, so that he could stand shoulder to shoulder with the proletariat. Orwell experienced what he took to be a truly socialist revolution in civil war Barcelona and was intoxicated by the atmosphere of equality and solidarity. If Barcelona fired his imagination about the possibilities of revolution, however, subsequent events, particularly the systematic harrying of Trotskyist and anarchist groups by the Spanish communists, made him pessimistic.

Although many critics have understood Orwell's work to offer an indictment of revolution as a process, he himself made no such claim, and there is overwhelming evidence that he both hoped for and expected a revolution in Britain in the early years of the Second World War. When this showed no signs of happening, and when indeed the government felt able to arm its citizens (the Home Guard), Orwell's own patriotism overcame his revolutionary fervor. Although he continued to believe that a working-class revolution would transform society hugely for the better—and that if there were any hope it lay with the "proles" (proletariat)—he came to accept that revolutions are likely to be dominated by intellectuals and to result in no tangible benefits for the working class. He became profoundly pessimistic about the prospects for socialist revolution as his health deteriorated, and he died in London in 1951 from his long-standing tuberculosis.

STEPHEN INGLE

BIBLIOGRAPHY

Crick, Bernard. *George Orwell: A Life.* Harmondsworth, England: Penguin, 1992.

Ingle, Stephen. *George Orwell: A Political Life.* Manchester, England: Manchester University Press, 1993.

Rodden, John. *The Politics of Literary Reputation.* Oxford: Oxford University Press, 1989.

Shelden, Michael. *Orwell: The Authorised Biography.* London: Heinemann, 1991.

THOMAS PAINE

A writer and activist, Thomas Paine (1737–1809) participated in the two most significant political revolutions of the early modern period: first in America, then in France. Born in Thetford, England, he spent his first thirty-seven years working in a variety of occupations until, in 1774, he emigrated to America, which was in ferment over acts of Parliament that the Americans thought were specifically designed to subjugate them. These acts, which placed high taxes on the American colonists without their consent, inspired Paine to write the first public pronouncement of why America must separate from Britain.

With the support of Benjamin Franklin, John Adams, and Benjamin Rush, in January 1776 Paine published *Common Sense,* an immediate bestseller in America and England. The pamphlet focused on British mistreatment of their American cousins by denying to them the historic rights of English citizens. Six months later, the Continental Congress, having revised Thomas Jefferson's draft, issued the Declaration of Independence. Paine thereafter was fully engaged in the Revolutionary War as a soldier (serving for a time as an aide-de-camp for Gen. Nathanael Greene) and more importantly as a writer. Between 1776 and the end of the war in 1781, he published several newspaper pieces, known collectively as *The American Crisis Series,* to rally the Continental Army to the American cause. George Washington read the first in the

THOMAS PAINE

series, with its heartstopping first line, "These are the times that try men's souls," to his troops on Christmas Day, just before they crossed the Delaware in a successful attack against the sleeping Hessian mercenaries whom King George III had hired from his German dominions.

In 1787, four years after the formal end of the war, Paine returned to England, but he eventually settled in France to sell his design for a pierless iron bridge, which he wanted to construct over the Seine. Although this effort failed, he was soon caught up in the French Revolution. He published his second-greatest work, the two-volume *Rights of Man* (1791–1792), which set forth the rationale for political revolution against tyranny and social revolution against inequality. Elected in 1792 to serve in the French National Convention, Paine helped draft a new constitution. France, the previous year, had become a constitutional monarchy, but it became a republic after Louis XVI was overthrown in August 1792. The constitution of 1793, although adopted by the Convention, was never implemented, because Maximilien Robespierre, the leader of the Committee of Public Safety, abolished it during the Reign of Terror (1793–1794). At the height of the Terror, for speaking out against the execution of Louis XVI and seeking the king's banishment instead, Paine was imprisoned for eleven months in the Luxembourg Prison.

In 1802 Paine returned to America, which he considered his true home, and seven years later died in New York City, largely alone, forgotten, and despised by his Federalist enemies, mainly John Adams, and others who never forgave him for his attack on organized religion in *The Age of Reason* (1793–1794). As a writer and activist for the freedom of all people everywhere, Thomas Paine inspired later generations to follow his example to transform the world from tyranny and privilege to liberty and equality.

See also *Adams, John; Jefferson, Thomas; Robespierre, Maximilien; Washington, George.*

JACK FRUCHTMAN JR.

BIBLIOGRAPHY

Foner, Eric. *Tom Paine and Revolutionary America.* Oxford: Oxford University Press, 1976.

Fruchtman, Jack, Jr. *Thomas Paine and the Religion of Nature.* Baltimore, Md.: Johns Hopkins University Press, 1993.

———. *Thomas Paine: Apostle of Freedom.* New York: Four Walls Eight Windows, 1994.

Keane, John. *Tom Paine: A Political Life.* Boston: Little, Brown, 1994.

Kramnick, Isaac, and Michael Foot, eds. *The Thomas Paine Reader.* Harmondsworth: Penguin, 1987.

MAXIMILIEN ROBESPIERRE

The most consistently radical of French revolutionary politicians, Robespierre (1758–1794) was the dominant figure during the Terror of 1793–1794. His downfall marked the end of the Revolution's most extreme and violent phase.

Born into a comfortably off legal family in Arras, northern France, Robespierre won a scholarship to a leading school in Paris, returning home in 1781 to practice law. He defended a handful of poor clients but spent most of his time in polite literary pursuits. His thinking was much influenced, then and later, by the writings of Jean-Jacques Rousseau. After writing radical pamphlets in the spring of 1789, he was elected to the Estates-General. When that body became the National Assembly in June, he became one of the most frequent speakers but was little heeded until 1791. He was even more assiduous in the Jacobin Club, soon the leading political circle in Paris, which proved to be his main power base throughout his revolutionary career. While fellow deputies derided the impracticality of Robespierre's opposition to the death penalty, slavery, and restrictions on popular political participation, his steady devotion to his principles and suspicion of those in power won him the nickname "the Incorruptible." Excluded from election to the subsequent Legislative Assembly by a law he had himself proposed, he was carried shoulder-high from the National Assembly on its last day by the Parisian populace.

During the Legislative Assembly (October 1791–September 1792), he devoted most of his political activity to the Jacobin Club, which his efforts had largely kept alive after its membership had split in July 1791. There he warned in vain of the perils of war against the Austrians, incurring the enmity of war's leading advocates, whom he called Girondins. Welcoming the overthrow of monarchy on August 10, 1792, he was elected to represent Paris in the Convention. In the Convention he argued for the execution of Louis XVI without a trial and was much execrated by the Girondins for his supposed dictatorial ambitions. In fact, he acquiesced only reluctantly in the purge of Girondins from the Convention on June 2, 1793, and later protected their supporters from prosecution.

Elected to the Committee of Public Safety on July 27, Robespierre soon became its main theoretical spokesman, defending the suspension of normal constitutional life until the return of peace and advocating resolute action against traitors. But he was alarmed by the de-Christianization that swept the country over the winter of 1793–1794, and he sought to restore religious practice in May 1794 with a very personal "Cult of the Supreme Being." Concerned lest indiscriminate Terror alienate more people than it punished, in March 1794 he orchestrated the execution of its leading advocates, the so-called Hebertistes. But by then the personal corruption of some who had warned him against

IN THIS PERIOD ETCHING (1794), MAXIMILIEN ROBESPIERRE LIES MORTALLY WOUNDED ON A TABLE IN THE ANTEROOM OF THE COMMITTEE OF PUBLIC SAFETY.

1794), Robespierre was guillotined without trial the next day.

Although no more responsible than many others for the Terror, Robespierre prolonged it unrepentantly and was made a scapegoat by those who survived to dismantle it. His bloody association with the Terror has always vitiated attempts to commend his earlier humanitarianism, commitment to social justice, and personal probity. He remains deeply controversial, but his admirers and detractors are curiously united in regarding him as the most complete personification of the French Revolution, a classic model (or warning) to all subsequent revolutionaries.

See also *Rousseau, Jean-Jacques.*

terrorist excesses had disgusted him equally, and they too, including the redoubtable Georges Jacques Danton, were executed a few weeks later. Thus began the "great" Parisian Terror, whose necessity Robespierre defended to the last, and whose processes he accelerated with the notorious law of 22 Prairial (June 10), which deprived those accused before the Revolutionary Tribunal of defense counsel. Alarmed that any of them might fall victim to the impossible demands of Robespierre's republic of virtue, his fellow deputies and committee members turned against him. Outlawed on 9 Thermidor (July 28,

WILLIAM DOYLE

BIBLIOGRAPHY

Hampson, Norman. *The Life and Opinions of Maximilien Robespierre.* London: Duckworth, 1974.

Haydon, Colin, and William Doyle, eds. *Robespierre. History, Historiography and Literature.* Cambridge: Cambridge University Press, 1998.

Jordan, David P. *The Revolutionary Career of Maximilien Robespierre.* New York: Free Press, 1985.

Rude, George. *Robespierre. Portrait of a Revolutionary Democrat.* London: Collins, 1975.

Thompson, James M. *Robespierre.* Oxford: Blackwell, 1935.

JEAN-JACQUES ROUSSEAU

Perhaps to no other French writer has so much political influence and inspiration been ascribed as to Rousseau (1712–1778). Revered as the champion of democracy, denounced as the theoretician of the totalitarian state, even credited with an important apology of aristocracy, Rousseau produced texts that remain today as emotionally gripping, yet intellectually ambiguous, as when they were published. The principal concepts associated with his name are a "social contract" among citizens, legitimizing government; a "general will," in which all citizens participate; an innate equality of men, which the state must respect; a critique of the ethical value of private property; and a civic mission of educating the citizenry to "virtue."

Rousseau passed abruptly from bohemian obscurity to literary fame when he published the *First Discourse* (1750), on the question of "whether the reestablishment of the arts and sciences has contributed to purifying morals." Rather than the predictable praise of civilization, Rousseau put forth a savage indictment of European society as denatured, effeminate, and degenerate, a set of denunciations that he turned into a posture of moral superiority from which to castigate the monarchy in the name of simple, primitive virtue and to call for violent measures of purification. The *Second Discourse* (1754), on the origins of inequality, consecrated his new identity as the "sage of Europe." In that essay, equating technical progress and artistic refine-ment with moral decay, he presented an original theory of how the means of production shaped not only man's economic life but his political and private existence as well.

"Man is born free, but everywhere he is in chains," Rousseau proclaimed in the *Social Contract* (1762), his major political work. Rousseau attempted to describe what kind of state would be legitimate and how it could be achieved. Rousseau's ideal state constituted a "moral being," a true body politic, absorbing its citizenry like cells in the human body. This unified state would have but a single source of motivation, the general will, and the citizen's virtue would consist of internalizing it: "Each man is virtuous when his private will conforms totally to the General Will" (Oeuvres, *completes,* 1964, 3:254). Aiming to fuse religion, patriotism, and self-interest into one set of beliefs, thus eliminating the fragmentation and contradictions inherent in European societies, Rousseau would substitute adoration of the state for traditional ethical values. Citizens would be obliged to swear a "civil profession of faith," and if someone betrayed that credo, "let him be put to death" (3:468). The tone of his ideal polity was resolutely virile; women were to be strictly relegated to a domestic, subservient mode.

The "common will" was not to be ascertained by elections, or party politics, or other democratic procedures. Rather, it could be voiced only by a superior being, the "legislator," a foreigner to

JEAN-JACQUES ROUSSEAU

turn its back to the world and form a self-absorbed entity, totally engrossed in its own exalted devotion to the body politic.

Rousseau's ideas, as well as his posture of virtuous accusation, were assumed and made use of during the French Revolution by leaders of opposing factions. Although he was cited as an authority by monarchists and moderate deputies alike, perhaps his most important disciples were Maximilien Robespierre, Louis-Antoine-Léon Saint-Just, and numerous other Jacobin leaders, who described themselves as the legislator and constantly invoked the authority of Rousseau.

Because of Rousseau's insistence on man's virtually total malleability, his distrust of representative democracy, and his espousal of manipulation in the interests of civic virtue, he has been charged with laying the intellectual groundwork for the modern totalitarian state.

See also *Robespierre, Maximilien*.

CAROL BLUM

BIBLIOGRAPHY

Cobban, Alfred. *Rousseau and the Modern State*. Hamden, Conn.: Archon, 1964.

Cranston, Maurice. *Jean-Jacques: The Early Life and Work of Jean-Jacques Rousseau, 1712–1754*. Chicago: University of Chicago Press, 1991.

Masters, Roger. *The Political Philosophy of Rousseau*. Princeton, N.J.: Princeton University Press, 1968.

Starobinski, Jean. *Jean-Jacques Rousseau, Transparency and Obstruction*. Chicago: University of Chicago Press, 1988.

Talmon, J. L. *The Origins of Totalitarian Democracy*. New York: Praeger, 1960.

the state who would see to it that the people were "instituted" (a form of political, religious, and social conditioning) to virtue, as Moses had instituted the Jews or Lycurgus the Spartans.

Rousseau applied his ideas to two real European peoples, the Corsicans (in 1764) and the Poles (in 1772), for whom he created constitutions. In both instances his advice was largely consistent with the principles of the social contract, insisting on the necessity for the nation to

JOSÉ FRANCISCO DE SAN MARTÍN

San Martín (1778–1850) was born in an Argentine town and joined the Spanish army in 1789. He saw action in Africa, Spain, and France. However, after Napoleon Bonaparte took the Iberian Peninsula, San Martín retired from the Spanish army and returned home in 1812. In Buenos Aires, he built an army out of militia elements and led his army to victories over the Spanish in Chile and Peru, earning for himself the appellation "Liberator."

As South American struggles against Spanish colonial rule intensified in the 1810s, the role of the military became ever more important. Aware that Spanish armies in the Andes and Lima threatened South American freedom, and that a direct attack on the strong Spanish positions in Upper Peru, and especially Buenos Aires, would be dangerous, San Martín began the long but less risky strategy of crossing the Andes to the south and moving on Lima from the Pacific.

His efforts converted the Argentine military into a professional fighting force. Many of his officers would eventually rise to dominate Argentine, Bolivian, and Chilean politics for the next fifty years. The 4,000 soldiers and 1,000 militiamen of his liberating Army of the Andes began marching out of Mendoza to Santiago, Chile, in early 1817. After a grueling Andean crossing, San Martín's forces saw action at Chacabuco (February 12), where they triumphed. Two days later, they entered Santiago. The general quickly prepared for the expedition on Lima, but bogged down by local rivalries in Chile and having to rout Spanish holdouts at Maipú (April 5, 1818), San Martín took several years to muster financial help from Buenos Aires and to secure the help of the English mercenary Lord Thomas Alexander Cochrane to lead a navy.

In 1819 San Martín left local political consolidation in Santiago to one of his generals, Bernardo O'Higgins, and the patriot forces aimed for the South American Spanish bastion of

JOSÉ FRANCISCO DE SAN MARTÍN

Peru. Lord Cochrane cornered the royalist fleet at Callao; San Martín, with 4,400 Argentine and Chilean soldiers, aimed for Lima. The enemy, however, boasted an army of 23,000. San Martín, ever prudent, sought to avoid the expense and turmoil of open battle. After almost a year of encirclement and only a few skirmishes, San Martín's army entered Lima on July 19, 1821; on July 28 a local council of notables declared Peruvian independence.

The Liberator issued a flurry of reforms (ending Indian tribute, freeing the new-born children of slaves, and abolishing press censorship), but consolidating constitutional rule was no easy task. Besides, royalist forces retained control of the highlands. San Martín chose to enlist the support of Gen. Simón Bolívar, now poised in the Ecuadorean port of Guayaquil. There, the two Liberators held a summit in July 1822 to discuss the final phase of the independence struggle. The proceedings of their three meetings remain shrouded in controversy. San Martín trumpeted a constitutional monarchy for the new countries; Bolívar wanted a republic. Bolívar refused to place his larger force under San Martín's command. His resources exhausted and personally dismayed at creole bickering over the constitutional makeup of the fledgling countries and military conspiracies, San Martín returned to Lima in September, where he resigned as Protector of Peru. Shortly thereafter he left for permanent exile in France, leaving the last stage of the wars to his rival, Bolívar.

See also *Bolívar, Simón.*

JEREMY ADELMAN

BIBLIOGRAPHY

Lynch, John. *The Spanish American Revolutions, 1808–1826.* New York: W.W. Norton, 1973.

Mitre, Bartolomé. *Historia de San Martín y de la emancipación sudamericana.* 2d ed. 3 vols. Buenos Aires: F. Lajouane, 1890.

Piccirilli, Ricardo. *San Martín y la política de los pueblos.* Buenos Aires: Gure, 1957.

AUGUSTO CÉSAR SANDINO

Sandino (1895–1934) waged successful rural guerrilla warfare against U.S. troops and surrogate native forces in Nicaragua over a quarter century before the Cuban revolutionary victory of 1959 popularized guerrilla-based insurgency. A poor, self-educated man, Sandino was a fervent nationalist, a spiritualist, and a socialist—in some senses, even a communist. He acquired a distaste for foreign intervention when U.S. marines suppressed Benjamin Zeledón's nationalist rebellion of 1912. Later, as a laborer for multinational corporations in Costa Rica and Mexico, he came to abhor the underside of capitalism.

In the mid-1920s, during a brief interlude in the direct U.S. occupation of Nicaragua (1912–1925, 1926–1932), he joined a Liberal revolt against the pro-United States Conservative government. When Washington reintroduced the marines, Sandino stood alone among Liberal commanders in refusing to negotiate—choosing instead to fight until the invaders left.

After failed attempts at conventional warfare, Sandino improvised rural guerrilla techniques. The ensuing struggle between Sandino's "crazy little army" and the U.S. marines and their surrogate Nicaraguan National Guard would foreshadow aspects of the Vietnam conflict decades later. The United States developed counterinsurgency tactics such as the aerial bombardment of "enemy" population centers, the establishment of rural free-fire zones, and the

AUGUSTO CÉSAR SANDINO (WITH HIS FOOT ON THE BUMPER) AND HIS STAFF, JUNE 1929.

creation of the equivalent of "protective hamlets." Sandino's forces engaged in hit and run as well as ambush tactics. While the homesick marines saw and referred to Nicaraguans as "Gooks," Sandino cultivated the support of locals who acted as his eyes and ears. The marines, under orders not to bring Sandino back alive should they capture him, were continuously frustrated in that quest.

As U.S. casualties mounted, the war became unpopular at home. Sandino metamorphosed into an international folk hero through a series of interviews he gave to American reporter Carlton Beals. Published in *The Nation* in 1928, the interviews were subsequently translated and published worldwide. An antiwar movement developed in the United States, which eventually gathered such strength that Congress cut off funding for the Nicaragua war. At the turn of 1932–1933, U.S. troops withdrew, leaving real control of Nicaragua to Anastasio Somoza García, the first native commander of the National Guard. Though Sandino and the nominal civilian government of Nicaragua worked out a peace settlement, Somoza—the first Somoza in a dynastic dictatorship that would last until 1979—ordered the arrest and summary execution of his foe in 1934.

Sandino's immediate legacy to Nicaragua and the world was the U.S. withdrawal and, to a large degree, the forced birth of Franklin Roosevelt's policy of the "Good Neighbor." Later, his name and image became the historical point of reference for the Sandinista Front for National Liberation (FSLN), an organization founded in 1961 to overthrow the Somozas. Though an attempt to implement Sandino's rural guerrilla strategy ironically led to their near obliteration at Pancasán in 1967, the Sandinistas eventually developed techniques of insurgency that would bring their revolution to power for eleven years (1979–1990). Dozens of aged veterans of Sandino's struggle marched proudly in the first victory parade.

THOMAS W. WALKER

BIBLIOGRAPHY

Hodges, Donald C. *Sandino's Communism: Spiritual Politics for the Twenty-First Century.* Austin: University of Texas Press, 1992.

Macaulay, Neill. *The Sandino Affair.* Chicago: Quadrangle Books, 1967.

Ramirez, Sergio, and Robert Edgar Conrad, eds. *Sandino: The Testimony of a Nicaraguan Patriot, 1921–1934.* Princeton, N.J.: Princeton University Press, 1990.

Selser, Gregorio. *Sandino, General de Hombres Libres.* Segunda edicion. San Jose: Editorial Universitaria Centroamericana, 1979.

GEORGES SOREL

Sorel (1847–1922) was committed, at least in his early years, to the notion of revolution, arising naturally from a general strike, as an energizing agency that would galvanize the industrial proletariat into a genuinely socialist force. Sorel was born in Cherbourg, France, and was educated at the École Polytechnique. In 1870 he became an engineer in the employment of the French government. He retired from his profession at the age of forty-five and devoted the rest of his life to reading and writing.

Sorel began his political writing career as a revolutionary syndicalist, believing that the control of production and distribution should be transferred to groups of industrial workers, but although he was greatly influenced by Marx, he rejected Marx's belief in the historical inevitability of class war and the triumph of the proletariat. There were no inexorable laws for him, only the ceaseless and unflinching pursuit of moral goals that might, through the application of communal energy and will, bring into being a creative, energized, and equal society. His most celebrated works were *The Disintegration of Marxism* (1906), *Reflections on Violence* (1908), and *The Illusions of Progress* (1908).

Sorel adopted an eclectic doctrine, deriving inspiration from the philosopher Henri Bergson, who gave prominence to the *élan vital* (life force) in the development of humanity. Reformist socialists, he came to believe (especially after the Dreyfus affair), were traitors. They shared with the capitalists a belief in progress, and this belief inevitably led to the further decadence of Europe. There was no place for Fabian-style gradualism or parliamentarianism in Sorel's thought. He abhorred compromise and the inevitable gradualness of compromise building. The moral rebirth he sought lay outside progressivism and the social institutions that claim to foster it. Only through action could people discover their virtue. So Sorel advanced instead the myth of the general strike. He used the notion of myth to imply not an illusion but a galvanizing vision. The myth would prove a potent force in persuading the proletariat of its potential for action. But class war would prove to be a creative force in its own right, allowing people to rediscover their Homeric virtues. As Sorel famously put it: "The goal is nothing; the movement is everything." The general strike was an exercise of political will and the imposition of that will upon nature. In its violence, Sorel believed—like Friedrich Nietzsche—the strike was a force for creativity.

By 1910, however, Sorel had abandoned syndicalism and extended his sympathies toward others who sought to use violence to reestablish traditional moral authority, namely those on the extreme right in France and elsewhere, and he became linked to the right-wing patriotic group Action Française. Mussolini was later to claim that Sorel had contributed the most to the "discipline, energy and power" of his fascist cohorts. Sorel's hopes for moral regeneration, all but killed by the First World War, were rekindled by the Russian Revolution, and he remained hopeful up to his death that the Soviet Communist Party would be the agent of the moral transformation of society he had sought to bring into being.

Sorel's influence was widespread, linking right-wing Catholics and conservatives, but also pacifists and anarchists. His influence stretched as far as the anticolonialist writers of the modern era, such as Frantz Fanon. More directly, his doctrines inspired revolutionary anarchosyndicalists and fascists in the 1930s: indeed, it has been said that the Spanish Civil War was fought between the supporters of the two branches of Sorel's thought!

See also *Fanon, Frantz Omar.*

STEPHEN INGLE

BIBLIOGRAPHY

Jennings, Jeremy. *Georges Sorel: The Character and Development of His Thought.* Basingstoke, England: Macmillan, 1985.

Roth, Jack. *The Cult of Violence: Sorel and the Sorelians.* Berkeley: University of California Press, 1980.

Vernon, Richard. *Commitment and Change: Georges Sorel and the Idea of Revolution.* Toronto: University of Toronto Press, 1978.

JOSEPH STALIN

Iossif (Joseph) Vissarionovich Dzhugashvili (1879–1953), who later took the name Stalin (the man of steel), was born of a poor family in Georgia, a part of the Russian Empire. Sent to a Christian Orthodox seminary to be trained as a priest, he instead converted to Marxism and became a revolutionary activist. In 1903 he was one of the relatively few Georgian Marxists who sided with Vladimir Ilyich Lenin's Bolsheviks against the Mensheviks. His activities included carrying out bank robberies to finance the party, and he came to Lenin's attention. Promoted to a leadership position in the party, he became its specialist on ethnic nationalism because of his experience in the diverse, contentious Caucasus. In 1913 he published a pamphlet, "Marxism and the National Question," which later became the guide to ethnic issues in the Soviet Union. In it he called for privileging the bigger linguistic groups, which ultimately meant Russian domination over the many minorities in Russia.

He was arrested and exiled to Siberia in 1913 and emerged in 1917 when the tsar was overthrown. He was one of Lenin's top aides in the Bolshevik Revolution and in the ensuing civil war. In 1922 he became general secretary of the Communist Party and proved to be skillful in filling crucial positions with his own followers. By the time Lenin died in 1924, Stalin was too entrenched to be removed, despite Lenin's explicit warning to the party that Stalin was too

brutal and had become too much a Russian nationalist.

In the succession struggle that followed Lenin's death, Stalin had three advantages. First, unlike his three top rivals, including Leon Trotsky, he was not a Jew. Second, he could talk

JOSEPH STALIN WAS ARRESTED AND DEPORTED TO SIBERIA ON SEVERAL OCCASIONS, THE FIRST TIME IN 1901, FOR HIS WORK IN PROPAGANDA AND MASS AGITATION FOR THE RUSSIAN SOCIAL DEMOCRATIC WORKERS' PARTY. THIS ARREST REPORT WAS MADE BY THE TSARIST GENDARMES IN MARCH 1908.

to less educated, more anti-Semitic, newer party members who found Lenin's other close associates too abstract, too intellectual, and too cosmopolitan for their own simpler tastes. Third, he proved to be an adept compromiser who could steer between the many factions in the party and appear as a moderate, practical man rather than as a wild-eyed extremist. But once he had gained absolute power in 1928, he relegated his former rivals to impotence, and then had almost all of them murdered in the 1930s.

In 1929 he set out to create a socialist, industrialized Soviet Union. First, he collectivized the land to make the peasants produce food for less compensation. This resulted in a famine and a war against the peasants, which ultimately killed some ten million. Then, to maintain discipline and absolute obedience to his will, he purged the Communist Party and anyone else suspected of disloyalty to the system. Finally, to ward off any military threat to his power, he destroyed most of his top army officers. By 1939 he had created an industrial, submissive society ruled by terror. Millions were in slave labor camps, and at least twenty million had died.

In 1939 he signed a treaty with Adolf Hitler dividing up Europe, but he was double-crossed when Hitler invaded the USSR in 1941. After suffering enormous losses, Stalin's armies pushed the Germans back, conquered eastern Europe, and occupied Berlin in 1945.

After the victory, Stalin's USSR became one of the world's two superpowers, along with the United States. But in 1946 Stalin resumed the purges and mass persecutions. He was planning to deport all Soviet Jews to Siberia and to execute most of his top aides when he died of a stroke in 1953.

Stalin was revered and praised by revolutionary Marxists all over the world during his lifetime. He was the chief architect of communism whose model was imitated by other communist leaders everywhere. With Hitler and Mao Zedong, he was also one of the greatest mass murderers in history.

See also *Lenin, Vladimir Ilyich; Trotsky, Leon.*

DANIEL CHIROT

BIBLIOGRAPHY

Kersahw, Ian, and Moshe Lewin, eds. *Stalinism and Nazism: Dictatorships in Comparison.* Cambridge: Cambridge University Press, 1997.

Tucker, Robert C. *Stalin as Revolutionary 1879–1929.* New York: W.W. Norton, 1974.

———. *Stalin in Power 1929–1941.* New York: W.W. Norton, 1990.

Volkogonov, Dmitri, *Stalin: Triumph and Tragedy.* New York: Grove, Weidenfeld, 1991.

SUKARNO

Sukarno (1901–1970), the leader of Indonesia's independence struggle against the Dutch, was born in Surabaya, the Dutch East Indies' largest port city. He attended an elite, Dutch-language high school, where he picked up notions of Indonesian nationalism. The late 1910s was a time of rapid change as the better educated natives were starting to become aware of their common Indonesian and anticolonial identity. As the Dutch Indies were a vast collection of different peoples with distinct languages and many religions, the awareness of a common identity was the requisite first step for the creation of an effective independence movement.

In 1926 Sukarno graduated from the Technical College of Bandung with an engineering degree. By then he had become deeply involved in political activity in behalf of the nationalist cause. In 1927 he was one of a small group of intellectuals who formed the Indonesia Nationalist Association (PNI), and he became its chairman. The PNI soon became the main nationalist party in the Indies.

Sukarno's doctrine rested on a vague combination of socialism, Gandhian passive resistance, respect for the many traditional religions of Indonesia, and a faith that somehow these could all be blended with a progressive, secular, Western approach to economic reform. In 1930, to control growing nationalist sentiment, the Dutch imprisoned Sukarno for two years. Then, in 1934, he was exiled by the Dutch to remote outer Indonesian islands. His reputation continued to grow, however, as without him the divided and fractious nationalist movement was repeatedly thwarted by the Dutch.

Sukarno's big chance came when Japan conquered the Dutch East Indies in 1942, during World War II, and set him up as president of a puppet nationalist government. Sukarno declared Indonesia independent on August 17, 1945, three days after Japan's surrender. The Dutch, however, tried to recapture Indonesia, and there followed a bloody war which ended on December 27, 1949, when Indonesian independence was recognized by the Dutch. Sukarno became president of the new nation.

Sukarno tried to steer a moderate path between the many political forces in his country. There were regional rebellions in many of the outer islands, an Islamic movement, and a powerful, growing Communist Party that demanded a genuine socialist revolution. Sukarno's attempt to tie together these various ideological strands proved unworkable. Indonesia's economy decayed as the Dutch left, and his socialist, autarkic policies discouraged both outside and internal investment. To compensate, Sukarno, like many other early nationalist leaders, turned to international affairs to rally his people and rekindle their revolutionary fervor. Internally, he tried to establish a dictatorship under the name of "guided democracy," but he never gained the absolute power he sought.

As Indonesian democracy collapsed into a corrupt, stalemated dictatorship, with Sukarno trying to maintain himself in power by balancing the competing interests of Indonesia's more conservative army and its now enormous Communist Party, he distracted the country by launching a series of foreign adventures and initiatives. He declared that he would destroy neighboring Malaysia because it was a British neocolonialist tool. He took Indonesia out of the United Nations; and he turned increasingly anti-American and procommunist.

By 1965 Sukarno was aging and ill, and his impoverished country was headed toward a civil war between the army and the communists. Sukarno increasingly sided with the communists; when some of them attempted to seize power in 1965, Sukarno was implicated. The army, however, quickly won the battle and annihilated the communists along with hundreds of thousands of their followers.

Sukarno was sidelined and pushed out of power in 1966. He died in semidisgrace in 1970, though more recently he has regained a posthumous status as Indonesia's great anticolonial hero and first president.

DANIEL CHIROT

SUKARNO

BIBLIOGRAPHY

Anderson, Benedict R. O'G. *Language and Power: Exploring Political Cultures in Indonesia.* Ithaca, N.Y.: Cornell University Press, 1990.

Legge, J. D. *Sukarno: A Political Biography.* New York: Praeger, 1972.

Mortimer, Rex. *Indonesian Communism Under Sukarno: Ideology and Politics, 1959–1965.* Ithaca, N.Y.: Cornell University Press, 1974.

SUN YAT-SEN

Sun (1866–1925) was the leader of an anti-monarchical revolution he could not control and the founder of a republic he could neither command nor fully support. As such, Sun embodied many of the contradictions and complexities that made the early stages of the Chinese revolution long, bloody, and indecisive.

The upwardly and outwardly mobile son of a farming family, Sun had followed the tide of the Chinese diaspora, joining his businessman-elder brother in Hawaii to attend a Christian school. Trained as a medical doctor in the southern coastal city of Guangzhou and in Hong Kong, Sun became a reformer and a nationalist. He tried to win the attention of Qing government reformers, but his Westernizing proposals were unexceptional and his lack of proper literary and examination credentials made him less than persuasive as a petitioner. Sun led an unsuccessful Guangzhou-based uprising against the Qing dynasty in 1895, pitching him from reform and anonymity to revolution and notoriety. He spent the next sixteen years in exile raising money for the revolutionary cause among overseas Chinese and planning a series of unsuccessful uprisings in China. Sun developed a powerful sense of his own destiny as China's leader, considerable skill as a public speaker, and a broad familiarity with foreign ideas and practices.

Sun's strategy of igniting small revolts in order to fire larger uprisings assumed the imminent

SUN YAT-SEN

collapse of the Qing dynasty. But the decisive blow was not directly delivered by Sun, who was traveling in the United States at the time of the 1911 revolution. Sun's status as a leading revolutionary won him the post of provisional president once he returned to China at the end of 1911. Sun had many assets: a name and face synonymous with revolution, impeccable republican credentials, a plan for national development (the "Three People's Principles" of nationalism, democracy, and people's livelihood), and the support of many revolutionaries. But he lacked military power and soon yielded the presidency to Yuan Shikai, a former Qing official with a modern army based in north China. Sun spent his remaining years trying to win back the post he gave away in 1912 through political campaigns, military expeditions, diplomatic initiatives, and propaganda efforts. In doing so he expanded the political repertoire of the modern Chinese leader.

Sun's many failures and his death in 1925 before he could regain national power make his acknowledged status as a Chinese revolutionary in a league with Hong Xiuquan, Chiang Kai-shek, and Mao Zedong somewhat surprising. Contemporaries accused Sun of stealing credit from more daring colleagues as well as being a politically naive blowhard whose deeds rarely matched his words. But Sun also captured the imagination of Chinese who had shifted their attention from the pattern of China's past to the promise of a brilliant future. Sun spoke of independence for China but also rhapsodized about rail lines, new harbors, paved roads, and a comfortable life in which Chinese would "get rich"

(*facai*). Sun called for a disciplined approach to revolution that countenanced sacrificing individual freedom in order to win freedom for the nation and to turn China from a disorganized "plate of sand" into a solid community with an "all-powerful state." His demand for sacrifice and discipline and the alliance of his Nationalist Party with the Communists in 1923 helped pave the way for the rise of Chinese Leninism and Maoist utopianism. Sun also pioneered the role of revolutionary Chinese leader as a potent but unstable mixture of populist rhetoric, statist ambitions, and imperial prerogatives.

DAVID STRAND

BIBLIOGRAPHY

Bergere, Marie-Claire. *Sun Yat-sen*. Paris: Fayard, 1994.
Schiffrin, Harold Z. *Sun Yat-sen and the Origins of the Chinese Revolution*. Berkeley: University of California Press, 1968.
Wei, Julie Lee, Ramon H. Myers, and Donald G. Gillin, eds. *Prescriptions for Saving China: Selected Writings of Sun Yat-sen*. Translated by Julie Lee Wei, E-su Zen, and Linda Chao. Stanford: Hoover Institution, 1994.
Wilbur, C. Martin. *Sun Yat-sen: Frustrated Patriot*. New York: Columbia University, 1976.
Wong, John Y. *Origins of an Heroic Image: Sun Yat-sen in London, 1896–97*. Oxford: Oxford University Press, 1986.

Josip Broz Tito

Tito (1892–1980) led the partisan resistance movement in Yugoslavia during World War II and was the unquestioned leader of socialist Yugoslavia from the war's end until his death. He also was one of the founders of the movement of nonaligned states, which sought to provide a third force in world politics in the era of cold war rivalry between the United States and the Soviet Union.

Born to a mixed Croatian/Slovenian family in northwest Croatia, Tito had completed his train-

Josip Broz Tito

ing as a locksmith by the time he was eighteen. In 1913 he entered the Austro-Hungarian army, where during World War I he was wounded and captured by the Russians. In Russia he participated in the Bolshevik Revolution and became a communist. Returning to newly created Yugoslavia in 1920, he rose steadily in the illegal communist party despite spending several years in prison. When Stalinist purges struck down other party leaders, in 1939 he became general secretary. After Hitler's armies invaded the Soviet Union in June 1941, Tito led his underground organization in vigorous resistance to the German occupation of Yugoslavia. Over the course of the war, his partisan movement not only fought the Germans but engaged in a three-way civil war with Croatian fascists and Serbian nationalists. Although later criticized after the war for mistakes of military judgment and other errors, his ability to lead and direct, and his acknowledged position as "the old man" of the movement, permitted him to guide the communist forces to victory in 1945.

Considered in the West as Soviet leader Joseph Stalin's most loyal ally in the years 1945 to 1948, Tito actually took initiatives of which Stalin did not approve, such as agreeing to a federation with Bulgaria. Having won their own revolution, Tito and his colleagues resented the overbearing way in which Russian advisers and functionaries treated them. In 1948, when they expressed these concerns, Stalin expelled Yugoslavia from the Cominform (Communist Information Bureau—the replacement for the disbanded Communist International, or Comintern). Until Stalin's death in 1953, the Soviet bloc pursued a relentless propaganda campaign against Yugoslavia. "Titoism," that is, questioning the leading role of the Soviet Union and Stalin, became a serious crime in Eastern Europe, and many Czechoslovaks, Hungarians, and Bulgarians went to their death as alleged Titoists.

To differentiate Yugoslav communism from the Soviet model, Tito adopted a system of worker self-administration. His willingness to permit somewhat more openness to the West, by letting people emigrate or work abroad, for example, along with the introduction of modest market mechanisms into the Yugoslav economy, permitted Yugoslavia to steer a middle course between East and West until his death in 1980. This policy was exemplified by his early leadership of the nonaligned movement, that is, the effort of states like Indonesia, India, and Egypt to create an alliance of countries committed neither to capitalism nor to communism.

Tito hoped that each of the many ethnic groups in Yugoslavia could retain its national identity while becoming loyal to a larger socialist community. But he was unwilling to open public debate on difficult issues, and he insisted that the party retain control despite rhetoric about self-administration. To try to solve ethnic tensions he did allow the Communist Party to decentralize into eight competing regional units, but this only worsened the problem. His personal, autocratic rule was an important factor in holding Yugoslavia together, but these qualities made it impossible for Yugoslavs to develop a level of civic consciousness sufficient to sustain them when socialism collapsed eleven years after his death.

GALE STOKES

BIBLIOGRAPHY

Auty, Phyllis. *Tito: A Biography.* Rev. ed. Hammondsworth: Penguin, 1974.
Dedijer, Vladimir. *Tito.* New York: Simon and Schuster, 1953.
Djilas, Milovan. *Tito: The Story from Inside.* New York: Harcourt Brace Jovanovic, 1980.
Maclean, Fitzroy. *The Heretic: The Life and Times of Josip Broz Tito.* London: Cape, 1949.

ALEXIS DE TOCQUEVILLE

lthough he participated briefly in the early stages of the French Revolution of 1848, Tocqueville (1805–1859) is chiefly important to the study of revolutions as one of the acutest analysts of the origins and significance of the French Revolution of 1789. Insofar as that revolution is a paradigm for the analysis of subsequent ones, his insights have a wider significance.

A nobleman and son of a distinguished Napoleonic administrator who wrote his own history of the French Revolution (having lived through it, unlike several guillotined relatives), Tocqueville embarked on a legal career. His legal research took him to the United States in the early 1830s, ostensibly on an official mission from the French government to study American prisons. Out of this visit came his first great masterpiece, *Democracy in America* (1835–1840), which is essential to understanding all his later thought.

In 1839 he entered politics as a deputy. The peak of his public career came after the 1848 revolution, when he served for five months in 1849 as foreign minister. Dismissed by President Louis Napoleon Bonaparte, he protested against Bonaparte's seizure of imperial power in 1851. Tocqueville, excluded in consequence from public life, devoted his remaining years to research and reflection on the Revolution amid whose consequences he had spent his life. The result was *The Old Regime and the French Revolution* (1856),

intended as merely the introductory volume to a work he never finished.

Although underpinned by unprecedented archival research, the work is famous for its factual errors. Far more important, however, are its broader insights. The Revolution, Tocqueville argued, was not the radical break that the French had sought and imagined they had achieved in 1789. Nor was it in any sense an accident. The Revolution was merely a phase in the inexorable development of two long-term and interconnected processes. One was the progress of democracy, which Tocqueville had first studied in America. Democracy meant an equalization of ranks, rights, and resources, and was the social pattern of the future. The other was bureaucratic centralization, which throve on democratic uniformity. Both processes were well advanced by 1789. The Revolution's historic destiny was to sweep away the remaining obstacles to their progress in the form of privileges, institutional anomalies, and social distinctions and exceptions of all kinds. The great casualty of the Revolution was liberty, which lost its last institutional underpinnings; and it was in no way surprising that the result should be the dictatorship of Napoleon. The Revolution had left nothing to stand in his way, or in that of his nephew, who had destroyed the revolution of Tocqueville's own lifetime. America, by contrast, had a free press and high levels of public involvement in government; Great Britain retained a powerful aristocracy; and

ALEXIS DE TOCQUEVILLE

so in both the spirit of liberty remained vigorous. Tocqueville's analysis minimized the religious significance of the Revolution, so central in the perceptions of most of his contemporaries. But his emphasis on the destructive results of hitherto untested Enlightenment ideology is once more fashionable among those revolutionary historians who have turned away from socioeconomic explanations of the Revolution.

WILLIAM DOYLE

BIBLIOGRAPHY

Brogan, Hugh. *Tocqueville.* London: Collins Fontana, 1973.
Furet, Francois. *Interpreting the French Revolution.* Cambridge: Cambridge University Press, 1982.
Herr, Richard. *Tocqueville and the Old Regime.* Princeton, N.J.: Princeton University Press, 1962.
Palmer, Robert R. *The Two Tocquevilles. Father and Son.* Princeton, N.J.: Princeton University Press, 1987.
Tocqueville, Alexis de. *The Ancien Regime.* Introduction by Norman Hampson. London: Dent, Everyman's Library, 1988.

LEON TROTSKY

Trotsky (1879–1940), born Lev Davidovich Bronshtein, was a prominent leader and theorist of the Russian revolutionary movement and Marxist socialism and a founder of the Soviet state. During his exile from the Soviet Union, his was a powerful voice in the anti-Stalinist opposition within the international left.

As a student in Odessa and Nikolaev, Trotsky was attracted to the revolutionary politics of social-democracy in the Russian Empire. He began his career as a journalist, pamphleteer, and orator to worker and student groups in 1896. Following his arrest in 1898, he served two years in prison and was sentenced to four additional years of exile in Siberia, but he escaped to London in 1902. There he met Vladimir Ilyich Lenin and attended the Second Congress of the Russian Social-Democratic Workers' Party in 1903, where he engaged in fierce polemics with Lenin about the character of the Russian revolutionary party. Trotsky prophesied that Lenin's vision of a professional, underground organization carried within it the seeds of future dictatorship.

In fall 1905 he chaired the Petersburg Soviet of Workers' Deputies, the center of revolutionary socialist politics during the brief experiment with quasi-constitutional monarchy. Following the crushing of the 1905 uprising, his arrest, and exile, Trotsky again fled abroad, where he edited social-democratic newspapers and occupied a middle ground between the Bolshevik and Menshevik fractions of the party. During this period he elaborated a theory of permanent revolution, which anticipated a rapid telescoping of the bourgeois-democratic and proletarian-socialist revolutions in the special conditions of Russia's uneven development.

With the outbreak of the First World War, Trotsky became a leader of the internationalist, antiwar wing of social democracy. After the March 1917 revolution in Petrograd, Trotsky returned from exile in America to play a promi-

LEON TROTSKY

nent role in the faction (the Interdistrict group) that steered a course between the Bolshevik and Menshevik parties. In July, following his arrest by the Provisional Government, he cast his lot with Lenin's Bolsheviks and became a powerful ally of Lenin during the months before the Bolshevik seizure of power in November 1917; he was elected chairman of the Petrograd Soviet and headed its Military Revolutionary Committee. In the first Bolshevik-dominated Soviet government he served as commissar of foreign relations and negotiated the short-lived peace of Brest-Litovsk. When the Germans resumed their offensive against Soviet Russia, Lenin appointed Trotsky military commissar (1918–1925); he built the Red Army and led the military campaigns of the civil war (1918–1921).

After the war, he withdrew from engagement in military affairs to economic planning and Communist Party politics. When Lenin was incapacitated by a series of strokes, Trotsky became one of the key figures in the succession struggle for leadership of the Soviet state and Communist Party. He criticized the bureaucratization of the once-revolutionary underground party and the concentration of power in an ever narrower circle of party leaders, especially Joseph Stalin. In 1927, however, Stalin defeated his opponents, expelled Trotsky from the party, and exiled him to Kazakhstan. While in Alma-Ata, Trotsky began writing his *History of the Russian Revolution,* a classic of eyewitness–participant history.

From exile in Turkey and later Mexico he waged an untiring campaign against Stalin's policies in the pages of *The Bulletin of the Opposition.* During his final years, he developed his theory of the degeneration of the proletarian revolution and its usurpation by the Thermidorian bureaucracy, which was presiding over counterrevolution. Trotsky still believed that Stalin's dictatorship would be overthrown by a newly assertive working-class movement. He was tried in absentia during the Moscow show trials of the 1930s, accused of spying for foreign powers, and assassinated on orders from Stalin in 1940.

See also *Lenin, Vladimir Ilyich; Stalin, Joseph.*

MARK VON HAGEN

BIBLIOGRAPHY

Deutscher, Isaac. *The Prophet Armed. Trotsky: 1879–1921.* New York: Oxford University Press, 1954.
———. *The Prophet Unarmed. Trotsky: 1921–1929.* New York: Oxford University Press, 1959.
———. *The Prophet Outcast. Trotsky: 1929–1940.* New York: Oxford University Press, 1963.
Knei-Paz, Baruch. *The Social and Political Thought of Leon Trotsky.* Oxford: Oxford University Press, 1978.
Trotsky, Leon. *My Life.* New York: Scribner's, 1930.

LECH WALESA

Walesa (1943–) was a charismatic leader of a social movement known as Solidarity, which attracted millions of adherents in Poland in 1980. He continued to nurture and preserve Solidarity's spirit despite fierce repression until 1989, when he seized and created opportunities that brought the rule of the Communist Party in Poland to an end. Walesa was lionized in the world media for effectively defying the Soviet Union's dominion over Eastern Europe and contributing to the demise of Soviet communism at large. Certainly, he worked in tune with broader historical forces, and he was not alone. But his agency was of great significance.

Walesa was born into a peasant family in central Poland. He completed a vocational education and, after compulsory military service, found employment as an electrician at the Lenin Shipyards in Gdańsk. Three years after his arrival in Gdańsk, food riots broke out in December 1970. Street demonstrations by shipyard workers were brutally repressed, and several dozen protesters were killed by security forces. He was driven into social activism by the memory of these events.

In the late 1970s Walesa ran afoul of the authorities by joining a group of early advocates of independent labor unions on the Baltic coast. He was dismissed from his job, and when the August 1980 strike broke out in the shipyards, he had to "jump over the wall" in order to join it.

LECH WALESA

Walesa at once established himself as a leader of the strike. He had a formidable stage presence when addressing large audiences, and he was a persistent, tough negotiator, with a brilliant sense for public relations. During the two-week-long strike of August, Walesa catapulted himself to worldwide fame.

Solidarity, an independent labor union, was established at the conclusion of the August strike. Within two months a majority of all working men and women in Poland had joined Solidarity.

Walesa presided over this vast social movement for the next sixteen months. After the government of Gen. Wojciech Jaruzelski imposed martial law on December 13, 1981, and banned Solidarity, Walesa was held in isolation for over a year. Upon release the security police kept him under close surveillance. But Walesa remained in the public eye—as when he received the Nobel Peace Prize in 1983, for example—and he kept in touch with the clandestine structures of Solidarity.

When a new wave of strikes erupted in the summer of 1988, General Jaruzelski balked at Walesa's demand for relegalization of the labor union. The issue was forced, however, after the leader of government-sponsored labor unions, Alfred Miodowicz, challenged Walesa to a television debate. With the whole country watching the debate, Walesa restored Solidarity to its role of unquestionable mouthpiece for the working people of Poland.

In the spring of 1989 roundtable negotiations between the government and opposition leaders concluded with the relegalization of Solidarity. In return, the union reluctantly agreed to put up candidates in the forthcoming parliamentary elections, thereby lending token legitimacy to the regime. Fearing co-optation, Walesa chose not to run. Electoral support for Solidarity in June 1989 exceeded the most optimistic expectations. In September a Solidarity-sponsored candidate, Tadeusz Mazowiecki, became prime minister. Ironically, the success of Solidarity in ending Communist Party rule in Poland put Walesa on the sidelines.

Walesa grew increasingly impatient with what he perceived to be his former associates' slow pace of reform. But Walesa, as chairman of just a labor union, lacked a suitable base for participating in the process. He engaged in petty quarrels and instigated conflicts until he got himself elected as the country's president in 1990. By then he was perceived as responsible for deep rifts among Solidarity activists-cum-politicians.

The four years of his presidency were uninspiring. The carelessness and internal contradictions of his public pronouncements became proverbial. He played personal favorites; promoted his former chauffeur to the most important position of minister of state in presidential chancellery; and kept changing his entourage in a capricious game of musical chairs. He acquired the reputation of a spoiler, able to undermine any initiative but incapable of constructive collaboration with others. In the end, he brought upon himself the indignity of losing a reelection bid in 1995 to a former second-tier Communist politician, Aleksander Kwaśniewski. Walesa accepted the voters' verdict with dignity.

Following the September 1997 parliamentary elections (in which he was not a candidate for office), he established the Christian Democratic Party of the Third Polish Republic, planning to attract "some of the 52 percent of eligible voters who did not participate in the 1997 elections." Thus, a great, charismatic movement leader and a mediocre, lackluster statesman, Walesa embarked on a new career as a party politician going after hearts and minds of a silent majority.

JAN T. GROSS

BIBLIOGRAPHY

Boyes, Roger. The Naked President. A Political Life of Lech Walesa. London: Secker and Warburg, 1994.

Walesa, Lech. The Struggle and the Triumph: An Autobiography. New York: Arcade, 1992.

GEORGE WASHINGTON

Washington (1732–1799) was a Virginia planter who commanded the American Revolutionary Army and later became the first president of the United States. Unlike many modern revolutionary leaders, Washington displayed no traits of asceticism. He was not culturally alienated from England, the mother country, nor did he suffer from a dysfunctional family. He failed to display narcissistic characteristics in an adult life filled with praise and adulation. Solid, steady, and focused, he brought to the national stage extensive military experience as the commander of Virginia's forces from 1755 to 1758 in the Seven Years' War (1756–1763) and seventeen years' legislative service in his colony. His background, as well as his qualities of persistence and tenacity, made him ideally qualified to lead the eight-year struggle for independence against Great Britain (1775–1783).

In June 1775 the Continental Congress appointed Washington, one of its own members, commander in chief of the colonial forces besieging the British troops in Boston following the battles of Lexington and Concord; he was a man the delegates knew and could trust. Ever deferential to Congress even though it was an extralegal body until near the end of the war, Washington believed fervently in civil control of the military, just as he endeavored to strengthen Congress's hand in dealing with the American states after the declaring of independence in 1776.

Washington preferred to engage Britain in a fairly conservative, traditional form of warfare. He feared that a partisan or guerrilla conflict, although tempting because of wilderness condition in much of America, would spawn atrocities and wholesale destruction of cities and towns, leading to the unraveling of American society and institutions. His army steadily improved after suffering reversals in New York City in 1776 and southeastern Pennsylvania the following year. By the summer of 1778 the major fighting had shifted outside Washington's immediate theater of command to the Southern states. An effective organizer and administrator and an inspirational leader, he held his army together and kept the British in the North largely confined to the vicinity of New York City.

In 1781, cooperating with American troops in the South, Washington boldly moved most of his own army to Virginia, where, with French military and naval support, he besieged and captured Lord Cornwallis's army, which effectively ended the struggle in America. His generalship throughout showed a mixture of caution and aggressiveness. But keeping his army—the most meaningful symbol of the Revolution during the war—intact was always his first consideration. His own symbolic importance explains his appointment as president of the Constitutional Convention of 1787.

Washington was the preeminent military and political leader of the Revolution. Both as com-

GEORGE WASHINGTON

mander in chief and later as first president under the Constitution, he did not seek power but accepted it reluctantly and then voluntarily stepped down from it. As general and as president, he helped mold the new nation by setting lasting military and constitutional precedents.

DON HIGGINBOTHAM

BIBLIOGRAPHY

Cunliffe, Marcus. *George Washington: Man and Monument*. Boston: Little, Brown, 1958.

Freeman, Douglas S. *George Washington: A Biography*. 7 vols. New York, 1948–1957.

Higginbotham, Don. *George Washington and the American Military Tradition*. Athens, Ga.: University of Georgia Press, 1985.

WILLIAM OF ORANGE (KING WILLIAM III OF ENGLAND)

William Henry, prince of Orange, was born at The Hague in November 1650 and died King William III of England in March 1702. He is most famous for leading the revolution of 1688, in which he replaced his Catholic father-in-law James II as ruler of the British Isles. But he was at least as active in Dutch politics and in European warfare and diplomacy as he was in British affairs.

The rulers of the Dutch Republic, in which William grew up, were most often men of merchant families who were rich enough to devote their lives to politics. Since their successful rebellion against Spain in the 1570s they had established a virtually hereditary oligarchy. The "regents," as the rulers were called, controlled local and provincial administration and kept the central government weak. There were nobles, especially among the diplomats and the army officers, but except for the prince of Orange they had little money or influence. The prince not only was the largest landowner in the United Provinces, as captain-general he was the head of the army, and as *stadhouder,* or governor, of the union and many of its individual provinces he was its leading political figure. He provided what little centralization there was in the system.

In 1650 William II attempted a coup against the great city of Amsterdam, failed, and then died eight days before the birth of his son. In 1651 the regents in a constitutional convention called the Great Assembly took away the offices of the House of Orange, and the boy was brought up almost as a private citizen. This too failed. William the Silent, William Henry's great-grandfather, had been the founder of the republic and its great hero; the family still had immense prestige. The regents were unwilling to keep up the army or the frontier fortifications. When France and England attacked the Dutch in 1672, five of the seven provinces were occupied and the regent party collapsed. William Henry, at age

WILLIAM OF ORANGE (KING WILLIAM III OF ENGLAND)

twenty-two, was given the offices of his ancestors and called on to save the republic.

He did save it, substantially freeing the republic in two years while also leading a political revolution to reestablish the position of his family and his party. The oligarchic scheme did not disappear; pro-Orange regents replaced republican ones, and in time Amsterdam learned to work with the prince if not to like him. William Henry, the grandson of Charles I of England, married his cousin, the English princess Mary, in 1677 and from then on was likely to inherit the English throne. At the least, William might make his Dutch position hereditary; if he became king of England, he might unite the two countries, at Dutch expense.

Yet when he went to lead the English Revolution in 1688 he went with the blessing of Amsterdam. During the ten years between wars (1678–1688) the Protestant Dutch had learned to take the French threat seriously. The English did so too, for after 1685 they had in their Catholic king James II a French client. When Louis XIV of France invaded Germany rather than the Dutch Republic in 1688 William seized his opportunity and, in command of a fleet of almost five hundred ships and an army of some forty thousand men, took England in six weeks with very little bloodshed. France fought back in the Nine Years' War (1688–1697), but she had lost momentum and was to lose both that war and its sequel, the War of the Spanish Succession (1702–1713).

Although England became a great military and economic power during his reign, the royal office grew weaker after the death of his Queen Mary II in 1695, and weaker still on William's own death. In the Dutch Republic the very office of *stadhouder* disappeared for two generations. William was the last king of England to lead its armies in battle or to be in full control of its foreign policy. His reign is noted for a substantial increase in civil liberties; for toleration and freedom of the press; for great architecture, including Hampton Court and Kensington Palace; and for the music of Henry Purcell, the science of Isaac Newton, and the philosophy of John Locke.

STEPHEN B. BAXTER

BIBLIOGRAPHY

Baxter, Stephen B. *William III and the Defense of European Liberty.* New York: Harcourt, Brace and World, 1966.
Jones, James R. *The Revolution of 1688 in England.* New York: W.W. Norton, 1972.

WILLIAM THE SILENT

William the Silent, prince of Orange (1533–1584), was the unlikely leader of the Netherlands Revolt. The richest noble in the Netherlands after the unexpected death of a relative made him prince of Orange at age eleven, he enjoyed the special favor of Holy Roman Emperor Charles V and, at first, of his son King Philip II of Spain. In 1555 he took a prominent part in the ceremony transferring power from Charles to Philip, and he helped negotiate the Treaty of Cateau-Cambrésis with France in 1559. Orange next served as the king's *stadhouder,* or chief executive officer, in the provinces of Holland, Zeeland, and Utrecht, where he presided over provincial assemblies, controlled military forces, and made official appointments.

Protestantism, a major cause of discord in the Netherlands, was persecuted vigorously by central government officials. Since many Netherlanders wanted to maintain local privileges, they opposed centralized persecutions and plans for ecclesiastical reform and increased taxation. Until 1564 Orange was careful about expressing his concerns. His political enemy, Antoine Perrenot de Granvelle, called him *le taciturne* ("the silent one").

William's religious views may be described as Erasmian: he preferred freedom of conscience. Born to Lutheran parents, he had been raised as a Roman Catholic at the emperor's insistence and continued to practice Catholicism while married to a Protestant. He thought that rulers could not control the faith of their subjects, but when other nobles conspired against the government in 1565, Orange stood aside. Yet when the opposition turned to violent iconoclasm and revolt and the government resorted to brutal repression in 1566–1567, William belatedly broke with Spanish rule.

After the revolt failed, Orange fled to Germany and resigned his stadhouderships. The Council of Troubles, a special court appointed to punish the rebels, issued a summons for him, seized his lands, and kidnapped his son. From exile Orange organized military campaigns to seek personal justice and liberate the Netherlands, but his land forces were poorly coordinated and had little success until the multiple invasions of 1572. Even then, the rebels' military situation remained weak except in Holland and Zeeland.

In October 1572 the States of Holland, an assembly of delegates from the towns and nobility, chose Orange as *stadhouder* without the king's permission. For four years they held out against Spanish invasions and sieges. William had few resources but popular support from urban regents, lower-middle classes, and Calvinists. Although he lobbied for religious toleration, he nevertheless joined the Calvinist Church. He sought foreign help and exploited Spanish atrocities, blunders, financial crises, and troop mutinies. By 1576 Orange could take advantage of the breakdown of Spanish control and the desire for peace to call a meeting of the States-General, which included delegates from seventeen provinces. The delegates agreed to stop fighting each other and to work together against the Spaniards.

The general union did not last, however. Internal stresses surfaced between strongly Catholic southern provinces and militant Calvinists of the north. Orange's proposals for freedom of worship met opposition from both sides. Meanwhile he had to contend with a formidable Spanish commander, Alexander Farnese. The Spaniards declared the prince an outlaw in 1580 and placed a price on his head. William responded with the *Apology,* a masterpiece of self-justification and political propaganda. He recalled the oaths the sovereign had sworn and listed Philip's violations of traditional privileges. Orange's view of the monarchy as a contract between ruler and ruled legitimized resistance when the sovereign failed in his obligations toward his subjects. He pleaded for Protestant worship to be allowed and declared that he was motivated more by patriotism than personal interest.

Yet Orange's vehemence masked his desperation. He thought the revolt would fail without a foreign prince as sovereign to take the place of Philip II. William's choice, the French duke of Anjou, proved a disappointment, and the military situation deteriorated. In 1584 the States of Holland proposed to offer Orange the title count of Holland so that he might hold power independently, but on July 10, 1584, he was murdered by Balthasar Gérard, a Catholic. But William's death did not end the revolt, which continued until 1609, when Spain agreed to the Twelve Years Truce. For the Dutch, William's death raised him to martyrdom as "father of the fatherland."

MAARTEN ULTEE

BIBLIOGRAPHY

Rowen, Herbert H. *The Princes of Orange: The Stadholders in the Dutch Republic.* Cambridge: Cambridge University Press, 1988.

Swart, Koenraad W. *William the Silent and the Revolt of the Netherlands.* London: Historical Association, 1978.

Wansink, Harm, ed. *The Apologie of Prince William of Orange against the Proclamation of the King of Spaine.* Leiden: E.J. Brill, 1969.

EMILIANO ZAPATA

Zapata (1879–1919) led the most radical agrarian movement within the Mexican Revolution from 1910 until his assassination. After death, he became the political and cultural symbol of the rights of Mexico's rural peoples and their demands for land, justice, and local autonomy.

Zapata was born to a modestly prosperous family in the sugar region of Morelos, south of Mexico City. His family owned lands, leased others, raised crops for sustenance and sale, and ran mule trains in the rugged country of southern Mexico. Young Emiliano's skills as a horseman became legendary.

As sugar production became industrialized around 1900, Morelos estates began to invade villagers' lands. Elected mayor of Anenecuilco in 1909, Zapata stood up against the encroaching estates. His defense of community lands made him an outlaw even before Francisco Madero called for revolt against the regime of Porfirio Díaz late in 1910. Zapata and his allies joined Madero, seconding the call for democracy and justice and insisting that justice meant the return of lands to Mexico's villagers. When Díaz fled and Madero became president in 1911, Zapata demanded, unsuccessfully, that village lands be returned immediately.

Zapata broke with Madero in 1911 and produced a "platform" of his group's political demands. This Plan of Ayala demanded a government rooted in autonomous communities and

EMILIANO ZAPATA

committed to returning land to villagers. When Victoriano Huerta and the military ousted Madero in 1913, Zapata remained in rebellion and joined the Constitutionalist coalition led by Venustiano Carranza. When Huerta fell in 1914, Zapata joined the northern populist Pancho Villa in a revolutionary coalition committed to popular rights and land redistribution. By fall, the radical coalition led by Villa and Zapata ruled the

Mexican interior, while Carranza and Gen. Alvaro Obregón clung to opposition in the port of Veracruz.

Early in 1915 Carranza marshaled arms and other supplies from the United States, secured earnings from booming oil and henequen fiber exports in coastal regions he controlled, and adopted—perhaps cynically—Zapata's agrarian platform to revive his fortunes. Meanwhile, the radical coalition was divided between Villa's emphasis on popular concerns in the commercializing northern borderlands and Zapata's program and strategies to serve the peasant villagers of central and southern Mexico. The power of the Constitutionalists rose while the radical coalition split. Obregón defeated Villa in the key battles of the revolution in the summer of 1915.

Zapata still remained powerful, at times dominant, in his home region of Morelos. As the Constitutionalists began to consolidate the new state, President Carranza returned lands to elite estate owners even while incorporating the promise of land reform in the constitution of 1917. Zapata led a guerrilla struggle in defense of the unfulfilled promise of agrarian justice until he was ambushed and assassinated in 1919 by Carranza's military.

Death did not end Zapata's influence. The demand for land remained strong into the postrevolutionary years. As postrevolutionary governments faced persistent opposition, land distribution—and the invocation of Zapata's legacy—repeatedly proved the key to mobilizing popular support. President Lázaro Cárdenas consolidated the postrevolutionary state in the 1930s with a massive land reform and a political consolidation built on its rural beneficiaries. Zapata and the villagers of Morelos, though defeated in the contest for state power, made land reform essential to the revolutionary settlement in Mexico.

JOHN TUTINO

BIBLIOGRAPHY

Brunk, Samuel. *Emiliano Zapata: Revolution and Betrayal in Mexico.* Albuquerque: University of New Mexico Press, 1995.

Warman, Arturo. *"We Come to Object": The Peasants of Morelos and the National State.* Baltimore, Md.: Johns Hopkins University Press, 1980.

Womack, John Jr. *Zapata and the Mexican Revolution.* New York: Alfred A. Knopf, 1968.

CREDITS FOR PHOTOGRAPHS

John Adams / *Library of Congress*

Samuel Adams / *Library of Congress*

Susan B. Anthony / *Library of Congress*

Kemal Atatürk / *Library of Congress*

Stephen Biko / *Reuters/Bettmann*

Simón Bolívar / *Library of Congress*

Edmund Burke / *Library of Congress*

Fidel Castro / *National Archives*

Chiang Kai-shek / *Library of Congress*

Oliver Cromwell / *Library of Congress*

Deng Xiaoping / *Gerald Ford Library*

Benjamin Franklin / *Library of Congress*

Mahatma Gandhi / *Library of Congress*

Giuseppe Garibaldi / *Library of Congress*

Mikhail Gorbachev / *United Nations Photo*

Antonio Gramsci / *no credit*

Ernesto "Che" Guevara / *UPI/Corbis-Bettmann*

Václav Havel / *Congressional Quarterly*

Patrick Henry / *Library of Congress*

Adolf Hitler / *Library of Congress*

Ho Chi Minh / *AP/Wide World Photos*

Thomas Jefferson / *Library of Congress*

Mohammad Ali Jinnah / *Courtesy Embassy of Pakistan*

Benito Juárez / *Corbis-Bettmann*

Jomo Kenyatta / *Library of Congress*

Ayatollah Ruhollah Khomeini / *UPI/Corbis-Bettmann*

Kim Il Sung / *no credit*

Martin Luther King, Jr. / *UPI/Corbis-Bettmann*

Gilbert du Motier de Lafayette / *Library of Congress*

Juan Lechín Oquendo / *Reuters*

Vladimir Ilyich Lenin / *Library of Congress*

John Locke / *Library of Congress*

François-Dominique Toussaint L'Ouverture / *Library of Congress*

Patrice Lumumba / *National Archives*

Martin Luther / *Library of Congress*

Rosa Luxemburg / *Hoover Institution Archives*

James Madison / *Library of Congress*

Nelson Rolihlahla Mandela / *United Nations Photo*

Mao Zedong / *National Archives*

Jean-Paul Marat / *Library of Congress*

José Martí / *Library of Congress*

Karl Marx and Friedrich Engels / *both images Library of Congress*

Rigoberta Menchú Tum / *Reuters*

Mohammad Mosaddeq / *UPI/Corbis-Bettmann*

Robert Gabriel Mugabe / *Peter Turnley/©Corbis*

Benito Mussolini / *National Archives*

Gamal Abdel Nasser / *Hulton-Deutsch Collection/Corbis*

Jawaharlal Nehru / *Library of Congress*

Kwame Nkrumah / *National Archives*

Julius Kambarage Nyerere / *Library of Congress*

George Orwell / *Corbis/Bettmann*

Thomas Paine / *Library of Congress*

Maximilien Robespierre / *Library of Congress*

Jean-Jacques Rousseau / *Library of Congress*

José Francisco de San Martín / *Library of Congress*

Augusto César Sandino / *National Archives*

Joseph Stalin / *Library of Congress*

Sukarno / *National Archives*

Sun Yat-sen / *Library of Congress*

Josip Broz Tito / *National Archives*

Alexis de Tocqueville / *Library of Congress*

Leon Trotsky / *National Archives*

Lech Walesa / *Courtesy Embassy of the Republic of Poland*

George Washington / *Library of Congress*

William of Orange (King William III of England) / *Library of Congress*

Emiliano Zapata / *Hulton-Deutsch Collection/Corbis*

Index

A

Academy of Fine Arts (Czechoslovakia), 43
Accumulation of Capital, The (Luxemburg), 84
Achimota Teachers College (Ghana), 113
Action Française, 129
Adams, John, 1-2, 32, 55, 119
Adams, Samuel, 3-4
Address to the Christian Nobility (Luther), 82
Africa. *See* Biko, Stephen; Cabral, Amílcar; Lumumba, Patrice; Nkrumah, Kwame; Nyerere, Julius Kambarage; individual countries
African National Congress (ANC), 11, 88, 89
African Party for the Independence of Guinea and Cape Verde (PAIGC), 19, 20
Age of Reason, The (Paine), 120
Albany (Ga.), 67
Al-e Ahmad (Iran), 63
Algeria, 29, 88
Alien and Sedition Acts (1798), 54-55
Ali Shariati (Iran), 63
Alvarez, Juan, 58
American Crisis Series, The (Paine), 119
American Republic. *See* United States
American Revolution
    Adams, John, 3
    Adams, Samuel, 3
    Franklin, Benjamin, 32
    Henry, Patrick, 46
    Jefferson, Thomas, 54
    Lafayette, Gilbert du Motier de, 69
    Madison, James, 87
    Paine, Thomas, 119-120
    Washington, George, 145
Amin, Idi, 116

Amsterdam. *See* Netherlands, The
Anatolia, 8
ANC. *See* African National Congress
ANC Youth League (ANCYL), 88
Andropov, Yuri, 38
Angola, 19, 22, 115
Animal Farm (Orwell), 118
Anthony, Susan B., 5-7
Antirevolutionary movements. *See* Revolutions
Apartheid, 11, 12, 88
Apology (William the Silent), 150
Arab-Israeli war (1967), 110
Arab Socialist Union, 110
Arbenz Guzmán, Jacobo, 41
Argentina, 41, 125, 126
Armistice of Mudros (1918), 8
Articles of Confederation (U.S.), 4, 32, 46
Arusha Declaration on Socialism and Self-Reliance, 116
Assassinations. *See also* Executions; Murders
    Cabral, Amílcar, 19
    Chitepo, Herbert, 105-106
    Gandhi, Mahatma, 34
    Hitler, Adolf, 49
    King, Martin Luther, Jr., 68
    Lumumba, Patrice, 80, 81
    Marat, Jean-Paul, 93, 94
    Menchú family, 101
    Smith, Ian, 105
    Trotsky, Leon, 142
    Zapata, Emiliano, 151, 152
Atatürk, Kemal, 8-10
Attlee, Clement, 112
Austria, 35-36, 47, 121
Axelrod, Pavel, 73
Ayutla, revolt of, 58
Azad, Maulana, 56-57
Azerbaijan, 103

B

Babeuf, Gracchus, 15
Barrientos, René, 42
Batista, Fulgencio, 21, 41
Baudouin (king; Belgium), 80
Bay of Pigs (Cuba), 22
Bazargan, Mehdi, 63
Beals, Carlton, 128
Belgium, 81
Bergson, Henri, 129
Bernstein, Eduard, 84
Biafra, 116
Biko, Stephen, 11-12
Bill of Rights (U.S.), 54
Birmingham (Ala.), 67
Black consciousness movement, 11-12
"Black Skin, White Mask" syndrome, 29-30
Blair, Eric Arthur. *See* Orwell, George
Bolívar, Simón, 13-14, 126
Bolivia, 13, 41, 42, 71-72, 125
Bolivian Federation of Miners (FSTMB), 71
Bolivian Revolution (1952), 71
Bolivian Workers Center (COB), 71-72
Bolsheviks (Russia), 73, 131, 141, 142
Bonaparte, Charles-Louis-Napoléon, 59, 139
Bonaparte, Napoleon, 15, 69-70, 79, 125
Boston (Mass.), 3, 31, 145. *See also* Massachusetts
Boston Tea Party (1773), 3
Boston University, 67
Botha, P.W., 88
Bourbons (France), 70
Brazil, 35
Bréda, Toussaint. *See* L'Ouverture, François-Dominique Toussaint
Brest-Litovsk, peace of, 142
Brezhnev, Leonid, 38
Britain. *See* Great Britain

Bronshtein, Lev Davidovich. *See* Trotsky, Leon
Brown Shirts (Germany), 47, 48
Buddhism, 52
Bulgaria, 137
Bulletin of the Opposition, The (Trotsky), 142
Buonarroti, Filippo Michele, 15-16
Burgos-Debray, Elisabeth, 102
Burke, Edmund, 17-18
Burmese Days (Orwell), 117

C

Cabral, Amílcar, 19-20
Calvinism, 149, 150
Cape Verde, 19
Cárdenas, Lázaro, 152
Carranza, Venustiano, 151-152
Casa de las Américas prize, 102
Castro, Fidel, 21-22, 41, 95
Catavi tin mines (Bolivia), 71
Catholic Church, 25, 59, 76, 82, 116, 149, 150
Cavour, Camillo, 35, 36
Central Intelligence Agency (CIA), 81
Chaco War (1932-1935), 71
Chains of Slavery, The (Marat), 93
Charles I (king; England), 25
Charles II (king; England), 25, 76
Charles V (Holy Roman Emperor), 149
Charter 77 (Czechoslovakia), 43
Chernenko, Konstantin, 38
Chiang Ching-kuo, 24
Chiang Kai-shek, 23-24, 91, 136
Chicago (Ill.), 67-68
Chile, 125
China. *See also* Revolutions; individuals by name
    civil wars, 23, 24
    Communist Party, 23, 24, 27, 65, 91, 92, 136
    economy, 27
    India and, 112
    People's Republic of China, 91
    Qing dynasty, 52, 53
    Soviet Union and, 23, 65, 91, 92
Christian Democratic Party (Poland), 144
Christianity, 29, 52-53, 116
Chuch'e (self-reliance; North Korea), 66
Churchill, Winston, 24

CIA. *See* Central Intelligence Agency
Cinco de Mayo (May 5th; Mexico), 59
Civic Forum (Czechoslovakia), 44
Civil Rights Act (1964; U.S.), 67
Civil rights movement, 67
Civil wars
    China, 23, 24
    Great Britain, 25
    Guatemala, 101
    Indonesia, 134
    Russia, 74-75, 131, 142
    Spain, 107, 117, 118, 130
    United States, 6
    Yemen, 110
Class issues
    China, 91
    Germany, 47
    India, 34
    Mussolini, Benito, 107
    revisionism, 84
    in revolution, 97, 99, 100
    Sorel, Georges, 129
    working class, 85, 100
Class Struggles in France, The (Marx), 100
COB. *See* Bolivian Workers Center
Cochrane, Thomas Alexander, 125-126
Coercive Acts (1774; Great Britain), 32
Cold war, 137
College of New Jersey, 86
Colombia, 13
Colonialism, 98-99
Cominform (Communist Information Bureau), 138
Comintern (Communist International), 39, 50, 138
Committee for Peasant Unity (CUC; Guatemala), 101
Committee for the Defense of the Unjustly Persecuted (Czechoslovakia), 43
Committee for Union and Progress (Turkey), 8
Committee of Public Safety (France), 120, 121
Committee of Safety (Va.), 86
Committees of correspondence (U.S.), 45
Committee to Draft the Declaration of Independence (U.S.), 32
Common Sense (Paine), 32, 119
Communism. *See also* Socialism

Cuba, 22
Czechoslovakia, 43, 44
Egypt, 110
Ho Chi Minh and, 50-51
India, 34
Russia, 73
Sandino, Augusto César, and, 127
Soviet Union, 16, 143
Spain, 118
Yugoslavia, 137-138
Communist Information Bureau. *See* Cominform
Communist International. *See* Comintern
Communist Manifesto, The (Marx and Engels), 99-100
Communist Party
    China, 23, 24, 27, 65, 91, 92, 136
    Cuba, 22, 41
    France, 50
    Germany, 85
    Indonesia, 133, 134
    Iran, 104
    Italy, 39
    Poland, 143, 144
    Russia, 37, 75, 131, 142
    South Africa, 11
    Soviet Union, 130
    Vietnam, 50
    Yugoslavia, 137-138
Communist Youth League (Komsomol; Russia), 37, 38
Comonfort, Ignacio, 58
Complete Works (Martí), 96
Confucianism, 52, 53
Congo. *See* Democratic Republic of the Congo
Congolese National Movement (MNC), 80
Congress of the International (Russia), 99
Conspiracy for Equality (Buonarroti), 16
Constitutional Convention (1787; U.S.), 2, 32, 46, 86, 145
Constitutionalism, 69
Constitutions
    Egypt, 110
    France, 69
    Iran, 63-64
    North Korea, 66
    United States, 6, 31, 87

Continental Association for
Nonimportation, 3
Continental Congress (U.S.)
Adams, John, 1
Adams, Samuel, 3
Declaration of Independence, 119
Franklin, Benjamin, 32
Henry, Patrick, 45-46
Lafayette, Gilbert du Motier de, 69
Madison, James, 86, 87
Washington, George, 145
Convention People's Party (CPP;
Ghana), 113, 114
Cooper, Anthony Ashley, 1st Earl of
Shaftesbury, 76-77
Corday, Charlotte, 94
Cornwallis, Charles, 1st Marquis
Cornwallis, 145
Corporatism, 107-108
Corsica, 124
Council of Europe, 44
Council of State (Va.), 87
Council of Troubles (Netherlands), 149
Coups d'état
Egypt, 109
England, 25
Germany, 47
Ghana, 114
Iran, 103
Netherlands, The, 147
Portugal, 19
CPP. See Convention People's Party
Critique of the Gotha Program (Marx), 99
Croatia, 137
Croce, Benedetto, 39
Cromwell, Oliver, 25-26
Crozer Theological Seminary (Pa.), 67
Cuba, 21-22, 41, 95
CUC. See Committee for Peasant Unity
Cult of the Supreme Being (France),
121
Cults of personality. See also Leadership
Garibaldi, Giuseppe, 35
Kim Il Sung, 66
Mao Zedong, 66, 90
Marat, Jean-Paul, 94
Martí, José, 95
Stalin, Joseph, 66
Czechoslovakia, 43
Czech Republic, 43, 44

D

Danton, Georges Jacques, 122
Daoism, 52
David, Jacques-Louis, 93
Declaration of Independence (U.S.), 2,
4, 31, 54, 86, 119
Declaration of the Rights of Man
(France), 54
Defence of the Constitutions of the United
States (Adams), 2
de Klerk, F.W., 88, 89
Democracy and democratization
according to Luxemburg, Rosa, 84,
85
according to Tocqueville, Alexis de,
139
in Germany, 47, 48
in Indonesia, 133-134
influence of Rousseau, Jean-Jacques,
123, 124
in Italy, 107
in the United States, 2, 4
Democracy in America (Tocqueville), 139
Democratic People's Republic of Korea,
65
Democratic Republic of the Congo, 80-
81
Democratic Republic of Vietnam, 50.
See also Vietnam
Deng Xiaoping, 27-28, 92
Dessalines, Jean-Jacques, 79
Development of Capitalism in Russia, The
(Lenin), 73
Dexter Avenue Baptist Church
(Montgomery, Ala.), 67
Díaz, Porfirio, 151
Discourses, First and Second (Rousseau),
123
Discovery of India (Nehru), 111
Disintegration of Marxism, The (Sorel), 129
Dissertation on Canon and Feudal Law
(Adams), 1
Dreyfus affair, 129
Duke of Gloucester, 69
Dutch. See Netherlands, The
Dutch Indies, 133
Dutch Republic, 147, 148
Dzhugashvili, Iossif Vissarionovich. See
Stalin, Joseph

E

École Polytechnique (France), 129
Economic issues
capitalism, 74, 84, 99, 127, 129
corporatism, 107-108
revolution, 97
Russia, 74, 75
Economic reforms
Cuba, 41-42
Deng Xiaoping, 27, 28, 92
Gramsci, Antonio, 40
Kim Il Sung, 66
King, Martin Luther, Jr., 68
Mao Zedong, 91
Mussolini, Benito, 107
Ecuador, 13, 126
Education, 6, 9, 10
Egypt, 108
El-Moudjahid (Algeria), 29
Emancipation, 6-7
Engels, Friedrich, 16, 97-100
England. See Great Britain
Enlightenment, European, 13, 140
Ethiopia, 22, 108
Europe, 7, 123
Europe, Eastern, 143
European revolutions (1848), 35, 97-98,
139
Executions. See also Assassinations;
Murders; Terror and terrorism;
Violence
China, 23
Cuba, 22
France, 121
under Stalin, Joseph, 132
Executions, specific
Babeuf, Gracchus, 15
Guevara, Ernesto "Che," 41, 42
Maximilien of Habsburg, 59
Robespierre, Maximilien, 122
Sandino, Augusto César, 128
Ulyanov, Alexander, 73

F

Facing Mount Kenya (Kenyatta), 60
Falange (Spain), 107
Famines, 91
Fanon, Frantz Omar, 29-30, 130
Farnese, Alexander, 150
Fascism, 39, 47, 107, 129-130, 137

Federalist Party (U.S.), 55
Federalist Papers, 87
Fichte, Johann Gottlieb, 83
First Discourse (Rousseau), 123
FLN. *See* National Liberation Front
Foundation for the Disinherited (Iran), 63
France
    Algeria and, 29
    Alliance of 1778, 31
    attack on the Dutch, 147
    Communist Party, 50
    Franklin, Benjamin, and, 32
    Garibaldi, Giuseppe, and, 36
    Mexico, 59
    Saint-Domingue, 78
    wars, 148
Franco, Francisco, 107, 108
Franklin, Benjamin, 2, 31-32, 54, 119
Freedoms. *See* Rights
Free Officers (Egypt), 109-110
French Guiana, 79
French National Convention, 120
French Revolution (1789)
    Buonarroti, Filippo Michele, and, 15
    Burke, Edmund, and, 17
    Jefferson, Thomas, and, 54
    Lafayette, Gilbert du Motier de, 69
    Madison, James, and, 87
    Paine, Thomas, and, 119-120
    Robespierre, Maximilien, and, 121-122
    Tocqueville, Alexis de, 139
FSLN. *See* Sandinista Front for National Liberation
FSTMB. *See* Bolivian Federation of Miners

G

Gandhi, Indira Priyadarshini Nehru, 111, 112
Gandhi, Mahatma Mohandas Karamchand, 33-34, 56, 67, 111
Garden Party, The (Havel), 43
Garibaldi, Giuseppe, 35-36
General Staff College (Turkey), 8
Geneva Conference (1954), 50
George III (king; England), 17, 32, 45, 119
Gérard, Balthasar, 150

German Democratic Republic, 82
German Social Democratic Party, 73
Germany. *See also* Hitler, Adolf
    Communist Party, 85
    invasion of Soviet Union, 137
    Luther, Martin, and, 82-83
    Marx, Karl, and, 100
    nationalism, 47
    Protestant Reformation, 82
    revolution in, 98
    Weimar Republic, 85
Ghana. *See* Republic of Ghana
Girondins (France), 120, 121
Good Neighbor Policy (U.S.), 128
Gorbachev, Mikhail, 37-38
Government of National Unity (South Africa), 89
Gramsci, Antonio, 39-40
Granvelle, Antoine Perrenot de, 149
Great Britain
    Adams, John, 2
    Adams, Samuel, 3
    antirevolutionary attitude, 17-18
    attack on the Dutch, 147
    Black Acts, 33-34
    civil war, 25
    Cromwell, Oliver, 25-26
    Egypt and, 109
    Germany and, 49
    in India, 33-34, 56-57
    Jefferson, Thomas, 54
    liberty in, 139-140
    national church, 26
    Orwell, George, and, 118
    Pakistan, 57
    revolutions, 25, 26, 99, 147, 148
    treaty with U.S. (1783), 31, 32
    World War II, 118
Great Depression, 9, 47, 67
Great Leap Forward (China), 91-92
Great Proletarian Cultural Revolution (China), 66, 92
Greece, 70, 108
Greene, Nathanael, 119
Guadeloupe, 79
Guatemala, 41, 101-102
Guerrillas and guerrilla warfare
    Chinese, 91
    foco theory of, 42
    Garibaldi, Giuseppe, 35-36
    Kenyan, 61

    in Mozambique, 106
    Nicaragua, 127, 128
    Palestinian, 110
    Washington, George, 145
    Zapata, Emiliano, 152
Guevara, Ernesto "Che," 41-42
Guinea-Bissau, 19
Gypsies, 48

H

Hamilton, Alexander, 54
Harvard University, 3
Havel, Václav, 43-44
"Heavenly Kingdom of Great Peace." *See* Taiping Tianguo
Henry, Patrick, 45-46
Hinduism, 34, 56, 112
History of the Russian Revolution (Trotsky), 142
Hitler, Adolf, 47-49, 107, 132
Ho Chi Minh, 50-51
Holy Roman Empire, 82, 83
Homage to Catalonia (Orwell), 117
Hong Kong, 28
Hong Xiuquan, 52-53, 136
House of Burgesses (Va.), 45, 54
House of Representatives (U.S.), 86
Hua Guofeng, 27-28
Huerta, Victoriano, 151
Hutchinson, Thomas, 3

I

Il Duce. *See* Mussolini, Benito
Illusions of Progress, The (Sorel), 129
Imperialism (Lenin), 74
"Incorruptible, the." *See* Robespierre, Maximilien
Increased Difficulty of Concentration, The (Havel), 43
Independence
    Africa, 80
    Congo, 81
    Cuba, 95-96
    Greece, 70
    Haiti, 79
    Indonesia, 133
    Kenya, 61
    Korea, 65
    Latin America, 13
    Peru, 126

Poland, 70
Turkey, 8-10
United States, 1-4
India, 33-34, 56-57
Indonesia, 133-134
Indonesia Nationalist Association (PNI), 133
Industrial Revolution, 5
Inkatha Freedom Party (South Africa), 89
Inonu, Ismet, 10
International Year of Indigenous Peoples, 102
Iran, 62-64, 103-104
Iran-Iraq War (1980-1988), 64
Iraq, 62-63
Ireland, 25
I, Rigoberta Menchú: An Indian Woman in Guatemala (Menchú), 102
Iskra ("Spark"; Switzerland), 73
Islam. See Muslims
Islamic Republic, 63
Italy, 15, 35, 39, 100, 107-108

J

Jacobin Club and Jacobins (France), 69, 99, 121, 124
James II (king; England), 76, 77, 147, 148
James, Duke of York. See James II (king; England)
Japan, 24, 65, 91
Jaruzelski, Wojciech, 144
Jay, John, 32
Jefferson, Thomas, 2, 32, 46, 54-55, 77
Jews, 47, 48, 131-132
Jinnah, Mohammad Ali, 56-57, 112
Johannesburg (South Africa), 88
Johnson, Lyndon B., 50, 68
Jordan, 110
Juárez, Benito, 58-59

K

KANU. See Kenya African National Union
Kasavubu, Joseph, 81
KAU. See Kenya African Union
Kaul, Kamala, 111
Kautsky, Karl, 73

KCA. See Kikuyu Central Association
Kemalism (Turkey), 9-10
Kentucky Resolutions (U.S.; 1798), 54
Kenya, 60-61, 115, 116
Kenya African National Union (KANU), 61
Kenya African Union (KAU), 60
Kenyatta, Jomo, 60-61
KGB (Soviet Union), 38
Khomeini, Ayatollah Ruhollah, 62-64
Khrushchev, Nikita, 38, 42
Kikuyu Central Association (KCA; Kenya), 60
Kim Il Sung, 65-66
King, Alberta Williams, 67
King, Martin Luther, Jr., 67-68
King, Martin Luther, Sr., 67
Korea, 65-66
Korean War (1950-1953), 65, 91
Kuomintang (China), 23
Kurds, 9
Kwaśniewski, Aleksander, 144

L

Labor and trade unions, 108, 129, 143-144
Labriola, Antonio, 39
Lafayette, Gilbert du Motier de, 54, 69-70
Land Ordinance of 1784 (U.S.), 54
Language issues, 10, 30, 115, 131
Latin America, 13. See also South America
Leadership. See also Cults of personality
    Khomeini, Ayatollah Ruhollah, 62-64
    Mandela, Nelson Rolihlahla, 89
    Nkrumah, Kwame, 113-114
    Walesa, Lech, 143-144
    Washington, George, 145-146
League for the Independence of Vietnam (Vietminh Front), 50
Lechín Oquendo, Juan, 71-72
Leclerc, Victor Emmanuel, 78, 79
Left Book Club (England), 117
Lenin, Vladimir Ilyich, 50, 73-75, 84-85, 131, 141, 142
Leopold, Grand Duke, 15
Leopoldville (Kinshasa; Democratic Republic of the Congo), 80
Les Damne's de la terre (Fanon), 30

Letters to Olga (Havel), 43
Lexington (Mass.), 145
Ley Juárez (Mexico), 58
Liberation Movement of Iran, 63
"Liberator." See San Martín, José Francisco de
Libya, 108
Lincoln, Abraham, 6, 36
Little Red Book (Mao), 90
Living in Truth (Havel), 43
Locke, John, 76-77, 148
London School of Economics, 60
Long March (China), 91
Louis XIV (king; France), 148
Louis XVI (king; France), 120, 121
Louis-Philippe, Duke of Orleans (king; France), 70
L'Ouverture, François-Dominique Toussaint, 78-79
Lumumba, Patrice, 80-81
Luther, Martin, 82-83
Lutheranism, 82, 149
Luxemburg, Rosa, 84-85

M

Machel, Samora, 106
Madero, Francisco, 151
Madison, James, 46, 86-87
Mahmud II (sultan of Turkey), 8
Malaysia, 134
Mandela, Nelson Rolihlahla, 88-89
Mann, Thomas, 83
Mao Zedong, 27, 42, 51, 90-92, 132, 136
Marat, Jean-Paul, 93-94
Martí, José, 95-96
Martinique, 29, 79
Marxism and Marxism-Leninism
    in Bolivia, 71
    Deng Xiaoping, 27
    development of, 98-100
    Ho Chi Minh, 51
    in Zimbabwe, 106
"Marxism and the National Question" (Stalin), 131
Marxists
    Axelrod, Pavel, 73
    Cabral, Amílcar, 19-20
    Engels, Friedrich, 16
    European, 51, 74

Gramsci, Antonio, 39–40
Guevara, Ernesto "Che," 41–42
Labriola, Antonio, 39
Lenin, Vladimir Ilyich, 73–75
Luxemburg, Rosa, 84–85
Mao Zedong, 91
Marx, Karl, 16
Mugabe, Robert Gabriel, 105
Nehru, Jawaharlal, 111–112
Plekhanov, Georgii, 73
Stalin, Joseph, 131
Trotsky, Leon, 73
Zasulich, Vera, 73
Marxist Workers Party (POUM; Spain),
    117
Marx, Karl, 16, 39, 97–100
Mary II (wife of William III), 77, 148
Massachusetts, 1, 2, 3, 4, 5. *See also*
    Boston
Massacres, 33–34, 88, 94
Mass Strike, Party, and Trade Unions
    (Luxemburg), 85
Mau Mau movement (Kenya), 61
Maximilian of Habsburg, 59
Mayans, 101
May Fourth Movement of 1919
    (China), 91
May 5th. *See* Cinco de Mayo
Mays, Benjamin E., 67
Mazowiecki, Tadeusz, 144
Mazzini, Giuseppe, 35
Mein Kampf (Hitler; My Struggle), 47
Memorandum, The (Havel), 43
Menchú Tum, Rigoberta, 101–102
Menchú, Vicente, 101
Mendive, Rafael Maria de, 95
Mensheviks (Russia), 73, 131, 141, 142
Mexico, 58–59, 151–152
MIA. *See* Montgomery Improvement
    Association
Michaelangelo, 15
Miodowicz, Alfred, 144
MNC. *See* Congolese National
    Movement
MNC-Lumumba, 80
MNR. *See* Nationalist Revolutionary
    Movement
Mojahedin-e Khalq, 63
Montgomery Improvement Association
    (MIA), 67

Morehouse College, 67
Mosaddeq, Mohammad, 103–104
Moscow State University, 37
Mountbatten, Louis (1st Earl
    Mountbatten of Burma), 112
Mozambique, 106, 115
Mugabe, Robert Gabriel, 105–106
Murders. *See also* Assassinations;
    Executions; Terror and terrorism;
    Violence
    under Hitler, Adolf, 48–49, 132
    under Mao Zedong, 132
    in Poland, 143
    under Stalin, Joseph, 132
Murders, specific
    Biko, Stephen, 11–12
    Luxemburg, Rosa, 85
    Martí, José, 95, 96
    Mussolini, Benito, 108
    William the Silent, 150
Muslim Brotherhood, 109, 110
Muslim League, 56
Muslims, 56–57, 112, 116, 133
Mussolini, Benito, 39, 47, 107–108, 129–
    130

N

NAACP. *See* National Association for
    the Advancement of Colored
    People
Nanjing (China), 52
Napoleon I. *See* Bonaparte, Napoleon
Napoleon III. *See* Bonaparte, Charles-
    Louis-Napoleon
Nasser, Gamal Abdel, 42, 109–110
Nation, The, 128
National Association for the
    Advancement of Colored People
    (NAACP), 67
National Charter (Egypt), 110
National Congress Party (India), 56, 112
National Democratic Party (Zimbabwe),
    105
National Front (Iran), 104
Nationalism
    according to Luxemburg, Rosa, 84
    according to Mussolini, Benito, 107
    according to Sun Yat-sen, 135–136
    of Stalin, Joseph, 131
    violence and, 29

Nationalism, specific countries
    China, 23, 135–136
    Congo, 80
    Cuba, 21
    Egypt, 109
    Germany, 47
    Ghana, 113
    India, 34, 56
    Indonesia, 133
    Mexico, 58, 59
    South Africa, 11
    Tanganyika, 115
    Vietnam, 50–51
    Zimbabwe, 105
Nationalist Party (China), 136
Nationalist Revolutionary Movement
    (MNR; Bolivia), 71, 72
Nationalization, 59
National Liberation Front (FLN;
    Algeria), 29
National Pact (Turkey; 1919), 8
National Party (South Africa), 89
National Reconciliation Committee
    (Guatemala), 102
National Socialist German Workers'
    Party (Nazi), 47–49
National Union of South African
    Students, 11
NATO. *See* North Atlantic Treaty
    Organization
Nazi Party (Germany). *See* National
    Socialist German Workers' Party
Nehru, Pandit Motilal, 111
Nehru, Jawaharlal, 42, 56–57, 67, 111–
    112
Netherlands, The, 2, 99, 147–148, 149–
    150
New Order, The (Gramsci), 40
Newton, Isaac, 148
New York, 145
Nguyen Tat Thanh. *See* Ho Chi Minh
Nicaragua, 127–128
Nice (Italian kingdom of Sardinia-
    Piedmont), 35–36
Nicholas II (tsar; Russia), 73–74
Nietzsche, Friedrich, 129
Nigeria, 116
Nineteen Eighty-Four (Orwell), 118
Nixon, Richard, 92
Nkomo, Joshua, 105
Nkrumah, Fathia, 114

Nkrumah, Kwame, 80, 113-114, 115
Nobel Peace Prize, 89, 101, 102, 144
Nonaligned movement, 66, 110, 137, 138
Nonviolence, 33, 67. *See also* Violence
North Atlantic Treaty Organization (NATO), 44
Northeast Anti-Japanese United Army (China), 65
Northern Expedition (China), 23, 24
Notes on the State of Virginia (Jefferson), 54
"Novanglus" (John Adams), 1
Nuri, Shaikh Fazlullah, 62
Nyerere, Julius Kambarage, 115-116

O

Oaxaca Institute of Sciences and Arts, 58
Obregón, Alvaro, 152
O'Higgins, Bernardo, 125-126
Oil, 104
Old Regime and the French Revolution, The (Tocqueville), 139
Oliver, Andrew, 3
On Temporal Authority (Luther), 82
Opium War (1839-1842), 52
Order of the Augustinian Hermits, 82
Organizational Questions of Social Democracy (Luxemburg), 84-85
Organization of African Unity, 114
Orwell, George, 117-118
Ottoman Empire, 8. *See also* Republic of Turkey

P

Pahlavi, Mohammad Reza Shah, 62, 103, 104
Pahlavi, Reza Shah, 62, 103
PAIGC. *See* African Party for the Independence of Guinea and Cape Verde
Paine, Thomas, 32, 119-120
Pakistan, 34, 56-57, 112
Pakistan Resolution, 56
Palach, Jan, 44
Palestine war (1948), 109-110
Pan-Africanist Congress, 11, 88
Pan-African movement, 113, 114, 115
Panama, 13

Papacy, 82. *See also* Catholic Church
Paraguay, 71
Paris Commune (1871), 97-98, 99
Parks, Rosa, 67
Parliament (England), 1
"Parsons' Cause (U.S.)," 45
Paz Estenssoro, Víctor, 72
Peasant wars (1524-1526; 1929), 82, 132
Peking University, 91
Pennsylvania, 31-32, 145
Penn, Thomas, 31
People's Friend, The (Marat), 93
People's Party (Turkey), 9
People's Republic of China. *See* China
Perestroika (restructuring), 37, 38
Perón, Juan Domingo, 107
Peru, 13, 125, 126
Petrograd. *See* St. Petersburg
Philadelphia (Pa.), 31
Philip II (king; Spain), 149, 150
Piedmont (Italian kingdom), 35
Plan of Ayala (Mexico), 151
Plekhanov, Georgii, 73
PNI. *See* Indonesia Nationalist Association
Poland, 70, 84, 100, 124, 143-144
Political parties. *See* individual parties
Poor People's Campaign (Washington, D.C.), 67-68
Popular Front (Iran), 104
Popular Movement of Iran, 103
Populism, 71, 93, 114, 136
POR. *See* Revolutionary Labor Party
Portugal, 19, 115
POUM. *See* Marxist Workers Party
Prison Notebooks (Gramsci), 39-40
Privatization, 59
Proletariat
    Bolivian Revolution and, 71
    Lenin, Vladimir Ilyich, and, 73, 75
    Marx, Karl, and Friedrich Engels, 97, 98, 99, 100
    Mussolini, Benito, and, 107
    Orwell, George, and, 117, 118
    Sorel, Georges, and, 129
    Trotsky, Leon, and, 142
Protestant Church, 25, 76, 82-83, 149, 150
Prussia, 36
Purcell, Henry, 148
Purges, 27, 41, 94, 121, 132, 137

Q

Qing dynasty, 52, 53, 135
Qur'an, 10, 34

R

Racial and minority issues. *See also* Apartheid
    Hitler, Adolf, and, 47, 48-49
    King, Martin Luther, Jr., and, 67-68
    Menchú Tum, Rigoberta, 102
    Stalin, Joseph, 131
    Tito, Josip Broz, 138
Radicals and revolutionaries. *See* individuals by name
Rebellions and revolts
    Ayutla revolt (Mexico; 1855), 58
    Shays's Rebellion (Mass.; 1786), 2, 4
    Sheikh Said Rebellion (Turkey; 1925), 9
    Taiping Rebellion (China; 1851-1864), 52-53
Reconciler, The (Kenya), 60
Reflections on the Revolution in France (Burke), 17, 18
Reflections on Violence (Sorel), 129
Reformation, 82-83
Reign of Terror (1793-1794; France), 94, 120, 121-122
Religion, 26, 29, 140. *See also* individual religious groups
Republicanism, 69, 70
Republican Party (U.S.), 55
Republic of Ghana, 29, 105, 113-114
Republic of Turkey, 8-10
Revisionism, 84
Revolutionary Armed Forces (Cuba), 41
Revolutionary Labor Party (POR; Bolivia), 71
Revolutionary Party of the Nationalist Left (Bolivia), 72
Revolutions
    antirevolutionary thought, 17-18
    in Asia, 51, 57
    communist, 15, 90
    Marxist ideas, 97-100
    Orwell, George, and, 118
    patron saints, 83
    role of intellectuals, 73
    role of women, 30
    Tocqueville, Alexis de, 139

Revolutions, specific
America (1776), 2, 32, 46, 54, 69, 87,
119
Bolivia (1952), 71
China (1921-1949; 1965), 27, 28, 66,
90, 92, 135
Cuba (1953-1959), 21, 41
Czechoslovakia (Velvet; 1989-1993),
44
England (1638-1660, 1688), 25, 26,
147, 148
Europe (1848), 35, 97-98, 139
France (1789), 15, 17, 54, 69, 87, 119,
121-122, 139
Iran (1906-1911), 62, 103
Mexico (1910-1940), 151-152
Muslim in South Asia, 57
Russia (1905, 1917), 37, 73-74, 85,
98, 130, 137
Young Turk (1908), 8
Rhodesia. *See* Zimbabwe
Rights
according to Locke, John, 76
according to Luther, Martin, 82
civil rights, 67-68
freedom of religion, 26, 86, 149
freedom of expression, 26
natural rights, 1
revolution and, 97
Rights of Man (Paine), 120
Rigoberta Menchú Tum Foundation,
102
Rivonia trial (1963-1964; South Africa),
88
Road to Wigan Pier (Orwell), 117
Robespierre, Maximilien, 15, 120, 121-
122, 124
Romania, 107
Roman republic, 35
Rome, 36
Roosevelt, Franklin, 24, 128
Rousseau, Jean-Jacques, 15, 121, 123-
124
RUOG. *See* Unitary Representation of
the Guatemalan Opposition
Rush, Benjamin, 119
Rushdie, Salman, 64
Russia, 37, 73-75, 131, 142. *See also*
Engels, Friedrich; Lenin, Vladimir
Ilyich; Marx, Karl; Trotsky, Leon;
Union of Soviet Socialist Republics

Russian Revolutions (1905, 1917), 37,
73-74, 85, 98, 130, 137
Russian Revolution, The (Luxemburg), 85
Russian Social Democratic Workers'
Party, 73, 141

S

Sadat, Anwar al-, 110
St. Augustine (Fla.), 67
Saint-Domingue, 78
Saint-Just, Louis-Antoine-Léon, 124
St. Petersburg (Russia), 74, 141
Sandinista Front for National Liberation
(FSLN; Nicaragua), 128
Sandino, Augusto César, 127-128
San Domingo, 78
San Martín, José Francisco de, 125-126
Santa Anna, Antonio Lopez de, 58
Sardinia, 39
Sarvodaya ("the uplift of all"; Gandhi),
34
Satyagraha ("hold fast to the truth";
Gandhi), 33-34, 111
School of Law and Politics (Iran), 103
Schucht, Tatiana, 39
SCLC. *See* Southern Christian
Leadership Conference
Scotland, 25
Second Discourse (Rousseau), 123
Selma (Ala.), 67
Seneca Falls Convention (1848), 6
Serbia, 137
Seven Years War (1756-1763, U.S.), 145
Sharpeville massacre (South Africa), 88
Shaw, George Bernard, 111
Shays's Rebellion (Mass.; 1786), 2, 4
Sheikh Said Rebellion (Turkey; 1925), 9
Shi'ism, 62-63
Sicily, 36
Siles, Zuazo, Hernán, 71-72
Sinn Fein, 111
Sisulu, Walter, 88
Sithole, Ndabaningi, 105
Slavery, 6, 32, 54, 78-79
Slovakia, 44
Smith, Ian, 105
Social Contract (Rousseau), 123
Social democracy, 89
Social Democratic Party (Germany), 73,
100

Socialism. *See also* Communism
Ghana, 113
Indonesia, 133
Kenya, 61
Latin America, 41
Nehru, Jawaharlal, 112
Nyerere, Julius Kambarage, 116
Orwell, George, 117-118
Sorel, Georges, 129
Soviet Union, 38, 42
Trotsky, Leon, 141-142
worldwide, 74
Yugoslavia, 138
Socialism and the New Man in Cuba
(Guevara), 42
Socialist Party (Italy), 39, 40
Social Reform or Revolution (Luxemburg),
84
Social reforms
Anthony, Susan B., 5-7
Atatürk, Kemal, 8, 9-10
Bolívar, Simón, 13
Cabral, Amílcar, 19
Castro, Fidel, 21-22
Gandhi, Mahatma, 34
Garibaldi, Giuseppe, 36
Guevara, Ernesto "Che," 41
Kenyatta, Jomo, 61
King, Martin Luther, Jr., 67
Mussolini, Benito, 107
Nasser, Gamal Abdel, 109, 110
Nyerere, Julius Kambarage, 115
San Martín, José Francisco de, 126
Stalin, Joseph, 37
Zapata, Emiliano, 151, 152
Society for Humanity (Iran), 103
Solidarity (Poland), 143-144
Somalia, 22
Somoza García, Anastasio, 128
Sons of Liberty, 3
Sorel, Georges, 129-130
South Africa, 11, 22, 33, 88-89, 115
South African Student Organization
(SASO), 11
South America, 35, 125. *See also* Latin
America
Southern Christian Leadership
Conference (SCLC), 67
Soviet Union. *See* Union of Soviet
Socialist Republics
Soweto (South Africa), 11, 12

Spain
civil war, 107, 117, 118, 130
Cuba, 95-96
Napoleonic invasion, 13
Orwell, George, and, 117
Saint-Domingue, 78
South America and, 125
War of Spanish Succession, 148
Stalingrad, 49
Stalin, Joseph
biography, 131-132
communist state of, 49, 107
de-Stalinization, 38
expulsion of Yugoslavia, 137-138
Lenin, Vladimir Ilyich, and, 75
social reforms, 37
Trotsky, Leon, and, 141, 142
Stamp Act (1765), 1, 3, 32, 45, 86
Stamp Act Resolves, 45
Stanleyville (Kisangani; Democratic
Republic of the Congo), 80
Stanton, Elizabeth Cady, 6
Statute for Securing Religious Freedom
(Jefferson), 54
"Stolen lands." *See* White Highlands
Strikes, 129. *See also* Labor and trade
unions
Suez Canal, 110
Suez War, 110
Sukarno, 133-134
"Summary View of the Rights of British
America, A" (Jefferson), 54
Sun Yat-sen, 23, 135-136
Suppression of Communism Act, 88
Syndicalism, 129
Syria, 110

T

"Taciturne, le." *See* William the Silent
Taiping Rebellion (1851-1864), 52-53
Taiping Tianguo ("Heavenly Kingdom of
Great Peace"), 52-53
Taiwan, 24
Tambo, Oliver, 88, 89
Tanganyika, 115
Tanganyika African National Union, 115
Tanzania, 115-116
Technical College of Bandung, 133
Tekere, Mugabe, 106

Terror and terrorism. *See also*
Executions; Murders; Violence
France, 94, 120, 121-122
Marx, Karl, and, 99
Russia, 37
Stalin, Joseph, and, 132
Thailand, 107
Theocratic government, 63
"Theses on the National and Colonial
Questions" (Lenin), 50-51
Thoughts on Government (John Adams), 2
"Three People's Principles" (Sun Yat-
sen), 135-136
Tiananmen Square (China), 27, 91
Tin mines, 71-72
Tito, Josip Broz, 137-138
Titorenko, Raisa, 37
Tocqueville, Alexis de, 139-140
Totalitarianism, 107, 123, 124
Touré, Ahmed Sekou, 80
Townshend Acts (1767), 3, 86
Treaties and agreements
Anglo-Iranian (1919), 103
Armistice of Mudros (1918), 8
Brest-Litovsk (1918), 142
French Alliance (1778), 31, 32
Geneva Conference (1954), 50
Treaty of Cateau-Cambrésis (1559),
149
Treaty of Paris (1783), 2, 87
Twelve Years Truce (1609), 150
U.S.-Great Britain (1783), 31, 32
Trinity College, 111
Troeltsch, Ernst, 83
Trotsky, Leon, 73, 74, 131-132, 141-142
Truth and Reconciliation Commission
(South Africa), 12
Tudeh Party (Iran), 104
Turkey. *See* Republic of Turkey
Twenty-sixth of July Movement (Cuba),
21
Two Penny Act, 45
Two Treatises of Government (Locke), 76,
77

U

Uganda, 115, 116
Ujamaa (Africa), 116
Ulyanov, Alexander, 73

Ulyanov, Vladimir I. *See* Lenin, Vladimir
Ilyich
Umhonto we Sizewe (South Africa), 88
Union of Soviet Socialist Republics
(USSR). *See also* Gorbachev,
Mikhail; Russia; Stalin, Joseph
China and, 23, 65, 91, 92
Communist Party, 130
Cuba and, 22
Czechoslovakia and, 44
dissolution of, 38
Germany and, 49, 137
Korea and, 65-66
Nehru, Jawaharlal, and, 111
Spain and, 117
Stalin, Joseph, and, 132
Suez Canal and, 110
Unions. *See* Labor and trade unions;
Solidarity
Unitary Representation of the
Guatemalan Opposition (RUOG),
101-102
United Nations, 102, 115, 134
United Republic of Tanzania, 115
United States. *See also* individual states
antiwar movement, 128
China and, 91
civil war, 6
Cuba and, 21, 22, 41-42
Czechoslovakia and, 44
Good Neighbor Policy, 128
independence of, 1-2, 139
Iran and, 63-64
Korea and, 65
Nicaragua and, 127-128
revolution in, 99
Suez Canal and, 110
as a union of states, 54
University of Erfurt, 82
University of Fort Hare, 105
University of London, 105
University of Lyon, 29
University of Natal, 11
University of Neuchâtel, 103
University of Wittenberg, 82
University of Zurich, 84
Uruguay, 35
USSR. *See* Union of Soviet Socialist
Republics

V

"Velvet Revolution" (Czechoslovakia), 44
Venezuela, 13
Vergennes, Charles Gravier, 32
Victor Emmanuel II (king; Italy), 36
Vienna (Austria), 47
Vietminh Front. *See* League for the Independence of Vietnam
Vietnam, 50-51, 127
Vietnam War, 68
Villa, Pancho, 151-152
Violence. *See also* Assassinations; Executions; Murders; Nonviolence; Terror and terrorism
    according to Fanon, Frantz Omar, 29, 30
    according to Sorel, Georges, 129-130
    in France, 69
    in Hitler Germany, 48
    in Iran, 64
    in Kenya, 60, 61
    in revolutions, 99
Virginia, 145
Virginia Convention, 46, 86
Volta Dam, 114
Voting rights, 6-7
Voting Rights Act (1965), 67

W

Walesa, Lech, 143-144
War of 1812, 87
War of Spanish Succession (1702-1713), 148
Wars. *See also* Civil wars; Revolutions; World War I; World War II
    Algeria (1954-1962), 29
    Arab-Israeli (1967), 110
    Chaco War (1932-1935), 71
    Indonesia-The Netherlands (1949), 133
    Korean War (1950-1953), 65

Nicaragua-U.S. (1925-1933), 127-128
Nine Years' War (1688-1697), 148
Opium War (1839-1842), 52
Palestine War (1948), 109-110
Peasant wars (1524-1526; 1929), 82, 132
Seven Years' War (1756-1763), 145
Suez War (1956), 110
War of 1812, 87
War of Spanish Succession (1702-1713), 148
Warsaw Pact, 43
Washington, D.C., 68
Washington, George, 32, 69, 119, 145-146
Washington (George) administration, 2, 54, 87
Weimar Republic, 85
Weydemeyer, Joseph, 99
Whampoa Military Academy (China), 23
What is to be Done? (Lenin), 73
Whig Party, 86
White Highlands (the "stolen lands"; Kenya), 60
William of Orange (William III; king; England), 77, 147-148
William the Silent (prince of Orange), 147, 149-150
Witherspoon, John, 86
Women's issues, 6-7, 10, 30, 53, 123
Women's National Loyal League, 6
Woman's rights movement, 5, 6
Workers' Party of Korea, 65
World War I
    Atatürk, Kemal, 8
    Bolsheviks, 74
    Hitler, Adolf, 47
    Luxemburg, Rosa, 84
    moral regeneration and, 130
    Mussolini, Benito, 107
    Tito, Josip Broz, 137
    Trotsky, Leon, 141

World War II
    Chiang Kai-shek, 23
    Gramsci, Antonio, 39-40
    Hitler, Adolf, 48, 49
    India and, 56-57
    Orwell, George, 118
    Russia, 37
    Sukarno, 133
    Yugoslavia, 137
Wretched of the Earth, The (Fanon), 29, 30
Writers Union (Czechoslovakia), 43

Y

Yemeni civil war (1962-1968), 110
Yoga, 33
Young Italy, 35
Young Turk Revolution (1908), 8
Yuan Shikai, 136
Yugoslavia, 137-138

Z

Zaire. *See* Democratic Republic of the Congo
Zambia, 88
ZANU. *See* Zimbabwe African National Union
ZANU-Popular Front (ZANU-PF), 106
Zanzibar, 115
Zapata, Emiliano, 151-152
ZAPU. *See* Zimbabwe African People's Union
Zasulich, Vera, 73
Zeledón, Benjamin, 127
Zhou Enlai, 27
Zia, Sayyed, 103
Zimbabwe, 105-106, 115
Zimbabwe African National Union (ZANU), 105-106
Zimbabwe African People's Union (ZAPU), 105, 106